GULLS
of
NORTH
AMERICA

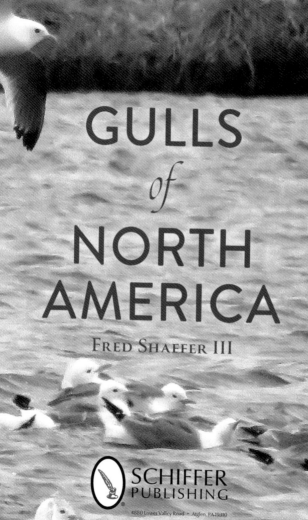

GULLS
of
NORTH
AMERICA

Fred Shaffer III

SCHIFFER
PUBLISHING

4880 Lower Valley Road • Atglen, PA 19310

Library of Congress Control Number: 2021931782

Designed by Ashley Millhouse
Type set in Adobe Caslon/Brandon Grotesque
ISBN: 978-0-7643-6294-1
Printed in India

Published by Schiffer Publishing, Ltd.
4880 Lower Valley Road
Atglen, PA 19310
Phone: (610) 593-1777; Fax: (610) 593-2002
Email: Info@schifferbooks.com
Web: www.schifferbooks.com

For our complete selection of fine books on this and related subjects, please visit our website at www.schifferbooks.com. You may also write for a free catalog.

Schiffer Publishing's titles are available at special discounts for bulk purchases for sales promotions or premiums. Special editions, including personalized covers, corporate imprints, and excerpts, can be created in large quantities for special needs. For more information, contact the publisher.

We are always looking for people to write books on new and related subjects. If you have an idea for a book, please contact us at proposals@schifferbooks.com.

Other Schiffer Books on Related Subjects:

An Illustrated Guide to the Common Birds of Cape Cod, Peter Trull, ISBN 978-0-7643-3877-9

Birds of Cape Cod & the Islands, Roger S. Everett, ISBN 978-0-7643-2461-1

Birds of Cape May, New Jersey, Kevin T. Karlson, ISBN 978-0-7643-3534-1

For most gulls it was not flying that matters,

but eating. For this gull, though, it was not

eating that mattered, but flight.

—Richard Bach

Contents

Preface

Let me begin with a few words about what this book is and isn't. First and foremost, it is a labor of love. I am not a professional ornithologist or photographer; however, over the last twenty years, watching gulls has brought me endless opportunities to learn, enjoy spectacular natural settings, and observe this magnificent group of birds at their diverse best. Like a lot of birders, I initially avoided gulls as too difficult to identify, but over time I came to appreciate their range of molt- and age-related plumages, adaptable habits, and engaging behavior. Long ago I set a goal of observing and photographing all the ages and plumages of North America's gulls. While I have yet to study some of the rarer species firsthand, I have experienced most of the species by visiting far-flung North American locations. I've tried to present what I've learned in an enjoyable and accessible format to encourage others to do the same.

This book isn't intended as the ultimate gull identification guide. That task is better left to true ornithologists. Several excellent books come far closer to summarizing all that is known about gull identification, and I've referenced them in the bibliography. Many books focus on feather-for-feather details that can be seen only with high-powered spotting scopes,

or after the fact by examining high-resolution photographs. Sometimes this approach is necessary to make a difficult identification, and several fine books cover this level of detail.

That said, gulls are attracted to areas where people live and play, and they aren't scared off when we get close to them. I used that my advantage as I kayaked on bays, lakes, and coastal waters; walked beaches; explored city parks and prairie potholes; and birded in and around landfills. The results are representative of what birders actually see in the field with a regular set of binoculars and spotting scope.

This book is an introduction aimed particularly at people who see gulls regularly and haven't paid much attention but want to learn more about what makes them unique. It is also for recreational birders who have dismissed gulls because of the effort it takes to learn unfamiliar terminologies. The tips I've picked up for identifying and aging gulls are meant for all skill levels.

My favorite books are written by authors who clearly love their subject matter, and if this book encourages one person to take a deeper interest in the gulls around them, I will have considered the effort well worthwhile. I have certainly enjoyed the process of compiling this information, and I hope this comes through in the pages and photos that follow.

Acknowledgments

Many people provided assistance, guidance, and encouragement as I worked on this book. First, I am grateful to my editor at Schiffer Publishing, Cheryl Weber, for her help in making a daunting and unfamiliar process seem achievable and enjoyable. I also thank Nancy and Pete Schiffer for believing that my rough species accounts showed promise, and for having faith that I could bring this book to fruition. Schiffer Publishing has given me the opportunity to pursue a longtime dream, and for that I am grateful.

Second, I'd like to thank all the birders and naturalists who have taken the time to talk to me about gulls, puzzle over an identification, or provide insights into the thornier identification challenges. Special thanks to Gene Scarpulla, who provided valuable assistance early on by giving feedback on some species accounts and sharing some of the many and varied references on gulls contained in his library. He also reviewed most of the photos, double-checked the identifications, and made sure that the captions made sense. Any mistakes that remain are solely my responsibility. Frank Marenghi took time to review species accounts and provided valuable input on terminology. Jim Stasz shared his contagious enthusiasm, providing insights into gull identification and being a sounding board when I had a particularly difficult gull to identify at Schoolhouse Pond.

Thank you to Phil Davis, Sean McCandless, Jeff Shenot, Peter Relson, and Bill Hubick for sharing their gull photos. Although my goal was to photograph all of the plumages myself, I needed other birders to fill the gaps in my collection, and their contributions greatly improved this book. Thank you to Jeff Shenot for the companionship on the long drives out to see the Black-Tailed Gull in Ohio and the Gray-Hooded Gull in New York. And thank you to George Shaffer for accompanying me to see the Ivory Gull in Plymouth, Massachusetts, and gulls at Niagara Falls.

The Maryland birding community has been incredibly generous with their knowledge, insights, photos, and countless hours of companionship.

I'd like to express my continued appreciation to my parents, Fred and Janet Shaffer, for their ongoing encouragement and the purchase of a camera after I dropped one in a river and wore out another. They also purchased the kayak from which I saw many, many gulls over the years (and dropped the previously mentioned camera).

Last but not least, thank you to my wife, Pam, and sons, Ben and Josh, for their patience and good humor. They endured countless stops over the years where I lingered far too long over a flock of gulls while hoping for a rarity or puzzling over a confusing bird. They put up with trips to the landfill, with only my vague assurances that the spectacular gulls we would see would far outweigh the noxious odors and unsightly rubbish. On Ben's first trip to a landfill, he was aghast that his father would go to a place like that and "know everybody there" (we ran into other birders). Ben also provided the captions on photos depicting gull topography. Pam encouraged my two trips to Alaska to see Ross's Gulls and Red-Legged Kittiwakes. Witnessing the annual fall migration of Ross's Gulls over the Arctic Ocean and seeing Red-Legged Kittiwakes at their Bering Sea home are memories that I'll always treasure (and hope to repeat).

Introduction

Gulls are an ideal group of birds for close study. They are widespread, approachable, and easy to view. They are also large, diverse, and prone to turning up in unexpected places. Many gulls take several years to reach maturity, so there is a seemingly endless variety of plumages, even within the same species. Gulls tend to congregate in large numbers; occur where people live, work, and play; and can at times appear personable, confiding, and even pushy or pugnacious. Even the most urban landscape is likely to hold a few gulls, be it at a fast-food parking lot, along an industrial river, or in a city park.

Gulls don't shy away from people, especially when a free meal might result. They are intelligent and adaptable, quick to take advantage of a new source of food, and frequently working cooperatively, be it at a breeding colony, in defense of their young, or searching for prey offshore. However, this spirit of cooperation does not stop them from squabbling endlessly over food, and it can be fun to watch them bicker and joust over a discarded leftover. Often these arguments are at their most animated when there is a seemingly inexhaustible food supply at hand, such as at a landfill or restaurant dumpster. Once, when I was observing a large group of gulls on the ice of Schoolhouse Pond in Maryland, I witnessed

an Iceland Gull sneak up behind a Herring Gull and swipe the food out of the larger bird's bill as smoothly as a seasoned pickpocket. The Herring Gull spun around and, in retribution, pecked the Iceland Gull in the back so hard that it drove the thief through the thin layer of ice. But it didn't succeed in retrieving its lunch, which the Iceland Gull had already gulped down.

Gulls are beautiful and elegant. They are masters of flight, quartering with ease in a strong wind or gliding effortlessly above the wake of a boat far offshore, changing direction or speed with an imperceptible shift of the wings or tail. Seeing a large group of these agile and maneuverable birds in flight over a windswept ocean, one cannot help but marvel at how effortlessly gulls negotiate a variety of weather conditions with speed, precision, and grace. Gulls are well adapted to handle the worst that nature can throw at them.

Up close, it can be thrilling to sift through large flocks of common species and find a rare species or unexpected stray. With their endless array of age-, molt-, and wear-related plumages, the opportunities for discovery never cease.

Gull Terms and Topography

The following photos include labels for the different parts of a gull and their markings. If you have a question about the field marks referenced in the species accounts, these photos indicate what you should be looking for (greater coverts, mantle, gonydeal angle, orbital ring, and so on). The glossary defines many of the terms referenced in the photos. The pattern and extent both of the white and black in the wingtips can often be useful when separating look-alike gull species in the field. If you see a gull you are unsure of, look at as many of the field marks as possible, as well as some more obvious features such as size, leg color, and the bill size and shape.

Crown

Nape

Hind Neck

Throat

Mantle

Breast

Scapulars

Lesser Coverts

Tertials

Median Coverts

Greater Coverts

Primaries

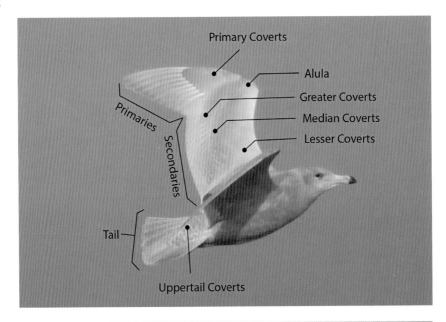

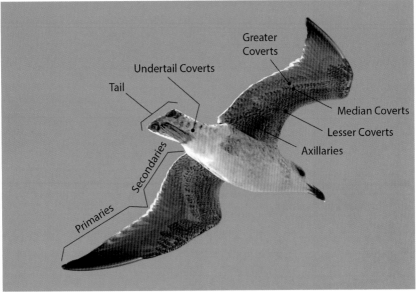

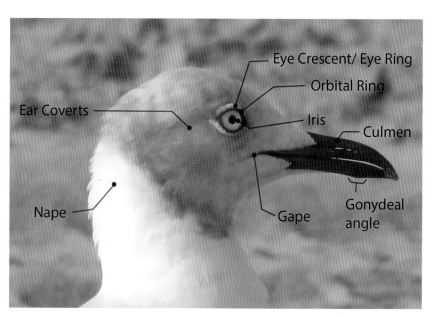

Eye Crescent/ Eye Ring

Orbital Ring

Ear Coverts

Iris

Culmen

Nape

Gape

Gonydeal angle

Ear Spot

Carpal Bar

Dark Tail Band

Black Trailing Edge

Glossary

albino: Total lack of pigmentation resulting in white plumage and pink bill and legs

alula: A small group of feathers near the base of the primaries at the bend of the wing

axillaries: The feathers covering the area where the wings meet the body

bleaching: The fading or whitening of feathers due to prolonged exposure to sunlight. Gulls tend to show significantly faded and worn feathers during the later spring and summer.

breeding plumage: The appearance of a gull during the breeding season (spring and early summer)

clinal: The gradual change in appearance or plumage within a population over a geographical area

concolor: Uniformly colored

coverts: Small feathers that cover the base of the major feathers of the wings (primaries and secondaries) and tail (rectrices)

distal: Toward the tip. On gulls, this can refer to dark markings near the tip of the bill, or markings toward the tip of the tail feathers or primaries.

ear spot: A contrasting black spot on the side of the head, seen on some gulls during the nonbreeding season (late fall and winter)

first-winter: Refers to a gull during winter (nonbreeding season) in its first year of life

first-year: Refers to a gull during its first year of life, without specifying a season or plumage

gape: The opening created when the bill is opened wide. Can also refer to the area where the maxilla and mandible meet. Some gulls show colorful bare skin in this area during breeding season.

gonydeal angle: The expansion of the lower mandible near the tip. This feature is prominent on many of the larger gulls. The bill of gulls with a large gonydeal angle looks swollen toward the tip.

flight feathers: The major feathers of the wings (primaries and secondaries) and tail (rectrices)

hind collar: Dark streaking or smudging on the lower hind neck or nape. This feature is prominent on juvenile Black-Legged Kittiwakes.

hooded gulls: A general term referring to small- to medium-sized gulls that have a black head (or "hood") in breeding plumage

immature: A general term for any gull that has not yet attained its adult plumage

inner primary panel: A paler area on the innermost primaries, seen on the extended wing of some immature gulls (such as first-winter Herring Gulls).

inner wing: The part of the wing between the bend of the wing and the body

juvenile: A first-year bird wearing its first coat of true (nondowny) feathers

juvenile plumage: The first plumage of true (nondowny) feathers; usually the plumage that a bird wears upon fledging. Sometimes termed the juvenal plumage.

kleptoparasitism: Foraging strategy involving stealing food from other birds

leading wedge: A contrasting white or black wedge seen on the leading edge of the outer wing. The white leading wedge is especially prominent on adult Bonaparte's and Black-Headed Gulls.

leucistic: A pale or white plumage due to a deficiency of pigmentation

M pattern: A contrasting black or dark-gray pattern seen on the upper wing of some gulls. The M pattern is formed by the dark outer primaries and primary coverts of the outer wing and the dark ulnar bar across the inner wing.

mandible: The lower portion of the bill, sometimes referred to as the lower mandible

mantle: The upper back

maxilla: The upper portion of the bill, sometimes referred to as the upper mandible

medial: Refers to the central portion of the feather. For example, the white medial band on the wings of adult Franklin's Gulls runs through the center of the primaries and separates the black primary tips with the gray of the upper wings.

mirror: A white spot enclosed with black, seen on the tips of the outermost primaries of many adult gulls

molt: The normal loss and regrowth of feathers. Molt can cause dramatic differences in the appearance of many gulls over the course of a year.

nape: The back of the gull's neck just below the top (or crown) of the head

nonbreeding plumage: The appearance of a gull during the nonbreeding season (late fall and winter)

orbital ring: The narrow band of bare skin surrounding the eye. Many gulls have bright orbital rings during breeding season that can be seen with close views.

pelagic: The deepwater marine environment beyond the continental shelf. Birds regularly found in this offshore environment are sometimes called "pelagic" species. Of all the gulls, only the Black-Legged Kittiwake, Red-Legged Kittiwake, and Sabine's Gull are regularly found in this environment.

primaries: The ten visible feathers of the outer half of the gull's wing. Primaries are numbered from the innermost (P1) to the outermost (P10). The innermost primaries are the ones closest to the body, while P10 is the very tip of the wing.

primary extension: The distance the longest primaries extend past the tertials on the folded wing

secondaries: The feathers on the inner half of the gull's wing

second-winter: Refers to a gull during winter (nonbreeding season) in its second year of life

second-year: Refers to a gull during its second year of life, without specifying a season or plumage

subspecies: A geographical subset of a species that differs in morphology or coloration (or both) compared to other members of the species. Subspecies (abbreviated "ssp.") may also differ by range, habitat, and voice.

subterminal: Immediately behind the tip or end of the feather

tertials: The innermost flight feathers closest to the body

third-winter: Refers to a gull during winter (nonbreeding season) in its third year of life

third-year: Refers to a gull during its third year of life, without specifying a season or plumage

ulnar bar: A dark diagonal bar across the inner wing, seen on some immature gulls

undertail coverts: Small feathers that cover the underside of the base of the tail feathers.

upper-tail coverts: small feathers that cover the upper side of the base of the tail feathers

"Venetian blind" pattern: Refers to the alternating light and dark pattern seen on the outer wings of some gulls, formed by the dark outer web and lighter inner web of the outermost primaries. Usually noticeable only when the gull is in flight or the wings are extended.

vagrant: A bird that appears well outside the known range for that species

white-headed gulls: A general term referring to the three- and four-year gulls that have a clean white head in breeding plumage

white-winged gulls: A general term that refers to gulls having white or mostly white primary tips

wing coverts: The feathers that cover the base of the flight feathers on the upper and lower sides of the extended wing

wingtip: The exposed tips to the outermost primaries. The primary tips of many adult gulls appear black with white tips or mirrors.

Identification

Perhaps nobody has simplified the identification process better than the late Rick Blom. His 2001 article "Identifying Gulls: Don't Panic!" in *Bird Watcher's Digest* was a revelation for me; any birder can use it to identify the vast majority of gulls. His article was subsequently incorporated into *Identify Yourself: The 50 Most Common Birding Identification Challenges* by Bill Thompson III and the editors of *Bird Watcher's Digest*. The chapters on gulls are essential, whether you are a serious birder or just want to learn about the gulls at your local park. I've tried to follow that approach.

Blom observed that too many birders are scared off by the most difficult identifications and have decided to ignore gulls altogether. In truth, identifying most gulls is no more difficult than for the other bird groups.

Roger Tory Peterson, too, was a genius at distilling bird identification to its essence, relying on readily observable field marks that could be seen on any bird with decent looks. He took bird identification beyond the "shotgun" method of identification, when even experts would identify a species only when they had a specimen in hand and feather-by-feather details to examine.

Much of recent gull identification has resorted back to feather-by-feather level of identification, with descriptions focusing on individual feathers or on marks that can be seen only with a high-powered telescope or by examining high-resolution photos. Only the most-difficult identifications require getting to this level of detail; the majority of gulls can be identified using a simpler approach.

When identifying gulls, there are a few key points to remember. Rare gulls are just as hard to come by as rare warblers or rare shorebirds. Just because you see a flock of 500 gulls does not mean a rarity will be present. If you become familiar with the gulls of your area, you will be in a much-better position to identify the out-of-place gull. Frequently, when I search through a gull flock, what draws my attention is some feature or mark that just doesn't look right. Also, remember that gulls are extremely variable within a species. A single-species flock of twenty gulls all can look identifiably different. This is because gulls molt at varying rates and can take three or four years to reach maturity. Blom encouraged birders to focus on the big similarities, not the small differences (Blom 2001).

AGING

The first step to identifying a gull begins with determining its age. Perhaps the definitive resource on aging birds in the field is the 2007 *Gulls of the Americas* by Steve N. G. Howell and Jon Dunn. This reference guide should be on the shelf of every gull enthusiast. The introduction contains thirty-three photos that illustrate all the ages, plumages, and molts of a Western Gull. The beauty of the book is its vast scope and attention to detail, with species descriptions including a feather-by-feather level of detail and in-depth discussion on how molt and wear affect a gull's appearance over its life span. Howell and Dunn use the Humphrey-Parkes system of naming molts and plumages. While technically accurate, this system can be cumbersome in the field and requires a slew of technical terminology, which can be difficult to master and apply.

For some difficult-to-identify immature gulls, this methodology may be necessary, but there is a simpler approach for the majority of gulls. In this book, I use the simplified life-year system, which calculates a bird's age the same way we think about our own age: a first-year gull applies to birds in their first year of life, from fledgling through their first spring. I also refer to "breeding" and "nonbreeding" plumage; the former term refers to how most gulls look during the warmer months (breeding season), while the latter refers to how gulls look throughout the rest of the year. These labels describe what a birder sees in the field, rather than referencing molt.

And, as noted in *Identifying Gulls: Don't Panic!*, there are shortcuts for aging the vast majority of gulls (Blom 2001). I've summarized some of these shortcuts in tables 1 and 2. However, some difficult first-year gulls or hybrids can stump even the experts. My rule of thumb is that if I have even one field mark or feature that is confusing or contradictory, I leave the bird unidentified. Rather than feeling discouraged, look at it as a learning opportunity. Some of the most enjoyable conversations I've had with other birders have been over gulls that we just couldn't figure out or agree on.

SMALL, MEDIUM, OR LARGE?

As noted by Blom, the aging and identification process can be simplified if we place gulls in one of three categories: small, medium, or large (Blom 2001). The small group includes species such as Bonaparte's, Black-Headed, and of course Little Gull. These birds usually achieve their adult plumage in their second year, which simplifies the identification process by reducing the number of plumages that they go through.

The medium-sized group includes species of "hooded" gulls such as Laughing and Franklin's Gulls, and "white-headed" gulls such as Ring-Billed Gull and Short-Billed Gull. These birds take three years to reach their adult plumage. Although they go through more changes in appearance before they reach maturity, these species are still straightforward and well covered in standard field guides.

Where things really get complicated is with the large gulls, which take four years to reach maturity and are more variable (particularly in immature plumages). What follows is a summary of these field-recognizable tips for aging gulls. Table 1 summarizes the shortcuts for aging each type of gull (small, medium, and large), and table 2 presents a pictorial summary of each type, using Bonaparte's, Ring-Billed, Laughing, and Herring Gulls as examples.

The size of each species is summarized in the species accounts, with wingspan, weight, and length given for each species. Sources for these measurements include Sibley 2014, Olsen and Larsson 2004, and *Birds of the World*. Males are generally larger and heavier than females, although much variation exists within each species.

TABLE 1: GULL-AGING TIPS

Size	Small Gulls	Medium-Sized Gulls (hooded)	Medium-Sized Gulls (white-headed)	Large Gulls (white-headed)
Species	Little, Bonaparte's, Black-Headed	Laughing and Franklin's	Short-Billed and Ring-Billed	California, Herring, Western, Great Black-Backed, Lesser Black-Backed
First-Year	Adultlike (gray) mantle acquired early in fall. Immature (brown or tan) wings and tail. Dark diagonal bar across upper side of the inner wing, seen in flight.	Adultlike mantle (gray) acquired in fall / early winter; Immature (brown or tan) wings and tail; Extensive black in the wingtips.	Adultlike mantle (gray) acquired in fall / early winter; Immature (brown or tan) wings and tail; Extensive black in the wingtips.	Brown overall, tail and rump dark; body and wings immature (brown or brown streaked); bill all black or mostly black.
Second-Year	Acquire adult plumage in second year; mostly whitish head (with ear spot or faint streaks) in winter; black hood in breeding plumage	Mostly adult; adultlike (gray) upperparts; trace of a tailband or dark markings on the tertials; more extensive black in primaries than on adults.	Mostly adult; adultlike (gray) upperparts; trace of a tailband or dark markings on the tertials; more extensive black in primaries than on adults.	Mostly brown, tail dark and rump light; bill dark with a pale base; begins to acquire adultlike (gray or black) mantle
Third-Year	NA	Acquire adult plumage in third year; hooded gulls have a black hood in breeding season and white head with ear spot or faint streaking in nonbreeding season;	Acquire adult plumage in third year. White-headed gulls have a clean white head in breeding season and streaked head in nonbreeding season	Mostly adult, tail mostly white and rump white. Bill pale with dark ring toward the tip; adultlike (gray or black) upperparts with some brown in the coverts or tertials; limited white in primaries
Fourth-Year	NA	NA	NA	Acquire adult plumage in fourth year. Tail and rump white. Adult upperparts (gray or black); bill pale with dark red or black (or both), head white in breeding season, can be streaked in nonbreeding season.

TABLE 2: GULL-AGING PICTORIAL SUMMARY

Size	Small Gulls	Medium-Sized Gulls (hooded)	Medium-Sized Gulls (white-headed)	Large "white-headed" Gulls
Species	Bonaparte's Gull shown below	Laughing Gull shown below	Ring-Billed Gull shown below	Herring Gull shown below
First-Year				
Second-Year (NB) (B)				
Third-Year (NB) (B)	NA			
Fourth-Year (NB) (B)	NA	NA	NA	

One approach to identification is to first focus on the adult gulls. They can usually be identified by mantle color and leg color alone. Then start sorting through the juvenile and first-year gulls. Try to figure out which immature gulls go with which adults. For example, first-year Ring-Billed Gulls will be similar in size and structure to adults, just as first-year Laughing Gulls will share the same structural features (size, long primary extension and long, drooping bill) with adults. The same can be said of the large white-headed gulls. Immature Great Black-Backed Gulls, while looking quite different in plumage, share the extremely large size, massive bill, and blocky head of their black-backed, adult relatives.

The first-year and adult plumages are the "beginning" and "ending" point for the appearance of a gull, while the ages and plumages of second- or third-year gulls will be intermediate between the two. One note of caution: while aging a gull as first-year or adult is usually straightforward, a more tentative approach should be taken with the intermediate ages. An "advanced" second-year white-headed gull can share many of the same features as a third-year gull, while a "retarded" third-year gull can show the plumage features more typical of a second-year gull. Some birds are best left as "second-year type" or "third-winter type." If you are really puzzling over the age of an individual gull, consult *Gulls of the Americas* by Steven Howell and Jon Dunn, which provides a wealth of photos of gulls at all ages and in all plumages and discusses the differences in detail. They also provide many tips for identifying or aging difficult species. For example, among the four-year white-headed gulls, second-year birds have immature (brownish) inner primaries while third-year birds have adultlike (gray or black) inner primaries (Howell and Dunn 2007). However, thinking "big picture," I like the synopsis presented in *Identifying Gulls: Don't Panic!* For large, four-year gulls, first-year birds are immature or brown overall, second-year birds are mostly brown, third-year gulls are mostly adult (mostly gray or black above, perhaps with some brown coverts or tertials and white below), and fourth-year gulls are adult (gray or black above and white below). Of course, some gulls that are "advanced" or "retarded" in plumage development will be exceptions to these generalities; for the most part, this sequence holds true.

In summary, there are some wonderful resources out there for identifying gulls. *Gulls of the Americas* provides a wealth of information and high-quality photos and is my first reference to consult with confusing immature gulls or possible hybrids. *The Gulls of North America, Europe and Asia* by Klaus Malling Olsen and Hans Larsson is a beautiful book and contains both large-format photos and beautifully done artwork of each species. More recently, the *Gulls of the World: A Photographic Guide* by Klaus Malling Olsen combines concise and readable species descriptions with world-class photos of all the species of gulls found worldwide. Due to its combination of beautiful, large-format photos and readable text, this is perhaps my favorite detailed reference on gulls.

Similarly, there are also multiple websites that contain a wealth of information. Anything Larus, by Amar Ayyash, includes current information on gull sightings, identification issues, and nomenclature. When a nationally significant rarity turns up somewhere, it is discussed here, and many of the thornier identification issues that people wrestle with are covered here as well. Also of interest is the monthly list of notable gull sightings from across North America. And the Gull Research Organization website includes an incredible number of scientific and identification-related gull articles. If you want to learn about the distribution, identification tips, or latest research on a particular species of gull, this is a great link to have bookmarked on your computer. A listing of many of the articles, books, and websites that I've found most helpful and informative is included at the back of this book. If you want additional information on just about any facet of this book, you will likely find a good reference listed here.

Chapter 1. Hooded Gulls

LITTLE GULL

Background

The diminutive Little Gull is the smallest gull species in the world, and only a rare breeder in North America. They are distinctive not only for their pint-sized dimensions, but also for the charcoal-black underwing of adults, which can be seen from a great distance on flying gulls. In flight they appear buoyant, fluttery, and almost mothlike as they flap erratically above a marsh or bay, changing direction or dipping to the water's surface seemingly on a whim.

Flying Little Gulls have been compared to marsh terns (such as black tern) due to their up-and-down (or yo-yo) motion. When resting on a river or lake, they bob on the water like a cork as they deftly pick at the surface or spin about in search of food, in a manner reminiscent of a phalarope. Their old Latin name of *Larus minutus* confirmed their status as the smallest of the gull tribe. However, more-recent genetic work has placed Little Gulls in their own genus, *Hydrocoloeus*. Due to their small size, round head, dinky bill, and large eyes, a variety of adjectives have been used to describe them, such as gentle, confiding, winsome, and just plain cute. In *Life Histories of North American Gulls and Terns*, Arthur Cleveland Bent described their flight:

Their flight is graceful and active, and it is said at times to be butterfly-like or to resemble that of swallows. Professor Liljeborg, quoted by Dressner, says that their graceful and quick evolutions in pursuit of insects "almost surpass goatsuckers." In a word, these gulls resemble terns in flight rather than the larger gulls (Bent 1921).

In North America, Little Gulls are most commonly seen along the eastern Great Lakes in the fall and along the East Coast during the winter or early spring with large flocks of Bonaparte's Gulls, with which they regularly associate both in winter and in migration. Little Gulls were first recorded breeding in North America in 1962 along Lake Ontario, and they have subsequently bred elsewhere in the Great Lakes region. Although they have not been documented as breeding in North America since 1989, it is suspected that they continue to breed in small numbers in the Hudson Bay region, a remote area poorly covered by birders or ornithologists. Their numbers appear to be stable or perhaps slightly increasing in North America, but information on breeding locations remains elusive.

In North America, most Little Gulls winter along the Atlantic coast between the mid-Atlantic region and New England, with smaller numbers remaining in the lower Great Lakes and Niagara River area. During the winter, some Little Gulls are found well offshore and can be quite adept at flying in strong winds over the ocean; in that environment their rapid, almost shearwater-like flight is different from their slow, erratic flight pattern.

Like the larger Black-Headed Gull, Little Gulls are native to Eurasia and only recent breeders in North America. Unlike Black-Headed Gulls, which first began occurring along the East Coast around 1930, reports of Little Gulls stretch well back into the 1800s. Bent reported that the first mention of Little Gulls in North America was by Swainson and Richardson in 1831, who say, "A specimen obtained on Sir John Franklin's first expedition was determined by Mr. Sabine to be a young bird of the first year of this species, exactly according to M. Temminek's description." Bent continues, "The first thoroughly authentic specimen is recorded by Dutcher (1888) of a bird shot by Robert Powell at Fire Island, Long Island, New York, about September 15, 1887" (Bent 1921).

The origin of the North American population is questioned, with some saying that the species has always occurred in North America in small numbers, others saying that they originated from across the Bering Sea, and still others saying that the North American population came from Europe, perhaps using Iceland and Greenland as "stepping stones" to North America. The later explanation may be most likely, with one Swedish-banded chick found in Pennsylvania and the vast majority of sightings occurring in eastern North America (Ewins and Weseloh 2020).

Some of my favorite Little Gull sightings have occurred while kayaking the Back River in Maryland. Several times an adult Little Gull glided tantalizingly close to my boat as I drifted on the water among a huge flock of Bonaparte's Gulls. When an adult Little Gull flies over your boat, its blackish underwing can be seen in all its glory. Indeed, whereas a swirling flock of Bonaparte's Gulls can seem a dizzying blur of gray and white, Little Gulls add a flash of black to the mix. When seen in proximity to Bonaparte's Gulls, the Little Gull's smaller size is evident, and when foraging on a mudflat, Little Gulls can appear barely larger than a Red-Winged Blackbird.

Structure and Field Markings

Little Gulls live up to the second half of their Latin name, "*minutus.*" Often, size alone is enough to distinguish Little Gulls from other species. However, size can be difficult to judge on lone or distant birds. Little Gulls have short, compact bodies; short tails; blunt-tipped wings; short legs; and a petite bill. The head is round with a steep forehead, which combined with the tiny bill gives the species a dovelike appearance. In flight these birds make surrounding Bonaparte's Gulls appear almost lanky in comparison.

First-Year Plumage

Although they lack the charcoal-black underwing of adults, first-winter Little Gulls have an equally distinctive dark blackish M pattern on the pale-gray upper wing. This pattern is visible on distant flying birds and is thicker than that of Bonaparte's and Black-Headed Gulls. First-year Black-Legged Kittiwakes have a similarly bold pattern but also have a blackish hind collar and a clean white triangle on the trailing edge on the extended wing. Little Gulls have a dark secondary bar in this area. In addition to the tailband and black ear spots, first-year Little Gulls have a black "cap" or crown, which further serves to separate them from Bonaparte's Gulls. During their first summer, the immature upper-wing coverts are gradually replaced by adultlike gray feathers, and some Little Gulls acquire a full or partial hood, while others retain a more winter-like head pattern.

Adult Plumage

As adults, their charcoal-black underwing and light-gray upper wing are visible even at significant distances. The entirely dark underwing is unique among regularly occurring North American gulls. The upper wing is all gray, but it includes a thick white border along the trailing edge that extends around the outermost primaries. This white border is also visible on the lower surface of the wing, where it contrasts with the black underwing. In a flock of perched gulls, Little Gull adults can be identified by the black cap that covers the top of the head or crown. Winter plumage Bonaparte's Gulls lack this feature and have a clean white head with dark ear spots. In breeding plumage, Little Gulls have a black hood and bill and lack the white eye crescents seen on many other hooded gulls. Some second-year Little Gulls can be distinguished from full adults by variable black markings on the end of the outermost primaries, slightly paler underwing coverts, and some black on the primary coverts.

Size

Little Gulls are the smallest of gulls in wingspan, weight, and length. The short tail, dinky bill, and rounded wings of adults add to this impression. Little Gulls have an average length to 11.4 to 11.8 inches and an average wingspan of 27 to 29 inches. They weigh between 3.5 and 5.3 ounces.

Even from a distance, the bold black M pattern on the upper wing of first-spring Little Gulls can be seen on flying birds. Merseyside, England, spring. *Photos by S. Young / VIREO*

The faint cap and small, fine bill is seen on this foraging first-summer Little Gull. Bombay Hook National Wildlife Refuge, Delaware, June 28, 2017.

The Little Gull's diminutive size is highlighted next to a Red-Winged Blackbird. Bombay Hook National Wildlife Refuge, Delaware, June 28, 2017.

A second-year Little Gull with two Bonaparte's Gulls. The Little Gull is on the far right, showing the dark-gray underwing, the even gray upper wing, and a small amount of black in the primary tips. Potomac River near Dyke Marsh, Virginia, April 11, 2014.

A second-year breeding-plumage Little Gull. This bird appears mostly as an adult but retains a blackish subterminal mark on P8, and the underwing coverts have a lighter tint. Back River, Maryland, April 25, 2015.

A hint of black can be seen in the tips of one or two of the outer primaries of this second-year Little Gull. Back River, Maryland, April 25, 2015.

This adult Little Gull in winter plumage shows the even gray upper wing and blackish underwing in flight. Back River, Maryland, March 30, 2013.

An adult Little Gull displays its characteristic black underwing and rounded wingtips in flight. Centennial Park, Maryland, April 6, 2014. *Photo by Bill Hubick*

This adult Little Gull passed right over my kayak, allowing great views of the blackish underwing. Back River, Maryland, March 30, 2013.

The blackish underwing and all-gray upper wing are visible on this flying adult Little Gull. Even from a distance, this pattern can be clearly seen on adult Little Gulls and stands out in a flock of flying Bonaparte's Gulls. Centennial Park, Maryland, April 6, 2014. *Photo by Bill Hubick*

On resting birds, the adult Little Gull is subtly but noticeably smaller than surrounding Bonaparte's Gulls. Centennial Park, Maryland, April 6, 2014. *Photo by Bill Hubick*

This beautiful breeding-plumage Little Gull shows the full black hood and white-tipped gray primaries typical of adults. Vaala, Finland, in July. *Photo by J. Peltomaki / VIREO*

BLACK-HEADED GULL

Background

Black-Headed Gulls are attractive and graceful small gulls that have only recently gained a foothold in North America. With their bright-red bill and legs, pearly-gray mantle, and distinctive wing pattern, adult Black-Headed Gulls are a striking species at rest and in flight. Native to Eurasia, they were first documented nesting in North America in 1977, when several adults were observed with a recently fledged young bird in Newfoundland. In the summer of 1982, the first Black-Headed Gull nest in North America was discovered on an island in the Gulf of St. Lawrence, Quebec. Since that time, they've continued to breed in Newfoundland and elsewhere in maritime Canada along the Atlantic and have bred or attempted to breed in Maine and Massachusetts.

They are often found in the company of Bonaparte's Gulls during the winter and in migration, but they seem just as likely to be spotted with groups of Ring-Billed Gulls. They are now fairly common in Newfoundland but rare to scarce elsewhere in maritime Canada and the northeastern United States. Also, it surprises many birders to learn that Black-Headed Gulls occur in small numbers in the Bering Sea region in spring, with sightings occurring in the Pribilof and Aleutian Islands. The source population for these gulls is probably the Kamchatka Peninsula or other areas in northeastern Russia. Birds seen in Alaska are presumably of the subspecies *sibiricus*, which averages slightly larger in size and has a different molt timing than birds found in Europe and eastern North America.

In North America, Black-Headed Gulls are generally found in coastal waters such as protected bays, estuaries, and inlets. Sometimes they can be seen migrating over the ocean with flocks of Bonaparte's Gulls. They also occur more rarely on inland bodies of fresh water. They are adaptable and opportunistic feeders and can be found feeding while walking on land, floating on the water, or snatching prey from the water's surface in flight.

In North America, wintering or migrant flocks of Bonaparte's Gulls should always be searched for this species. The slightly larger size, black on the underside of the middle primaries, and reddish bill and legs distinguish the Black-Headed Gull from the much more numerous Bonaparte's Gulls. These adaptable gulls can also be found with Ring-Billed Gulls in a variety of more-urban and more-developed habitats, where they can more than hold their own with these larger birds as they fight for fast-food handouts in parking lots. Black-Headed Gulls have been documented as hybridizing with Ring-Billed Gulls, producing one of the more unexpected hybrid combinations in eastern North America, with birds displaying features intermediate between these dramatically different species.

Like many other gull species, Black-Headed Gulls are not above stealing food from other birds (or kleptoparasitism). Barnard and Thompson provide a fascinating and exhaustive account of this behavior in their 1985 book *Gulls and Plovers: The Ecology and Behaviour of Mixed-Species Feeding Groups*. Barnard and Thompson found that Black-Headed Gulls in Europe victimize Lapwings and Golden Plovers with this behavior. Often, the shorebirds will capture an earthworm or other prey from an agricultural field, and one or more Black-Headed Gulls will give chase, frequently causing the shorebird to drop or abandon its meal.

As with gulls as a whole, kleptoparasitism is just one of many ways that the adaptable and opportunistic Black-Headed Gull finds food. However, it has been calculated that Black-Headed Gulls can obtain in excess of their daily energy requirements simply by stealing earthworms from Lapwings! Kleptoparasitism in gulls is at least partially related to the size of the gull, with the behavior being common only in intermediate-sized species. In addition to Black-Headed Gulls, Laughing and Heermann's Gulls regularly engage in the behavior. Smaller species (such as Little and Ross's Gulls) tend to search for their own food, while larger species (such as Great Black-Backed and Glaucous Gulls) are more predatory (Barnard and Thompson 1985). However, all gulls like an easy meal, and most gulls can be seen engaging in this type of behavior from time to time. Black-Headed Gulls can be quite long lived, with a banded gull in England living more than thirty-three years in the wild and several other individuals exceeding thirty years in age (van Dijk et al. 2014).

I've been fortunate to see Black-Headed Gulls in a variety of settings, including the local pond near where I worked, along rivers and the Chesapeake Bay, while kayaking in a tidal marsh, and in a shopping-center parking lot. Some of my most memorable views of Black-Headed Gulls have come when I am kayaking. I have been able to paddle surprisingly close to the gulls, yielding unforgettable views of the brightly colored bill and the extent and shade of the hood on spring birds. When the gull flushes, the distinctive pattern of the extended wings is seen. What first draws your attention is the red bill and legs, but soon the attractive plumage, distinctive pattern of the extended wing, and graceful, tern-like flight can usually be noted.

Perhaps my favorite Black-Headed Gull sighting was on the frozen surface of Schoolhouse Pond in Maryland as a blizzard raged around me, the first part of the two-blizzard "snowmageddon" that beset the mid-Atlantic region in February 2010. The bird was perched stoically on the ice with Ring-Billed and Herring Gulls as the snow fell at a fantastic rate and was blown madly across the ice by the heavy wind.

Another Black-Headed Gull spotted in Maryland was the long-staying adult gull at the Hunt Valley Town Center just north of Baltimore. This bird appeared at the shopping-center parking lot for four winters in a row and treated birders to close views as it rested in the parking lot, perched on streetlights, or flew overhead. The bird provided an excellent case study for how fast Black-Headed Gulls can transition from winter (or nonbreeding) plumage to their hooded breeding-plumage appearance, and this transition could be observed for four consecutive springs.

Structures and Field Marks

Black-Headed Gulls are structurally similar to Bonaparte's Gulls, although decidedly larger. In flight they can have a somewhat tern-like general impression. In the field, they are noticeably larger than Bonaparte's Gulls, which is usually readily apparent at rest and in flight, at least with birds seen at close range. However, they share the grace of the smaller gulls, while perhaps lacking their maneuverability. When mingling with larger gulls, they are noticeably smaller than both Laughing Gulls and Ring-Billed Gulls and have a much-thinner, pointed bill lacking the gonydeal angle of the Ring-Billed Gull or the droop of the Laughing Gull. When seen in a swirling mass of flying gulls, the dark underside of the primaries usually stands out on the Black-Headed Gull, at least in good light. By contrast, the more common Bonaparte's Gull has a clean, white underwing. Black-Headed Gulls also have more-pointed wings in flight than the much-smaller Little Gulls, with which they are sometimes seen.

The gray of the upperparts is especially attractive on Black-Headed Gulls, at least to my eyes. While similar in gray tone to Ring-Billed Gulls, Black-Headed Gulls may be a shade lighter and have a slightly silver cast. And in all plumages, the color of the bare parts should include at least a hint of reddish tones that will be lacking on the similar Bonaparte's Gull, although the bill and legs of Black-Headed Gulls can appear quite dark in poor light.

First-Year Plumage

First-winter Black-Headed Gulls have flesh- or orange-toned bill and legs, decidedly paler than in adult birds. First-winter birds also show some brown on the wing coverts of the folded wings, some blackish brown on the tertials, and a narrow black tailband. The extended wing has a white leading edge on the outer wing, a brown ulnar bar on the inner wing, and a thick, brownish-black trailing edge. First-winter Black-Headed Gulls have the same dark underside on the middle primaries that is diagnostic on adults, although it can be less prominent on first-year birds.

Adult Plumage

Black-Headed Gulls are extremely attractive in adult plumage, having acquired their pearly-gray mantle; deep-red, black-tipped bill; white wedge to the upper wing, and contrasting black underside to the middle primaries. These last two marks are extremely helpful in separating distant flying Black-Headed Gulls from Bonaparte's and Ring-Billed Gulls. Winter-plumage Black-Headed Gulls also seem much more likely than Little, Bonaparte's, or Laughing Gulls to retain two faint black streaks or lines on the head—one extending from the dark ear spot to the crown and a second extending above the eye. There can be much variation in the color of the bill and legs, with most birds having bright-red bare parts, while others having much-duskier legs and bills, with only a hint of a reddish hue. Field marks that may indicate a second-year bird that has not achieved full adult plumage include some black on the alula, primary coverts, and tertials, or the retention of some black in the outer primaries. Some second-summer birds retain a winter-like head pattern during the breeding season.

Adult breeding-plumage birds acquire a black hood in late winter or early spring. The hood of the breeding-plumage Black-Headed Gull also has some subtle differences from other hooded gull species. The hood, when seen at close range and in good light, is actually brownish black, not a jet black as with other hooded species such as Laughing and Bonaparte's Gulls. This is generally not noticeable in the field. However, you can see the extent of the hood, which barely extends to the top of the nape, leaving most of the hind neck clean white. This gives the appearance that the hood has been "pushed forward" on the head of the Black-Headed Gull, leaving the back of the head white. Other hooded gulls have the hood extending farther onto the back of the head and nape.

Black-Headed Gulls acquire their hood several weeks to a month earlier than most Bonaparte's and Little Gulls. Therefore, when large flocks of Bonaparte's Gulls are migrating in late March or early April, most of them remain in winter or transitional plumage, with no or only a partial hood. A gull with a full hood in late winter or early spring should warrant a closer look, since frequently the full dark hood of a Black-Headed Gull is the first thing a birder notices when inspecting a flock of flying or perched winter plumage Bonaparte's Gulls. While the majority of Bonaparte's Gulls in late March or early April remain in winter plumage, the stray Black-Headed Gull will often stand out with its full breeding-plumage hood.

Size

Black-Headed Gulls are a small to medium size, larger than Bonaparte's Gulls but smaller than either Laughing or Ring-Billed Gulls, the species with which it most readily associates. They appear sleek and nimble in flight, although not as tern-like as the smaller Bonaparte's Gulls. Black-Headed Gulls average 13.4 to 15.4 inches in length and have a wingspan between 39.4 and 43.3 inches. Black-Headed Gulls can vary significantly in weight. Males vary from 6.6 to 14.1 ounces, while females range in weight from 5.9 to 12.4 ounces.

This first-summer Black-Headed Gull has a faint partial hood and mostly gray upperparts, and some dark markings in the wing coverts and tertials. St. Paul Island, Alaska, May 24, 2017.

This photo shows the black trailing edge to the entire wing, as well as a faint carpal bar typical of first-year Black-Headed Gulls. St. Paul Island, Alaska, May 22, 2017.

A first-year Black-Headed Gull has a black trailing edge to the wing and black within the white in the leading edge of the primaries. St. Paul Island, Alaska, May 22, 2017.

A dark underside to the middle primaries is seen on the winter plumage of an adult Black-Headed Gull. Hunt Valley Town Center, Maryland, December 12, 2011.

An adult Black-Headed Gull in winter plumage along the Patuxent River. Note the red legs and bill, pale-gray mantle, and dark ear spot. Jug Bay, Maryland, November 11, 2012.

An adult Black-Headed Gull molting into breeding plumage. Back River, Maryland, March 30, 2013.

An adult winter-plumage Black-Headed Gull in flight. Note the black on the underside of the middle primaries, plus the black tips to P9 and P10 (the two outermost primaries). The white leading edge to the upper side of the wing is also visible. Eagle Harbor, Maryland, August 20, 2008.

Adult Black-Headed Gull in winter plumage. Note the bright-red bill and legs and well-defined ear spot. Hunt Valley Town Center, Maryland, November 27, 2013.

Adult Black-Headed Gull molting into breeding plumage. Hunt Valley Town Center, Maryland, March 16, 2013.

Adult Black-Headed Gull in mostly breeding plumage. Hunt Valley Town Center, Maryland, March 21, 2013.

This adult Black-Headed Gull is easily identified by the bright-red bill and legs and black middle primaries on the underside of the wings. Wolfe Neck Wastewater Treatment Plan, Delaware, February 14, 2020.

Notice how the dark hood of the Black-Headed Gull stands out among the winter plumage Bonaparte's Gulls. Back River, Maryland, March 17, 2020.

The brownish hues to the hood, which can sometimes be noted in bright sunlight, can be seen on this breeding-plumage Black-Headed Gull. Hunt Valley Town Center, Maryland, March 21, 2013.

The distinctive upper and lower surfaces of the primaries are seen on this adult winter-plumage Black-Headed Gull. Wolfe Neck Wastewater Treatment Plan, Delaware, February 14, 2020.

An adult Black-Headed Gull that has acquired most of its full breeding-plumage hood. Hunt Valley Town Center, Maryland, March 21, 2013.

Notice how the hood of an adult Black-Headed Gull barely extends to the rear of the head, leaving the back of the head and nape clean white. On close view the brownish wash to the hood can be seen. Back River, Maryland, March 30, 2020.

This rare Black-Headed Gull × Ring-Billed Gull hybrid has a pale hood and upper-wing pattern indicative of the Black-Headed Gull lineage, while the size and bill shape are more reflective of a Ring-Billed Gull. Eagle Harbor, Maryland, August 13, 2008.

The white leading edge to the upper side of the wing is seen here, as is the partial hood and pale underwing. The mantle color of this presumed hybrid was pale, comparable in tone to either a Black-Headed or Ring-Billed Gull. A Black-Headed Gull and Laughing Gull hybrid would presumably show a darker mantle. Eagle Harbor, Maryland, August 13, 2008.

BONAPARTE'S GULL

Background

Bonaparte's Gulls are small, hooded gulls that are widespread across most of North America. These attractive gulls nest along northern ponds, bogs, and bays in the boreal zone; can be found virtually anywhere in southern Canada and the continental United States during migration; and winter along the Atlantic, Pacific, and Gulf coasts. They can often be seen in large numbers in the winter or during migration at favored coastal locations.

Because of their small size and graceful movements, they have frequently been described as more tern-like than the larger, more lumbering gulls. John James Audubon noted that "the flight of this gull is light, elevated, and rapid, resembling in buoyancy that of some of our terns more than that of most of our gulls, which move their wings more sedately" (Audubon 1844). Their quick, snappy wingbeats; nimble and fluid movement; and buoyant flight make Bonaparte's Gulls a delight to watch and set them apart from most other gulls. Although a social species that often gathers in large numbers with others of its kind, it usually does not mix with the larger gull species or gather at landfills.

Most North American birders see Bonaparte's Gulls in the winter along the coast as they fly by windswept beaches or rest on the water in sheltered bays. But they are equally at home above the open ocean, where they can be found over 10 miles offshore. In migration they also turn up along rivers and at lakes and are sometimes seen flying overhead in small-to-medium-sized groups early in the morning as they move north in the spring.

Large flocks can be impressive to behold as they swirl elegantly above the water or sit cork-like on the water, picking at prey. Arthur Cleveland Bent compared the flocks to "snowflakes wafted by the wind." He goes on to say that a gull "can rise and fall over the crests of the largest waves, and can go whither it will with the utmost ease and grace."

"I know of no prettier, winter, seashore scene than a flock of these exquisite little gulls hovering over some favorite feeding place, plunging into the cold gray water, unmindful of the chilly blasts and the swirling snow squalls" (Bent 1921). It is hard to disagree.

Bonaparte's Gulls can be found in large numbers along the coast during migration, and they frequently gather in large groups at staging areas before commencing spring migration. On many early-spring days, I've kayaked slowly along the Back River and found myself surrounded by Bonaparte's Gulls as they rest on the water, perch on nearby mudflats, and whirl overhead. Their nonstop activity and constant chatter make Bonaparte's Gulls memorable companions on any boating trip. During his travels, Audubon also noted the massive movement of Bonaparte's Gulls during spring migration in the Chesapeake Bay region:

> No sooner do the shad and old-wives enter the bays and rivers of our Middle Districts, than this Gull begins to shew itself on the coast, following these fishes as if dependent upon them for support, which however is not the case, for at the time when these inhabitants of the deep deposit their spawn in our waters, the Gull has advanced beyond the eastern limits of the United States. However, after the first of April, thousands of Bonapartian Gulls are seen gambolling over the waters of Chesapeake Bay, and proceeding eastward, keeping pace with the shoals of fishes. (Audubon 1844)

Other areas where Bonaparte's Gulls have been known to congregate (or gambol) in large numbers include San Francisco Bay, the southern shore of Lake Erie, and the lakes and marshes of the prairie region. Perhaps most impressively, flocks approaching 100,000 birds in size have been recorded in the Niagara region of New York (Burger and Gochfeld 2020). Sometimes fortunate sea watchers can view flocks of several hundred passing along the coast as the migrating birds fly low, appearing to be swept along effortlessly by the wind. They are attracted to rough, choppy waters, where the birds dart down deftly to capture food when the opportunity arises.

Bonaparte's Gulls use a variety of techniques to feed: plunging into the water from the air, dipping to the water to pluck prey from the surface, making shallow dives into the water from the surface, and picking at prey on the surface phalarope-like while wading in or floating on the water. They are also adept at snatching insects out of the air. At interior nesting locations, insects compose a substantial portion of their diet. Bonaparte's Gulls are one of the only gulls that regularly nest in trees, usually conifers near water in the boreal woods of the North.

Structure and Field Marks

This petite gull is the smallest of the gulls that occurs regularly over much of North America, being noticeably smaller than Laughing, Ring-Billed, and Short-Billed Gulls. In flight, they are also appreciably smaller than the other "common" gulls, with quick, snappy wing-beats. Adding to the tern-like impression is the small, narrow, and sharply pointed all-black bill. Bonaparte's Gulls have a short, plump body and straight and somewhat triangular wings, which are evident in flight. The white leading edge to the upper side of the wing is distinctive in all ages, although it is more muted in younger birds, when they retain some black edges to the outermost primaries. The wings of adult birds, when seen from below, are all white with a narrow, dark trailing edge to the outer primaries, similar to the trailing edge seen on sterna terns. Bonaparte's Gulls' wings also show a trace of translucency that is absent on the larger gulls. From below, both the underwing coverts and the flight feathers appear pale white, lacking the slightly darker flight feathers seen in many medium- and large-sized gulls.

First-Year Plumage

First-year Bonaparte's Gulls are distinguished from adults by the blackish- or brownish-centered tertials, a tannish wash to the upper-wing coverts, and narrow black tailband. Basically, first-winter Bonaparte's Gulls have adultlike bodies and juvenile wings and tails, with a narrow black tailband; dark-centered tertials; and brownish-black wash to the lesser coverts. The juvenile lesser coverts and tailband are retained into the first summer. On perched birds, the dark lesser coverts contrast with the pale-gray median and greater coverts. First-summer Bonaparte's Gulls can appear extremely bleached and worn. They also have a variable head pattern, with some birds appearing similar to winter adults and others attaining a partial hood.

First-year Bonaparte's Gulls are distinctive in flight, since the wing has a brown ulnar bar, mostly dark outer primary coverts, and dark outer webs to the outermost primaries, which combine to give first-year birds a characteristic M pattern across the mantle and extended wings in flight. However, this mark is not as dark and wide as on the immature of several other gull species such as Little Gull and Black-Legged Kittiwake. First-year Bonaparte's Gulls have the same white leading edge to the upper wing that adult birds have, although it is less prominent due to the dark primary coverts and the dark outer webs of the outermost primaries. They also have a narrow brownish-black border to the entire trailing edge of the wings. This mark is visible from above and below. Combined with the M pattern on the upper wings, this narrow trailing edge to the wing serves to make the upper surface appear pale gray overall, framed in a dark border.

Adult Plumage

Adult Bonaparte's Gulls have a black hood in breeding plumage, with narrow white eye crescents above and below each eye. In winter plumage, adult birds retain only a dark ear spot on an otherwise predominately white head. The mantle is a pale gray, sometimes with a bluish tint and always significantly paler than Laughing Gulls and perhaps a shade darker than Ring-Billed Gulls. The white wedge on the upper side of the wing is a distinctive mark that is visible from a great distance on flying birds. Unlike the other small gulls with which it sometimes occurs (Little and Black-Headed), Bonaparte's Gulls have a clean, white underwing, with only a narrow, black trailing edge to the primaries. The bill is straight and all black and the legs are reddish orange. Many winter plumage adults show a small black crescent in front of the eye. Although this mark is usually visible only at close range, it often makes the black eye appear slightly larger within the whitish face and head. Also, winter plumage adult Bonaparte's Gulls have a grayish wash on the hind neck and sides of the breast, which causes the mostly white head to stand out even more prominently. Some second-year birds may retain traces of black or brown in the tail, primary coverts, or tertials.

Size

Bonaparte's Gulls average between 12.3 and 13.8 inches in length and have a wingspan of 29.5 to 35.4 inches. They are the smallest of the regularly occurring gulls in most of North America, smaller than Franklin's, Mew, and Laughing Gulls. Bonaparte's Gulls are comparable in size to the much less frequently seen Sabine's Gull. When standing, it shows a plump body and short legs. Adult males weigh an average of 7.8 ounces, while adult females average 7.1 ounces.

Notice how early this Bonaparte's Gull has acquired its first-winter (as opposed to juvenal) plumage, with extensive gray on the mantle and wing coverts. Eastern Neck National Wildlife Refuge, Maryland, October 22, 2017.

The dark trailing edge to the wing and faint but distinct M pattern on the upper wing is evident on this first-winter Bonaparte's Gull. Assateague Island National Seashore, Maryland, November 16, 2014.

A first-winter Bonaparte's Gull with fairly heavily marked lesser coverts forages in a tidal marsh. Jug Bay, Maryland, April 14, 2016.

This is a darker, more heavily marked first-winter Bonaparte's Gull. Back River, Maryland, April 19, 2017.

Even at a distance, the distinctive upper-wing pattern of a first-winter Bonaparte's Gull is evident, with the pale wing "framed in black." Assateague National Seashore, Maryland, November 11, 2017.

This first-spring Bonaparte's Gull shows new feathers on the mantle and scapulars, which contrast with the worn tertials and wing coverts. Fort Smallwood Park, Maryland, April 12, 2014.

First-winter Bonaparte's Gull. Back River, Maryland, April 25, 2015.

The wing on this first-winter Bonaparte's Gull appears pale gray, framed by a narrow brownish-black margin. Assateague National Seashore, Maryland, November 16, 2014.

A first-winter Bonaparte's Gull rests in a marsh along the Patuxent River. Jug Bay, Maryland, April 14, 2016.

An adult Bonaparte's Gull gracefully picks prey items from the water's surface. Notice the clean, white underwing with the black trailing edge to the primaries. Back River, Maryland, March 28, 2014.

Note the white wedge on the leading edge of the upper wing and the black trailing edge to the primaries on this winter-plumage adult Bonaparte's Gull. Assateague National Seashore, Maryland, November 16, 2014.

This winter-plumage adult Bonaparte's Gull shows the black ear spot and vague black crescent in front of the eye. A bluish tint to the upperparts is also apparent. Sandy Point State Park, Maryland, December 15, 2013.

Two adult Bonaparte's Gulls, including a full adult (*back right*) with an adult still acquiring its full hood (*front center*). Back River, Maryland, April 25, 2015.

An adult Bonaparte's Gull on takeoff from the water. This bird is molting into breeding plumage. Back River, Maryland, March 30, 2013.

An adult Bonaparte's Gull in winter plumage. Port Deposit, Maryland, March 23, 2013.

An adult Bonaparte's Gull just starting to molt into breeding plumage. Back River, Maryland, March 25, 2017.

A vocalizing adult Bonaparte's Gull. Back River, Maryland, March 25, 2017.

An adult Bonaparte's Gull molting into breeding plumage. Port Deposit, Maryland, March 23, 2013.

An adult Bonaparte's Gull in mostly breeding plumage. Fort Smallwood, Maryland, April 12, 2014.

This adult Bonaparte's Gull shows the distinctive pattern of the upper wing in flight. Ocean City Inlet, Maryland, April 5, 2014.

This beautiful adult Bonaparte's Gull has fully acquired its black hood. Back River, Maryland, April 19, 2017.

Adult Bonaparte's Gull in mostly breeding plumage in flight. Back River, Maryland, April 25, 2015.

LAUGHING GULL

Background

Laughing Gulls are one of the symbolic species of the coastal Southeast, well known to beachgoers by the black hood, dark mantle, engaging behavior, and far-reaching, laughing cry. One of the few gulls best known by their vocalizations, their rambunctious call can be heard on coastal barrier islands as they forage on sandy beaches, fly over a nearby coastal marsh, or glide over near-shore ocean waters. As with most other gull species, Laughing Gulls are quite adaptable and approachable. They are a common sight at fast-food restaurant parking lots, landfills, and inland ponds on the coastal plain. They often gather in extremely large numbers, their nasal, laughing call making incessant background noise.

Even gulls circling so high above that they are barely specks in the sky can be well heard far below. Pete Dunne summarizes their call best as a "loud, strident, nasal, two-syllable belly laugh" (Dunne 2006). That Laughing Gulls are capable of belting out such a raucous vocalization in a seemingly endless stream is impressive. I have heard what I thought was a sizable flock of Laughing Gulls above, only to look up and see that all the commotion was being caused by a lone bird, seemingly belting out a maniacal cry just to hear the sound of its own voice.

This impression is only heightened when a large flock of Laughing Gulls get worked up (which happens often) and emit their cry at an especially strident, discordant, and fevered pitch. Once while kayaking along the Patuxent River on Maryland's coastal plain, I passed close to a large mudflat where hundreds (if not thousands) of Laughing Gulls were resting. Soon I was surrounded by these cantankerous birds as they stood on the nearby flats, floated on the water surrounding me, and flew directly above and around my small boat. The noise they generated can only be described as deafening, and their collective cries and calls could be heard long after I had floated out of sight.

Laughing Gulls are medium-sized gulls that seem partial to warm weather. Unlike many gulls, which are seen in the greatest numbers during the cold winter months at frozen ponds and frigid coastal inlets, Laughing Gulls retreat from the northeastern and mid-Atlantic states with the onset of winter weather.

They are noted kleptoparasites and have long been documented pirating food from terns, pelicans, and other birds. Audubon, Bent, and other observers have reported that Laughing Gulls sometimes land on the head of a Brown Pelican and take food from its beak. Audubon provided the following narrative of this process:

They were all busily engaged on wing, hovering here and there around the Brown Pelicans, intent on watching their plunges into the water, and all clamorously teasing their best benefactors. As with broadly extended pouch and lower mandible, the Pelican went down headlong, so gracefully followed the gay rosy-breasted Gull, which, on the brown bird's emerging, alighted nimbly on its very head, and with a gentle stoop instantly snatched from the mouth of its purveyor the glittering fry that moment entrapped! Is this not quite strange, reader? Aye, truly it is. The sight of these manoeuvres rendered me almost frantic with delight. At times, several Gulls would attempt to alight themselves on the head of the same Pelican, but finding this impossible, they would at once sustain themselves around it, and snatch every morsel that escaped from the pouch of the great bird. So very dexterous were some of the Gulls at this sport, that I have seen them actually catch a little fish as it leaped from the yet partially open bill of the Pelican. (Audubon 1844)

Biologist William Baldwin observed that the pelicans "never show anything but stoic calm during this procedure" (Baldwin 1946). However, a more recent study has indicated that the pelicans frequently take flight as soon as the water drains from their pouch, in order to avoid the surrounding gulls. And at times, the pelicans behave aggressively, clearly irritated by the gulls' behavior. Several times, the researchers saw a pelican use its bill to grab a gull and toss it aside.

Despite such retribution, the researchers concluded that kleptoparasitism was beneficial for the gulls (Schnell et al. 1983). Gulls tend to be more aggressive in their pirating when part of a group, and the rate of success increases when more gulls are involved in the chase. Although many species of gulls exhibit this behavior, Laughing Gulls seem to display it more than most, perhaps owing to their aerodynamic build and especially quick, agile flight. A dark juvenile Laughing Gull displaying this aggressive behavior is sometimes even mistakenly identified as a jaeger (the proverbial "laughing" jaeger)! Although most other kleptoparasites victimize only other species, gulls are notorious for harassing their own kind, often over the most marginal scrap of food.

Laughing Gulls use a variety of habitats for breeding. In the Southeast, they breed on sandy beaches. Although secluded areas such as barrier islands are chosen, breeding can also occur in proximity to human activity. Farther north, Laughing Gulls also use marshes and, in some cases, rocky islands for nesting. Laughing Gulls demonstrate a pattern of postbreeding dispersal, appearing at inland lakes and up coastal rivers and bays. This dispersal begins in late July and continues into the fall. Although as a short-distance migrant they are less prone to appear out of their range than other gulls, they have been known to breed at the Salton

Sea and are casual to the Pacific coast. They are annual in Great Britain, and an off-course Laughing Gull was even recorded at the cooling pond of a power station in Malaysia, a first Asian record! The most out-of-range Laughing Gull that I have seen was in Hawaii, where the species is annual in low numbers. This wayward gull provided a familiar reminder of the mid-Atlantic region as I birded many miles from my Maryland home.

Structure and Field Marks

Laughing Gulls are fairly distinctive in all plumages. The most characteristic structural feature is the long, "drooping" bill, which is a reliable way of separating the species from Franklin's Gulls and other smaller hooded gulls. The long bill, with the tip angled slightly downward, is decidedly different from the short, straight bill of Franklin's Gulls and the thinner, pencil-shaped bills of Bonaparte's Gulls and Little Gulls. Other structural features that are useful for separating Laughing Gulls from Franklin's Gulls are head and body shape. Laughing Gulls have a noticeably more elongated head with a more gradually sloping forehead than Franklin's Gulls. Resting Laughing Gulls also appear to have a slightly bulkier and elongated body than the more compact Franklin's Gull. The rounded head; shorter, straight bill; and compact body of Franklin's Gulls combine to give them a more dovelike appearance. In flight, Laughing Gulls appear especially lanky and have long wings that are slightly bent at the wrist. The body of Laughing Gulls is attenuated toward the rear, and they lack the pot-bellied appearance of many larger species, or even the fuller-bodied appearance of Ring-Billed Gulls.

Juvenile Plumage

Laughing Gulls have an attractive, if briefly held, juvenile plumage. Juveniles are warm, rich brown overall, except for the white belly and darker brownish-black primaries. The mantle, upper-wing coverts, and tertials are edged with white, giving the bird an attractive "scaled" appearance. Although the head and face have a brown base color, the area immediately around the base of the bill is white. In some regards this plumage is reminiscent of a juvenile Sabine's Gull with its warm-brown ground color and paler feather edges above, although it lacks the bold wing pattern in flight. Also, juvenile Laughing Gulls have a brownish-gray wash to the breast, while juvenile Sabine's Gulls have a clean white breast. The white belly is extremely noticeable on flying juvenile Laughing Gulls, since it contrasts strongly with the brown breast, head, and wings. The underwing is a mixture of brown and white and can include a brown line running from the rear of the wing at the body, near the axillaries, to the front of the wing at the "wrist." A broad, black tailband extends across the entire tail, including the outermost tail feathers, and contrasts with the white rump and base of the tail.

First-Year Plumage

Young Laughing Gulls quickly begin to acquire the gray mantle typical of first-winter gulls. Initially this is seen as a few gray feathers sprinkled on the brown upperparts, but the gray mantle comes in quickly and is seen on most late-fall or first-winter birds. The coverts fade with wear to a pale grayish tan, rather than the warm brown seen in juvenile birds. The head is white with a variable gray wash and dark streaking. Birds often show darker streaking around and behind the eye, forming a dark mask on the face. First-winter Laughing Gulls retain a grayish wash on the back of the head, nape, and flanks. In flight, first-winter Laughing Gulls are an interesting mix of a gray mantle, brown upper-wing coverts, white rump, and blackish primaries, primary coverts, and tailband. By their first summer, many Laughing Gulls obtain a partial hood, although usually heavily flecked with white, while others retain a mostly white winter head pattern.

Second-Year Plumage

Second-winter Laughing Gulls are usually fully gray above and in this regard are similar to adults. However, at this age Laughing Gulls show more extensive black in the wingtips while in flight. This can extend almost to the wrist or alula. Birds can also retain some dark feathers in the secondaries. At this age the folded wing shows little or no white in the primary tips. Other points of difference include a gray wash to the nape, flanks, and breast. This gray wash makes the birds appear a little messier, lacking the clear delineation of gray and white seen on adult Laughing Gulls. Approximately half of all second-year Laughing Gulls retain some black in the tail. There is much variation in the head pattern on second-year breeding-plumage Laughing Gulls, with some obtaining a full hood, others having a hood heavily flecked with white, and some retaining a more winter-like head pattern.

Adult Plumage

Laughing Gulls are attractive and distinctive birds, acquiring a full black hood with prominent white "arches" or crescents above and below the eyes, resembling a partial eye ring not meeting on the sides. During the peak of breeding season (May and June), birds can attain a deep-red or maroon bill. The legs usually appear black, but they can have a tinge of deep red during high breeding season. Adult birds in breeding plumage show small white tips on the primaries, but these are often lost through wear by summer or early fall. There is some variability in the amount of white in the primaries on adult birds, with most having very little.

The upperparts are a medium dark, slate gray, noticeably darker than either Ring-Billed or Herring Gulls. In flight, the wingtips appear all black, blending subtly into the slate-gray wings. The contrast between the black in the primaries and the dark gray of the wing is not as noticeable as in paler-winged gulls. Seen from below, Laughing Gulls have dark flight feathers (primaries and secondaries) that contrast with the white underwing coverts.

Laughing Gulls begin to lose their hood by mid-August or September. The winter head pattern has heavy streaking behind the eye (often appearing as a dusky mask), with less dense streaking on the crown and rear of the head. The fall head pattern is notoriously variable, and some birds retain a significant partial hood well into the fall. These birds are distinguishable from Franklin's Gulls by the long, downturned bill; dark flight feathers; and limited white in the primary tips. The body of nonbreeding adult Laughing Gulls is white, sometimes with a pale grayish wash to the hind neck and breast sides.

Size

Laughing Gulls are medium sized. Perched birds are slightly smaller than Ring-Billed Gulls, noticeably longer winged, and less bulky. Length ranges from 14.2 to 16.1 inches, with the wingspan ranging from 37.4 to 47.2 inches. Adult male Laughing Gulls weigh between 9 and 13 ounces, with an exceptional individual weighing 14.1 ounces. Adult females weigh 8 to 10 ounces.

A juvenile Laughing Gull perches on a piling along the Patuxent River. Eagle Harbor, Maryland, August 10, 2008.

Juvenile Laughing Gulls are quite attractive, with their sandy-brown plumage and pale feather edges. Sandy Point State Park, Maryland, September 25, 2013.

This first-fall Laughing Gull is beginning to acquire some gray feathers on the mantle. Sandy Point State Park, Maryland, September 24, 2016.

Juvenile Laughing Gull. Jug Bay, Maryland, August 10, 2017.

The white belly contrasts with the rest of the plumage on flying juvenile Laughing Gulls. Schoolhouse Pond, Maryland, August 2, 2017.

A juvenile/first-fall Laughing Gull in flight. The mottled underwing, dark coverts and axillaries, and dark head and upper breast contrast with white belly. Lewes, Delaware, August 15, 2008.

The pattern of the extended wing on a first-fall Laughing Gull. The blackish primaries and secondaries contrast with the pale-brown wing coverts. Sandy Point State Park, Maryland, September 24, 2016.

A fairly dark, heavily marked first-fall Laughing Gull. Sandy Point State Park, Maryland, September 22, 2016.

A first-fall Laughing Gull with wings spread. Note the black tail bar, dark primaries and secondaries, and contrasting lighter-brown wing coverts. Sandy Point State Park, Maryland, September 24, 2016.

A first-fall Laughing Gull with incoming gray feathers on the mantle. Schoolhouse Pond, Maryland, October 15, 2014.

This second-winter Laughing Gull's gray nape and upper breast and mostly black primary tips distinguish it from an adult. The all-gray upperparts separate it from a full-winter Laughing Gull. Sandy Point State Park, Maryland, September 17, 2017.

Laughing Gulls of different ages. The left two birds are first-winter gulls, the middle two birds are adults, and the rightmost bird is a second-winter Laughing Gull. Sandy Point State Park, Maryland, September 21, 2013.

The grayish wash to the nape, breast, and flanks is typical of a second-winter Laughing Gull. Sandy Point State Park, Maryland, September 17, 2017.

A second-winter Laughing Gull in flight. Note the small amount of black in the tail and the extensive black on the primaries, primary coverts, and alula. Sandy Point State Park, Maryland, September 24, 2016.

An adult Laughing Gull in breeding plumage is a stunning bird. Jug Bay, Maryland, April 23, 2010.

This breeding-plumage Laughing Gull displays the full black hood, white eye crescents, and dark-reddish tone on the bill and legs. Riley Roberts Road, Maryland, May 18, 2020.

An adult Laughing Gull (*at right*) is shown in flight with a first-year Bonaparte's Gull. The larger size of the Laughing Gull is evident, as are the dark upperparts and extensive black on the primaries of the extended wings. Ocean City Inlet, Maryland, May 19, 2020.

Adult breeding-plumage Laughing Gull. Jug Bay, Maryland, April 2012.

Adult winter-plumage Laughing Gull. Sandy Point State Park, Maryland, September 30, 2017.

Laughing Gulls can gather in massive flocks during the fall. Over 2,000 Laughing Gulls were counted in this flock—only part of it was captured here. Depot Pond, Maryland, November 11, 2010.

Laughing Gulls fly overhead. The dark upperparts and dusky underwing accentuate the black hood and contrast with the white belly. Schoolhouse Pond, Maryland, April 18, 2016.

FRANKLIN'S GULL

Background

Franklin's Gulls are a medium-sized gull of the north-central United States and south-central Canada. While many people associate gulls with the beach, Franklin's Gulls are common breeders on freshwater lakes and marshes in the northern plains. This gull has been called the "prairie dove" due to its propensity to visit agriculture fields to forage for insects stirred up by the plow. Arthur Cleveland Bent quotes a Mr. H. K. Job's colorful description of their return to the prairie each spring:

In late April or early May, when the rich black soil has thawed to the surface, the settler of the northwest prairies goes forth to plow.... Then comes a day of warm sunshine, when, as he plows, he is followed by a troop of handsome birds which some might mistake for white doves. Without sign of fear they alight in the furrow close behind him, and, with graceful carriage, hurry about to pick up the worms and grubs which the plow has just unearthed. Often have I watched the plowman and his snowy retinue, and it appeals to me as one of the prettiest sights which the wide prairies can afford. No wonder that the lonely settler likes the dainty, familiar bird, and in friendly spirit calls it his "prairie pigeon" or "prairie dove." (Bent 1921)

Franklin's Gulls can gather in staggering numbers at favored breeding colonies or in migration. Watching a large group of these pretty gulls bob on a prairie pothole or gliding over an endless sweep of prairie is a memorable sight. These attractive gulls enliven the midwestern countryside and provide avian diversity to our expansive prairies. In breeding plumage, they can acquire a deep rosy blush to the underparts, which led to its earlier name of Franklin's Rosy Gull. Franklin's Gulls usually nest over water on constructed floating mats of vegetation, muskrat houses, or other debris from inland marshes and lakes (Burger and Gochfeld 2020).

In *Life Histories of North American Gulls and Terns*, Bent poignantly portrays a breeding colony of this social species:

A breeding colony of Franklin's Gulls is one of the most spectacular, most interesting, and most beautiful sights in the realm of North American ornithology. The man who has never seen one has something yet to live for—a sight which once seen is never to be forgotten. No written words can convey any adequate idea of the beautiful picture presented by countless thousands of exquisite birds, of such delicate hues and gentle habits, in all the activities of their closely populated communities. (Bent 1921)

Franklin's Gulls are one of the few truly long-distance migrants among North American gulls, flying from their breeding grounds in the northern plains to winter along the Pacific coast of South America. However, they are quite rare away from their breeding grounds and migratory routes, and so it is a real treat for birders when one of these gulls shows up on either coast. Although they largely migrate through the central part of North America, they have even been documented migrating over alpine tundra and high mountain passes in the Rockies.

Due to their long-distance migration, they are prone to be driven to unexpected places by strong storms sweeping across the plains and the Midwest. In extremely rare instances, storm systems and migration will coincide to produce a major fallout of Franklin's Gulls beyond their usual migratory range. Franklin's Gulls have been recorded as far north as the Pribilof and Aleutian Islands. Franklin's Gulls are annual in Europe and have occurred across the globe, with sighting in Africa, Australia, and East Asia.

I've been fortunate to see Franklin's Gulls in large numbers on the prairie potholes of South Dakota. There is something sublime about being surrounded by waving grassland as far as the eye can see, and coming upon Franklin's Gulls in a small lake gleaming in the late-afternoon sun. Their allure illustrates why early settlers were so fond of this familiar prairie companion.

My Maryland sightings have usually consisted of a lone Franklin's Gull mixed in with a horde of superficially similar Laughing Gulls. These sightings provided side-by-side comparisons of the two species and are perhaps the best way to gauge the subtle differences under field conditions, when the uniqueness of each species is on full display.

Structures and Field Marks

Although superficially similar to Laughing Gulls, Franklin's Gulls are quite distinct in proportions and structure. Franklin's Gulls are decidedly more compact, lacking the long wings and tail, long bill, and generally lanky appearance of the larger bird. This compact form is best seen when the bird is in flight. The sum of these features tends to make the Franklin's Gull seem more like the smaller Little Gull, as opposed to the more lumbering Laughing Gull. The bird flies on quick and at times erratic wingbeats and can look almost mothlike as it forages for insects over marshes or wet fields.

First-Year Plumage

Franklin's Gulls are unique in that they have two complete molts each year. One result of this is that they tend to always have a fresh plumage, whereas similarly aged Laughing Gulls can appear heavily worn and bleached, particularly in mid- to late summer.

Overall, first-winter Franklin's Gulls are cleanly marked with a plumage of black, gray, and white, lacking the brown wing coverts and grayish-brown wash to the nape, neck, and underparts seen on Laughing Gulls. Franklin's Gulls have a clean white body and gray wing coverts. First-winter Franklin's Gulls show a bold half hood that is darker and more well defined along the edges than that of any immature Laughing Gull. The hood is further accentuated by a clean white nape. First-year Franklin's Gulls also have bold white crescents above and below the eye, as though they were wearing white goggles. This half hood, retained during the fall and winter, encompasses the area around the eye, highlighting the wide white crescents. First-winter Franklin's Gulls have a clean white underwing, including the flight feathers. This feature is best seen on flying gulls and is quite different from the mottled brown and white underwing of immature Laughing Gulls. First-winter Franklin's Gulls show a black tailband that contrasts with the white rump and does not extend to the outermost tail feathers.

Second-Year Plumage

At this age, Franklin's Gulls most closely resemble Laughing Gulls, owing to the more extensive black in the wingtips. Observers must rely even more heavily on the compact shape of the body and the thin, straight bill of Franklin's Gulls. However, some plumage features are still visible that distinguish the two species. Second-winter Franklin's Gulls have white flight feathers on the underside of the wings, while adult and second-year Laughing Gulls have dark flight feathers. The clean white underwings can be clearly seen in flight, even at a great distance. Second-winter Franklin's Gulls also have much-bolder white eye crescents and a bright, clean, white nape and body. Second-year Laughing Gulls are often washed with gray in these areas.

Adult Plumage

The breeding plumage of adult Franklin's Gulls consists of a bold black hood, prominent white eye crescents, and a medium-dark-gray mantle. They are noticeably white in the folded wingtips and have a compact build, lacking the long bill and wings of the Laughing Gull. Other field marks distinguish adult Franklin's Gulls both in breeding and nonbreeding plumage. The bold eye crescents of Franklin's Gulls almost join at the rear of the eye.

The black in the wingtips is much more restricted to the tip of the primaries in Franklin's Gulls than it is in Laughing Gulls. This difference is accentuated in Franklin's Gulls by the presence of white primary tips and a white medial band, which highlights the black in the primaries. Laughing Gulls lack this feature and usually give the appearance of having black wingtips that blend evenly into the dark flight feathers. These field marks make a lone Franklin's Gull easier to pick out of a horde of Laughing Gull in flight.

Size

Franklin's Gulls are slightly smaller and structured differently than the more coastal Laughing Gull. Franklin's Gulls average 13.3 to 15.0 inches long and have a wingspan between 33.5 and 36.2 inches. At rest, they appear to have shorter legs, although this might be owing to the fuller, more rounded belly. Birds from Minnesota ranged from 7.8 to 11.8 ounces in weight, with males averaging 9.9 ounces and females averaging 9.8 ounces.

This first-winter Franklin's Gull shows the half hood, gray mantle, and brownish-gray wing coverts. The white underparts and nape are in contrast to first-winter Laughing Gulls, which have a grayish wash to the underparts and nape. Ocean City Inlet, Maryland, November 13, 2015.

Notice the smaller bill and size of the Franklin's Gull at left, compared to the two Laughing Gulls on the right. The thinner, more petite bill is also evident on the Franklin's Gull. Dorchester County, Maryland, October 22, 2006. *Photo by Bill Hubick*

Note the clean white underparts on this first-winter Franklin's Gull. Ocean City Inlet, Maryland, November 13, 2015.

In flight, Franklin's Gulls are noticeably compact, with a small, plump body and short wings and tail. In many ways, flying Franklin's Gulls are more reminiscent of Little Gulls than the larger, lankier Laughing Gulls. Ocean City Inlet, Maryland, November 13, 2015.

Note the clean white rump and tail with a narrow black band on this first-winter Franklin's Gull. The black does not cover the two outermost tail feathers (or rectrices). Ocean City Inlet, Maryland, November 13, 2015.

This first-summer Franklin's Gull shows a round head and short, straight bill, which is quite different than the long, drooping bill of Laughing Gulls. Loss Lake, South Dakota, June 16, 2016.

Franklin's Gulls have limited black in the wingtips and a pale (whitish) underwing when compared to similarly aged Laughing Gulls. Lake Andes National Wildlife Refuge, South Dakota, June 17, 2016.

Note the blackish "half hood" of this nonbreeding adult Franklin's Gull. The hood contrasts strongly with the thick white crescents above and below the eye and the white nape. Concon, Chile, in December. *Photo by Rick and Nora Bowers / VIREO*

The black hood, bold white spots in the primary tips, and thin, straight bill are seen on this breeding adult Franklin's Gull. Los Angeles, California, in April. *Photo by J. Fuhrman / VIREO*

The limited and well-demarcated black in the wingtips is bordered by white on this flying adult Franklin's Gull. In flight, adult Franklin's Gulls show significantly less black in the wingtips than Laughing Gulls. Bowdoin National Wildlife Refuge, Montana, in June. *Photo by Greg Lasley / VIREO*

SABINE'S GULL

Background

A beautiful and unique small gull, Sabine's Gulls have a striking plumage at all ages and are particularly arresting in flight, when their three-tone wing pattern can be seen. The wing pattern is perhaps best described as a tricolored mix of triangles and wedges. Adults are black, white, and gray, and juvenile birds are black, white, and light brown.

This pattern is visible at great distances on flying birds. Several years ago, I saw a group of Sabine's Gulls in flight over the Bering Sea. They were beyond the distance where most gulls can be safely identified, yet the conspicuous wing pattern was easily visible.

Sabine's Gulls were not described to science until 1819, the year after Captain Edward Sabine discovered them on small islands in Melville Bay during explorer John Ross's first expedition along the west coast of Greenland. Both the islands and the gull were named after their discoverer (Blomqvist and Elander 1981). Originally, this bird was called a Fork-Tailed Gull—an apt name, because it is the only regularly occurring North American species of gull that has a forked tail.

As with other gulls of the High Arctic, much of what was initially reported about Sabine's Gulls was discovered during nineteenth-century expeditions in the Far North. Sir John Richardson provided the following description of the initial discovery of the species in 1818:

This interesting species of gull was discovered by Captain Edward Sabine. It was first seen on the 25th of July at its breeding station on some low rocky islands lying off the west coast of Greenland, associated in considerable numbers with the Arctic Tern, the nests of both birds being intermingled. It is analogous to the tern not only in its forked tail, and in its choice of a breeding place, but also in the boldness which it displays in the protection of its young. (Audubon 1844)

Sabine's Gulls have several behaviors more reminiscent of terns or shorebirds than other gulls. In their forked tails and manner of flight, they closely resemble terns. Sabine's Gulls are known to use a distraction display to draw potential threats from their nest, a ploy Killdeer are famous for. At low tide, Sabine's Gulls sometimes run about on mudflats, probing in the substrate for prey, behavior reminiscent of plovers. At other times, they spin on the surface of ponds like a phalarope, stirring up prey in the water below.

Like terns, during courtship males bring females whole prey items, rather than regurgitated food as other gull species do. Their young are remarkably quick to develop, perhaps an adaptation to nesting at or near the Arctic. They grow at approximately twice the rate of other similarly sized gulls, doubling their body mass within the first three days after hatching. Chicks leave the nest as soon as they are dry, and at that point they are able to run, swim, or hide from potential threats. Sabine's Gulls breed in marshy areas or the edges of small ponds in the tundra of the Arctic and can frequently be found with Arctic Terns and Long-Tailed Jaegers at this time of year.

They are agile and maneuverable in flight, flying with continuous wingbeats and making frequent banks and turns. When I saw a juvenile Sabine's Gull in flight over the Potomac River in Washington, DC, it was acrobatically coursing back and forth over the river, picking prey from the water's surface and sallying nimbly along the shore. At other times it rested on the hydrilla flats that cover the shallows of the river in late summer, searching for food. Its prominent wing pattern was seen in all its glory as the gull glided past my kayak, with the Washington Monument and the jets at National Airport serving as an impressive backdrop for this out-of-place gull.

Arthur Cleveland Bent includes the following observation from Mr. F. S. Hershey:

On the wing this species bears a closer resemblance to a tern than it does to other gulls. It flies with continuous wing beats, seldom, so far as I have observed, sailing, and its flight is direct though not straight. It may swoop to the earth to pick up a bit of food or hover a moment if something attracts its attention, but only for an instant does it delay before resuming its onward flight in the direction it was going. (Bent 1921)

Sabine's Gulls are truly the champion long-distance migrants among gulls, visiting the Arctic only to breed and then undertaking an extended migration over the open ocean to their wintering grounds in the Southern Hemisphere. They are similar to Arctic Terns in this regard and have an annual round-trip migration of approximately 15,000 miles.

Outside the breeding season, Sabine's Gulls are regularly seen off the West Coast of the US during August and September, when significant numbers can be observed migrating well offshore. They are seen much less frequently elsewhere in the Lower 48 states, where they are casual to very rare migrants off the East Coast and casual migrants in the interior of North America, with most inland migrants being seen in the fall. It is a very fortunate birder who sees one of these beautiful gulls during an East Coast pelagic. However, perhaps owing to their long-distance migration, they can sometimes be found well outside their normal range and migration route.

Structure and Field Marks

Sabine's Gulls have a highly visible and diagnostic tricolored wing pattern at all ages, which can be seen from great distances on flying gulls. The pattern of the wings is most visible from above, but a paler, washed-out version can also be discerned from below. This is the only regularly occurring gull in North America that has a forked tail.

First-Year Plumage

Juvenile Sabine's Gulls are a warm brownish gray on the upperparts, hindneck, and crown, appearing uniform brown at a distance when perched. Close views reveal the pale feather edges on the upperparts, which give them a distinctive scaly pattern. With their soft brown back and nape, small head, and petite bill, first-year birds have a gentle, winsome appearance. The brown of the upperparts extends onto the sides of the neck, but the underparts are a clean white, including the breast. The lower face around the bill is also white. First-winter birds appear superficially similar to juvenile Laughing Gulls, even down to the pale feather edges on the upperparts. However, the latter can be distinguished by their larger size, longer drooping bill, and gray (not white) breast. Also, the upper side of Laughing Gull wings are brown in flight, lacking the bold pattern of brown, white, and black of similarly aged Sabine's Gulls. The wing pattern on juvenile Sabine's Gulls consists of the black outer primaries, a white "triangle" on the trailing edge of the upper wing, and brownish-gray upper-wing coverts and back. The tail has a narrow black distal band. In their first winter, Sabine's Gulls acquire gray on the mantle and scapulars. They also have a white head with diffuse streaking on the nape and variable dark markings on the ear coverts.

Adult Plumage

Sabine's Gulls are especially elegant as breeding adults, with their medium-gray mantle, dark hood, unique tricolored wing pattern, and yellow-tipped black bill. Their slaty-gray hood has a darker, black border, which is noticeable with good views. Also, at close range the red orbital ring is visible around the eye, which adds to its striking beauty. The thin, delicate bill is black with a bright-yellow tip. Adults show a large amount of white on the folded primaries. However, it is their bold black, white, and gray wing pattern that sets them apart from other gulls in flight. This pattern is composed of the black outer primaries, white "triangle" on the trailing edge of the upper wing, and gray wing coverts. Adult Sabine's Gulls are exquisite birds of uncommon grace, not soon forgotten by those who see them. Fortunately for birders who reside in the Lower 48, most Sabine's Gulls do not molt into their full winter plumage until after arriving on their wintering grounds, which means that those lucky enough to see an adult during the fall migration can appreciate their full breeding-plumage glory. Features indicating a second-year Sabine's Gull that has not achieved full adult plumage include browner outermost primaries lacking the bold white tips, upperparts washed with brown, and a duller and less distinct yellow tip to the bill. Some birds also retain dusky fringes to the tail feathers and dark marks on the tertials.

Size

These gulls are very small —only the Little Gull is significantly smaller. Sabine's Gulls are similar in size to the Ross's Gull and slightly smaller than Bonaparte's Gulls.

In Alaska, males range in weight from 6.7 to 7.5 ounces, while females range from 5.6 to 6.7 ounces. Sabine's Gulls average 10.6 to 13.8 inches long and have an average wingspan between 35.4 and 39.4 inches.

Juvenile Sabine's Gull with a thin, straight black bill and scaled pattern to the upperparts. Poplar Island, Maryland, September 17, 2017. *Photo courtesy of Tim Carney and the Maryland Environmental Service / Maryland Department of Transportation / Maryland Port Administration*

Note the white face and throat on this juvenile/first-winter Sabine's Gull. Poplar Island, Maryland, September 17, 2017. *Photo courtesy of Tim Carney and the Maryland Environmental Service / Maryland Department of Transportation / Maryland Port Administration*

A juvenile/first-fall Sabine's Gull viewed in flight. The bold pattern of the upper wing and the more muted pattern of the underwing can be seen. Alexandria, Virginia, September 7, 2017.

Another view of the juvenile/first-fall Sabine's Gull. Note the bold black primaries, white "triangle" on the trailing edge of the wing, and gray smudging on the nape. Alexandria, Virginia, September 7, 2017.

The distinctive wing pattern, small black bill, and narrow tailband are evident on this juvenile/first-fall Sabine's Gull. Alexandria, Virginia, September 7, 2017.

Field marks rarely get more distinctive than the wing pattern on the Sabine's Gull. The subtle scales on the mantle can also be seen. Alexandria, Virginia, September 7, 2017.

The slaty-gray hood has a dark border, and the yellow-tipped bill is striking. Triadelphia Reservoir, Maryland, September 8, 2012.

An adult Sabine's Gull spreads its wings, showing the distinctive wing pattern and the slightly forked tail as it prepares to fly. Mispillion Harbor Reserve, Delaware, May 23, 2012.

This beautiful adult Sabine's Gull forages on a beach along the Delaware Bay. The red eye ring, bold white wingtips, and black border to the slate-gray hood are evident. Dupont Nature Center, Delaware, May 24, 2012. *Photo by Jeff Shenot*

An adult Sabine's Gull forages along a Delaware Bay beach with turnstones, sandpipers, and Laughing Gulls. The paler mantle, bold white wingtips, and yellow-tipped bill set the Sabine's Gull apart from the surrounding Laughing Gulls. Dupont Nature Center, Delaware, May 24, 2012. *Photo by Jeff Shenot*

Nonbreeding adult/ subadult Sabine's Gulls on the Pacific Ocean. Channel Islands, California, October 1, 2011. *Photo by Bill Hubick*

Chapter 2. Large White-Headed Gulls

HERRING GULL

Background

A familiar sight on beaches, Herring Gulls are the most widespread large white-headed gull in North America. In winter, many retreat to the Atlantic, Pacific, and Gulf coasts. However, some Herring Gulls winter in the interior of the continent where there is ice-free water. They are the most numerous large gull across eastern North America, and only slightly less numerous along the West Coast, where they are outnumbered by the larger and more-aggressive Western and Glaucous-Winged Gulls. With their pink legs, pale-gray mantle, black wingtips, and white head and body, Herring Gulls are what most people think of when they think of gulls.

Several subspecies are recognized, some of which may warrant full species status. The so-called American Herring Gull is the focus here (subspecies *smithsonianus*) because it is the only regularly occurring subspecies across most of North America. That said, European Herring Gulls (subspecies *argenteus* and *argentatus*) are occasionally reported in northeastern North America, particularly Newfoundland. And Vega Gulls (subspecies *vegae*) breed in western Alaska.

The Herring Gull has been described as the "epitome of the large white-headed gull complex: variable, adaptable, and complex" (Leukering 2010). Indeed, anyone who has spent time studying a group of Herring Gulls will notice how much they vary in appearance, particularly in their first two or three calendar years. Recent evidence seems to indicate that the American subspecies is distinctive enough from the European subspecies to warrant full species status, and that American Herring Gulls are, in fact, more closely related to a group of North American / Pacific Rim gull species than their European counterpart. Because American Herring Gulls are not as closely related to European Herring Gulls as previously thought, one author has proposed that the American subspecies be named the Smithsonian Gull—"a distinctly American name for a distinctly American Gull" (Leukering 2010).

However, not only are American Herring Gulls distinctive from other subspecies, they vary within their own population. Although these hard-to-quantify differences are to some degree clinal, East Coast adults tend to have a slightly darker-gray mantle than West Coast adults. Some recent studies have found significant differences between adult Herring Gulls at Niagara Falls and Newfoundland. Birds seen in Niagara Falls are smaller overall, with shorter legs, a more rounded head, and a thinner, less robust bill. They also have significantly more black in the wingtips, with limited white in the primaries.

Newfoundland birds, in contrast, are larger and have a heftier build, including a larger bill and barrel chest. They also have much less black in the wingtips and significantly more white in the outermost primaries. This pattern is especially evident on the lower side of the wing, where the black can be restricted to the leading and trailing edges of the outermost primaries (Jonsson and Mactavish 2001). Differences in plumage have also been noted in juvenile/first-year birds: classic dark-chocolate-brown birds predominate in the East, while birds in the Great Lakes region are paler, and West Coast birds are the palest of all, with whitish greater coverts and a white base color to the rump and tail (Olsen and Larsson 2004).

Audubon referred to subspecies *smithsonianus* as the Herring Gull or Silvery Gull. In *Birds of America*, he reported that on an 1833 trip to Nova Scotia, they were nesting not on the beach or other open ground, but high in the branches of fir trees (elsewhere described as pine woods).

I observed that many of the Gulls had alighted on the fir-trees, while a vast number were sailing around, and when we advanced nearer, the former took to wing, abandoning their nests, and all flew about uttering incessant cries. I was greatly surprised to see the nests placed on the branches, some near the top, others about the middle or on the lower parts of the trees, while at the same time there were many on the ground. (Audubon 1844)

A local observer had told Audubon that nesting in trees was a new development in response to egg collectors and other disturbances. One interesting side effect of this disturbance was that "the young which are hatched on the trees or high rocks, do not leave their nest until they are able to fly, while those on the ground run about in less than a week, and hide themselves at the sight of man among the moss and plants, which frequently saves them from being carried off" (Audubon 1844).

Fortunately, Herring Gulls no longer face many of these disturbances; they nest in colonies in natural locations such as beaches, lakeshores, and mudflats. Nests are built in flat, treeless areas that offer good visibility of the surrounding area. Herring Gulls demonstrate a remarkable adaptability in their nesting areas, ranging from Arctic tundra, to lakes in the boreal forests, to city rooftops, to windswept beaches and salt marshes, to offshore islands. This is one of the reasons Herring Gulls are so well known. Arthur Cleveland Bent noted the following colorful description of a nesting colony from the journal of Army major

Ralph Mayer from Great Duck Island, Maine, in 1913:

This is one of the most wonderful sights I have ever witnessed. The air is literally full of gulls. In sight there must be at least 4,000 gulls and all screaming. It is a weird sound. The air is so full of them that it looks like a snowstorm. They are perched on the trees and standing on the ground, where they resemble nothing so much as a national cemetery with its thousands of white stones. (Bent 1921)

Niko Tinbergen wrote about his early trips to a Herring Gull breeding colony in the introduction to his classic book *The Herring Gull's World*. He described what he saw and heard in vivid terms and related how these experiences led him to detailed studies of Herring Gulls later in life.

Through the years of my boyhood watching the life in the large gullery was complete happiness; and I derived a vague but intense satisfaction from just being with the gulls, feeling the sun upon my skin, enjoying the scents of the lovely dune flowers, watching the snow-white birds soaring high up in the blue sky, and assuming, or rather knowing, that they were feeling just as happy as I was. (Tinbergen 1960)

Tinbergen provided additional insights into his early years on the North Sea and his interactions with its most common bird (albeit the European variety). Anyone who has spent time at the seashore, searching through groups of gulls or studying Herring Gulls in particular, is sure to share his sentiments:

I have naturally come under the spell of [the North Sea's] most familiar bird, the sturdy and yet graceful Herring Gull. The beach is simply unthinkable without these ever-present fellow-beachcombers. I have spent many happy days watching them. (Tinbergen 1960)

Because they are so common, Herring Gulls are a good species to learn well. Only when we understand their variation and development are we in a position to identify an out-of-place straggler, such as a "Thayer's" Gull (now a subspecies of Iceland Gull) or a first-year California Gull. Furthermore, when searching through flocks of Herring and Ring-Billed Gulls, sometimes one is fortunate to come across a rare Glaucous or Iceland Gull.

Structure and Field Marks

Herring Gulls are significantly larger than both Ring-Billed and Laughing Gulls. Although four-year Herring Gulls show a bewildering array of plumages depending on time of year and molt, size alone is usually enough to distinguish a lone American Herring Gull from superficially similar Ring-Billed Gulls. Larger both in length and wingspan, Herring Gulls display a proportionally larger and bulkier body and appear more ponderous and full bodied in flight.

However, most Herring Gulls do not display the thick bill, square head, and barrel chest seen in Great Black-Backed, Western, or Glaucous-Winged Gulls. Only the largest male Herring Gulls approach the size and demeanor of these more aggressive species, and they tend to avoid areas where these more aggressive species are found.

The bill varies from thin, with a small gonydeal angle, to thicker, with a more pronounced gonydeal angle, but not matching the thick, powerful bill of these other large white-headed gulls. The long, angular head is accentuated by the long and narrow bill. So, although Herring Gulls are large, they lack the bulky structure and domineering presence of some of the other large white-headed gulls.

First-Year Plumage

Juvenile Herring Gulls have a sooty-brown plumage, pale panel on the inner primaries, and neat scalloping created by the pale feather edges of the upperparts. The impression is of a uniformly brown gull with darker tertials and blackish primaries. In fact, European gull watchers find first-year American Herring Gulls (subspecies *smithsonianus*) to be especially distinctive, since they have a more saturated tan or brownish color compared to the contrasting checkered pattern with a white ground color seen in subspecies *argenteus* and *argentatus*.

That said, first-winter Herring Gulls are extremely variable in appearance and can become worn, faded, and bleached toward the end of winter. While some birds retain a brown base color, most start getting progressively paler as the season progresses, with many birds first attaining a lighter white head that contrasts with the slightly browner body. The bill, which is all black in juvenile-plumage birds, soon acquires a paler pink or diffuse base, with some extreme examples attaining a pink bill with a well-demarcated black tip, much like a first-winter Glaucous Gull (with whom Herring Gulls sometimes hybridize).

Second-Year Plumage

Herring Gulls are variable at this age too. Some slow-developing individuals can appear similar to first-winter birds, retaining a brownish cast and attaining few, if any, gray feathers on the mantle. More-advanced birds have significantly more gray on the mantle, and sometimes on the wing coverts as well. Most have a light eye at this age. In flight, birds appear tannish white to light brown, with contrasting dark areas in the wings. The secondaries and outer primaries are the darkest areas of the wing, with a paler area in the inner primaries appearing from both above and below. The primaries and tail can appear even blacker at this age than on first-year birds, contrasting even more with the white rump and pale panel on the inner primaries. The bill can vary from dark with a diffuse base, to bright pink with a well-demarcated black tip, to pinkish yellow with a black ring.

Third-Year Plumage

Advanced third-year birds look much like an adult but retain some black on the tip of the bill, a trace of a black tailband, and more extensive black in the primary tips. Slow-developing birds may retain extensive brown in the wing coverts and tertials. As with other species, third-winter birds can be best distinguished from second-year gulls by the inner primaries, which will be brown (immature) for second-winter birds, and gray (adultlike) on third-winter birds.

Adult Plumage

Adult Herring Gulls are distinctive by virtue of their gray mantle, black wingtips, pale-yellow eyes, pink legs, and large size. The mantle is pale gray, similar to Ring-Billed Gulls, and significantly paler than Laughing or Western Gulls. In flight, birds display a moderate amount of black in the primaries, with adult birds showing less extensive black both above and below than either adult Ring-Billed or California Gulls. The outermost primary (P10) includes a large white mirror, while P9 has a smaller white mirror (shown only in eastern birds). Adults have an all-white tail and a clean white head in breeding plumage. In winter, adult Herring Gulls can have significant streaking on the head and nape in nonbreeding plumage. The majority of adult Herring Gulls have pale-yellow eyes, although some birds in the West have duskier eyes.

Size

Herring Gulls are large gulls with an average length between 20.9 and 25.6 inches and a wingspan between 47.2 and 59.1 inches. Males are larger than females, with heavier builds, thicker bills, a flatter crown, and a more sloping forehead. Smaller females can resemble Iceland Gulls in size and shape. Herring Gull range weigh between 1 pound, 12.2 ounces, and 2 pounds, 12.1 ounces, although large birds can exceed 3 pounds.

A chocolate-brown juvenile Herring Gull. Sandy Point State Park, Maryland, August 25, 2010.

A first-fall Herring Gull in flight. Note the all-dark bill and brownish plumage with a slightly whiter head. Lewes, Delaware, November 19, 2011.

This juvenile/first-fall Herring Gull retains much of its brown juvenile plumage. Sandy Point State Park, Maryland, September 22, 2012.

A juvenile/first-fall Herring Gull in flight shows the brownish plumage typical of this age. Ocean City, Maryland, November 16, 2013.

This juvenile/first-fall Herring Gull has a brownish color, all-dark bill, and pale area on the inner primaries. Sandy Point State Park, Maryland, September 21, 2013.

A faded and worn first-spring Herring Gull is shown next to some Bonaparte's Gulls. Note the extensive wear, especially on the coverts and tertials, and the extremely bleached appearance overall. Back River, Maryland, April 1, 2018.

First-winter Herring Gulls with a few older birds mixed in. Note the dark-brown tail, brown base color to the barred rump, and pale window on the inner primaries. Ocean City, Maryland, March 20, 2011.

A first-winter Herring Gull comes in for a landing. Notice the pale inner primaries and the brown base color overall. Schoolhouse Pond, Maryland, February 3, 2016.

This paler first-year Herring Gull has a white ground color and neatly patterned wing coverts and scapulars. Schoolhouse Pond, Maryland, February 11, 2016.

This extremely dark and mottled Herring Gull is just entering its second year. Note the pale eye and pink tip to the bill, which help separate the bird from a first-year gull. Sandy Point State Park, Maryland, August 25, 2010.

This advanced second-winter Herring Gull is separated from a third-winter gull by the extensive brown on the tail (*not visible in this photo*), dark-brown and finely patterned greater coverts, and brown primaries. Cecil County Landfill, Maryland, January 7, 2017.

The pale eye distinguishes this second-winter Herring Gull from a first-year gull. Lewes, Delaware, December 8, 2007.

This second-year Herring Gull shows an extensive amount of gray on the mantle, which contrasts with the pale-brown and white wing coverts. Sandy Point State Park, Maryland, September 25, 2011.

A small second-winter Herring Gull, probably a female. Its immature (brown) primaries and dark eye are different from those of a third-year bird. Sandy Point State Park, Maryland, September 26, 2015.

The small white tips of the blackish primaries distinguish this third-winter Herring Gull from a second-year gull. Schoolhouse Pond, Maryland, January 10, 2017.

A third-winter Herring Gull (*center*) is similar to an adult but retains a black ring around the dull, yellowish-pink bill, as well as dusky eyes and some brown on the tertials and wing coverts. Schoolhouse Pond, Maryland, January 2, 2013.

This third-winter Herring Gull looks much like an adult, except for the black in the tertials and the black toward the tip of the bill. Schoolhouse Pond, Maryland, February 7, 2017.

A third- or fourth-winter Herring Gull peers longingly into a McDonald's, waiting for fast-food scraps. This gull resembles an adult except for the black in the tertials, traces of black tailband (visible in the field), dark flecks in the iris, and extensive black on the bill. Ocean City, Maryland, March 28, 2009.

A bulky adult Herring Gull with dense streaking concentrated on the nape and upper breast. Chesapeake Beach Marina, Maryland, December 7, 2019.

Adult Herring Gull in flight has the white mirror in the outermost primary (P10) and extensive black in the primaries when viewed from above and below. Lewes, Delaware, December 8, 2007.

The pale-yellow eye of this adult Herring Gull contrasts strongly with the dense, dark streaking on the head and neck. Chesapeake Beach Marina, Maryland, December 7, 2019.

Winter adult Herring Gull. Chesapeake Beach Marina, Maryland, December 7, 2019.

A "northern" Herring Gull shows the extremely limited black in the primaries that is reminiscent of an adult "Thayer's" Gull (Iceland Gull, ssp. *thayeri*). Also note the white mirrors on the two outermost primaries. Ocean City, Maryland, February 1, 2014.

Adult Herring Gull (*center*). Note the large size relative to the surrounding Ring-Billed Gulls, the bright-yellow eye, and the streaking on the head and nape typical of winter plumage birds. Schoolhouse Pond, Maryland, February 1, 2018.

This Herring Gull shows the adult wing pattern. Ocean City, Maryland, November 19, 2011.

Adult Herring Gulls in flight over the Atlantic Ocean. Ocean City, Maryland, March 1, 2014.

These Vega Gulls (*Larus* [*argentatus*] *vegae*) are separated from "American" Herring Gulls by range (western Alaska), the darker mantle, and dark eye. St. Paul Island, Alaska, May 24, 2017.

GREAT BLACK-BACKED GULL

Background

Great Black-Backed Gulls are the largest gulls in the world and are often identifiable by size and structure alone. They are prominent on many East Coast beaches and harbors due to their contrasting plumage, large size, and domineering behavior. With their bulky body, wide wingspan, massive bill, and jet-black upperparts, adult birds are impressive to behold, and immature birds are equally distinctive with contrasting salt-and-pepper plumage. While they are opportunistic foragers like other gulls, these massive birds can be seen taking a wide assortment of natural prey, ranging from passerines and fish to young seabirds, small mammals, and marine invertebrates. Great Black-Backed Gulls are significantly heavier and have a longer wingspan than even a Red-Tailed Hawk and thus make a formidable foe. Their habit of taking chicks and eggs from other coastal nesting birds is particularly damaging to some species of shorebirds and terns. They have even been reported to take prey as large as an Atlantic Puffin in flight!

Arthur Cleveland Bent's classic *Life Histories of North American Gulls and Terns* contains an apt and passionate description of the largest of all gulls:

While cruising along the bleak and barren coasts of southern Labrador, I learned to know and admire this magnificent gull, as we saw it sailing on its powerful wings high above the desolate crags and rocky islets of that forbidding shore, its chosen summer home. Its resemblance to the bald eagle was striking, as it soared aloft and wheeled in great circles, showing its broad black back and wings in sharp contrast with its snow-white head and tail, glistening in the sunlight. It surely seemed to be a king among the gulls, a merciless tyrant over its fellows, the largest and strongest of its tribe. No weaker gull dared to intrude upon its feudal domain; the islet it had chosen for its home was deserted and shunned by other less aggressive waterfowl, for no other nest was safe about the castle of this robber baron, only the eider duck being strong enough to defend its young. (Bent 1921)

Audubon, too, included an animated description of prowess and behavior of Great Black-Backed Gulls:

High in the thin keen air, far above the rugged crags of the desolate shores of Labrador, proudly sails the tyrant Gull, floating along on almost motionless wing, like an Eagle in his calm and majestic flight. On widely extended pinions, he moves in large circles, constantly eyeing the objects below. Harsh and loud are his cries, and with no pleasant feeling do they come on the winged multitudes below. Now onward he sweeps, passes over each rocky bay, visits the little islands, and shoots off towards the mossy heaths, attracted perhaps by the notes of the Grouse or some other birds. As he flies over each estuary, lake, or pool, the breeding birds prepare to defend their unfledged broods, or ensure their escape from the powerful beak of their remorseless spoiler. Even the shoals of the finny tribes sink deeper into the waters as he approaches; the young birds become silent in their nests or seek for safety in the clefts of the rocks; the Guillemots and Gannets dread to look up, and the other Gulls, unable to cope with the destroyer, give way as he advances. (Audubon 1844)

Passerines also fall victim to this powerful predator. On one visit to a landfill, I witnessed a large group of gulls chasing an adult Great Black-Backed Gull, which had food in its bill. I assumed it was a small rodent or a piece of trash. However, when the gull dropped its prey, it fell halfway to the ground before taking flight and making its escape! The fortunate bird (and almost dinner) was a European Starling! On another landfill visit, I witnessed no fewer than three European Starlings fall prey to Great Black-Backed Gulls. An adult bird swallowed its starling whole, while two immatures picked at their small meals over a more extended period of time. During a visit to a coastal beach in New England, I saw an adult Great Black-Backed Gull attack a blue crab. Unable to flee the gull, the crab stood its ground and used its claws in a spirited though futile defense. A fellow birder relayed that his group had come across a very unhappy American Coot well offshore as their boat approached the pelagic zone. Great Black-Backed Gulls surrounded the hapless coot, diving at it relentlessly. Ultimately, the coot was "drawn and quartered and ripped to shreds." Merciless tyrant indeed!

While bulky and imposing at rest, Great Black-Backed Gulls can appear almost buteo or eagle-like in flight, particularly as adults, when the white tail, head, and body contrast strongly with the black upperparts and dark flight feathers. Their occasional habit of soaring only adds to this impression. Audubon summed it up aptly:

The flight of the Great Black-Backed Gull is firm, steady, at times elegant, rather swift, and long protracted. While travelling, it usually flies at the height of fifty or sixty yards, and proceeds in a direct course, with easy, regulated flappings. Should the weather prove tempestuous, this Gull, like most others, skims over the surface of the waters or the land within a few yards or even feet, meeting the gale, but not yielding to it, and forcing its way against the strongest wind. In calm weather and sunshine, at all seasons of the year, it is fond of soaring to a great height, where it flies about leisurely and with considerable elegance for half an hour or so, in the manner of Eagles, Vultures, and Ravens. (Audubon 1844)

Great Black-Backed Gulls nest coastally along the Atlantic seaboard from North Carolina to Labrador, and along the eastern Great Lakes. During the winter they can be found throughout most of their breeding range south to Florida. During the winter their range extends inland along major rivers and large interior lakes and landfills. Increasing numbers of these birds also winter along the Gulf coast and have generally expanded their range southward.

They are noticeably larger than other East Coast gulls, including Herring Gulls. They also tend to be more pelagic than other gulls along the Atlantic Seaboard, sometimes foraging far offshore along the continental shelf in winter. Due to their black-and-white plumage and domineering presence, Great Black-Backed Gulls have been given a number of playful names over the years, including Saddleback, Coffin-Bearer (perhaps owing to the somber black mantle), Pondy, and Minister (Goode 2020). However, my favorite is Pete Dunne's moniker for the species: Beach Master (Dunne 2006).

Structure and Field Marks

Great Black-Backed Gulls are large and bulky, with a thick and muscular body, massive wingspan, wide wings, and a large, blocky head. The bill has a substantial width even at the base, and a pronounced gonydeal angle. Often these structural features alone are sufficient to identify the gull; even the largest Herring Gulls rarely approach the structure and size of the Great Black-Backed Gull. The imposing size and build of Great Black-Backed Gulls can be seen in all ages and plumages. They can frequently be identified at quite a distance just by their slow, powerful wingbeats, which contrast with the quicker, snappier wingbeats of smaller gulls.

First-Year Plumage

Although first-year gulls can be difficult to identify in general, Great Black-Backed Gulls are not hard to pick out. They have a checkered pattern of black and white on the upperparts (mantle, scapulars, and coverts), which tends to be darker than on Herring Gulls. At this age, the plumage is similar to that of Lesser Black-Backed Gulls, but the smaller birds have a longer primary extension and uniformly dark greater coverts.

In flight, first-year Great Black-Backed Gulls have marbled underwing coverts with dark-gray flight feathers that contrast with the pale, lightly streaked body. The underwing coverts are off-white and finely marked with brownish-black bars and streaks. The marbled underwing coverts, gray flight feathers, and contrasting white body and head are good field marks for first- and second-year Great Black-Backed Gulls flying overhead. The rump is mostly white against the dark tailband. On the upper side of the wing, the dark secondaries contrast with the lighter greater coverts.

Second-Year Plumage

Second-winter Great Black-Backed Gulls can look similar to first-winter gulls. Key points of difference include a pale or diffuse base to the bill, pale tip to both the upper and lower mandible, and a few black feathers in the mantle, although these can be lacking. The greater coverts of second-winter Great Black-Backed Gulls appear plainer and more finely marked than first-year birds, with only thin, pale markings. The birds tend to look slightly "messier" than first-winter gulls, which exhibit the distinctive crisp, checkered black-and-white pattern. In flight, second-year Great Black-Backed Gulls have gray flight feathers, finely patterned underwing coverts, and sometimes a small white mirror on the outermost primary.

Third-Year Plumage

Third-winter Great Black-Backed Gulls look like adults but retain some black toward the tip of the bill, a trace of a broken tailband (evident in flight), and some brown feathers or a brownish wash in the upper-wing coverts. The white tips to the primaries also tend to be smaller than on adult birds or absent completely. Third-winter birds can be distinguished from more-advanced second-winter birds by the more extensive black in the greater coverts as well as adultlike (black) inner primaries.

Adult Plumage

Adult Great Black-Backed Gulls have a clean white head and tail and a black back and wings. Adult Great Black-Backed Gulls are distinguished from Lesser Black-Backed Gulls by pink (not yellow) legs, a heavier bill, a blocky head, and a darker mantle. In flight they have dark flight feathers on the lower surface of the wing. This is noticeable from a significant distance and can be useful separating Great Black-Backed Gulls from Herring Gulls. The large white tip of the outmost primary is also usually visible in flight, and the black wingtips contrast little with the dark-gray flight feathers from below.

Adult Great Black-Backed Gulls are perhaps most similar to Western Gulls, although they are extremely unlikely to be seen together because their ranges do not overlap. Western Gulls are slightly smaller, and the mantle is a paler slate gray, although these features can be difficult to gauge on lone birds. In Great Black-Backed Gulls the tip of the outermost primary (P10) is entirely white tipped, whereas on Western Gulls P10 has a white subterminal mark, with some black separating the white from the wingtip. Other areas of difference include the Great Black-Backed Gull's red or reddish orbital ring and pale-pink legs. Western Gulls have a bright-yellow orbital ring and brighter-pink legs.

Size

Great Black-Backed Gulls are the largest gulls in the world, with a wingspan of 57 to 64.9 inches and a length from 24 to 30.5 inches. In North America, females range in weight from 2 pounds, 10 ounces, to 3 pounds, 11 ounces. Males range in weight from 3 pounds, 5 ounces, to 4 pounds, 10 ounces. Their massive size is reinforced by their extremely thick bill, blocky head, muscular body, and wide wing base. If a gull could be said to resemble a middle linebacker, this would be the one.

This juvenile Great Black-Backed Gull's underparts are slightly more washed with tan than first-winter gulls later in the season. Sandy Point State Park, Maryland, September 22, 2016.

Note the all-black bill, white body contrasting with the marbled under-wings, and black tailband of this first-winter Great Black-Backed Gull. Ocean City, Maryland, November 19, 2011.

A first-winter Great Black-Backed Gull shows the marbled underwing, white belly, streaked flank, and hefty proportions of the species at this age. Lewes, Delaware, November 28, 2009.

First-year Great Black-Backed Gull. Sandy Point State Park, Maryland, September 21, 2013.

First-winter Great Black-Backed Gull with all-black bill and contrasting "checkered" upperparts. Sandy Point State Park, Maryland, September 26, 2015.

The differences between a first-year (*left*) and a second-year (*right*) Great Black-Backed Gull are evident. Sandy Point State Park, Maryland, September 22, 2012.

A first-winter Great Black-Backed Gull in flight shows the contrasting pattern above and mostly white underparts. Lewes, Delaware, November 19, 2011.

First-winter Great Black-Backed Gulls in flight have a pale rump and tail base, black tailband, and checkered wings and mantle. Sandy Point State Park, Maryland, September 21, 2013.

Note this second-winter Great Black-Backed Gull's heavy, dark bill with diffuse pink base. Sandy Point State Park, Maryland, September 22, 2016.

This bird is a more advanced second-winter Great Black-Backed Gull with more extensive black on the mantle and greater coverts. Schoolhouse Pond, Maryland, February 3, 2016.

A paler, less advanced second-winter Great Black-Backed Gull. Sandy Point State Park, Maryland, September 21, 2013.

A second-winter Great Black-Backed Gull shows some black, adultlike feathers coming in on the upperparts. The basal half of the bill is pale, unlike the all-black bill of first-year Great Black-Backed Gulls. The immature greater coverts distinguish it from a third-winter gull. Chesapeake Beach Marina, Maryland, December 7, 2019.

A second-year Great Black-Backed Gull (*left*) with a third-year Great Black-Backed Gull (*right*). Sandy Point State Park, Maryland, September 21, 2013.

This third-year Great Black-Backed Gull retains some immature (brownish-black) feathers on the wing coverts, a black ring toward the tip of the bill, and limited white on the folded primaries. Sandy Point State Park, Maryland, September 30, 2017.

This third-year Great Black-Backed Gull looks much like an adult, except for the bit of black on the bill and tail. Sandy Point State Park, Maryland, September 24, 2012.

This adult Great Black-Backed Gull shows the dark flight feathers, subterminal marking on P9, and large white tip to P10. Ocean City, Maryland, March 1, 2014.

Adult Great Black-Backed Gull with the red orbital ring, stout bill, blocky head, and bulky body typical of the species. Chesapeake Beach Marina, Maryland, December 7, 2019.

Perched on a piling along the Chesapeake Bay, an adult Great Black-Backed Gull shows black marks toward the tip of the bill and inconspicuous streaking on the hindneck, typical of nonbreeding adults. Chesapeake Beach Marina, Maryland, December 7, 2019.

Note the limited color contrast between the primaries and the rest of the flight feathers of this adult Great Black-Backed Gull. Lewes, Delaware, December 13, 2008.

LESSER BLACK-BACKED GULL

Background

Lesser Black-Backed Gulls are a recent addition to the North American avifauna; they were first recorded in 1934 in New Jersey. Adults have an attractive dark-gray mantle and striking, mustard-yellow legs. These features distinguish them within flocks of paler Ring-Billed and Herring Gulls and larger, darker-backed, pink-legged Great Black-Backed Gulls. Lesser Black-Backed Gulls have increased in North America in recent decades. Most of these North American gulls are from the *graellsii* subspecies, with fewer records of the darker *intermedius* subspecies.

Because of their long, narrow wings and streamlined body, flying Lesser Black-Backed Gulls look like a larger, lankier version of Laughing Gull. In 1852 William Macgillivray wrote, "The flight of this bird is particularly elegant, resembling, however, that of the Great Black-backed Gull, but more easy and buoyant, with the wings considerably curved" (Bent 1921).

Breeding has yet to be documented for Lesser Black-Backed Gull pairs in North America. Like other species from Europe, Lesser Black-Backed Gulls appear to have used Iceland and Greenland as stepping stones to North America. They were initially documented breeding in Iceland in the late 1920s and in Greenland around 1990. Lesser Black-Backed Gulls increased slowly in North America prior to 1980, but numbers have increased exponentially since then, especially from 1995 to 2015. It is interesting to note that 33 percent of all Lesser Black-Backed Gulls reported during winter counts from 1996 to 2006 were seen in Pennsylvania (Hallgrimsson et al. 2011). While most reports of Lesser Black-Backed Gulls are from October through May, numbers appear to be increasing during the summer months as well, adding to the likelihood that pairs will be found breeding in the future. The graph illustrates the dramatic increase in Lesser Black-Backed Gull as documented by annual Christmas Bird Count data.

Although breeding pairs of Lesser Black-Backed Gulls have yet to be found in North America, they have been found breeding with Herring Gulls. The first documented occurrence was in May 2007 on Appledore Island, about 10 miles off the coast of New Hampshire. The pair had two chicks, one of which survived and was banded (Ellis et al. 2007). The pair was found breeding at the same location the following summer and raised two chicks, which were also banded. The banded adult Lesser Black-Backed Gull was seen at several beaches in Volusia County, Florida, in January and February 2009.

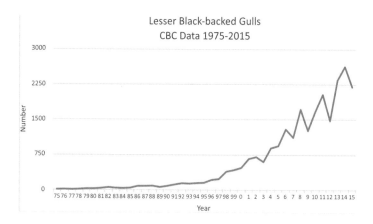

Lesser Black-backed Gulls
CBC Data 1975-2015

National Audubon Society. The Christmas Bird Count Historical Results [Online]. Available http://www.christmasbirdcount.org [April 26, 2017]

Source: birds.audubon.org/historical-results

These pairings are reported with increasing frequency—something to consider when spotting paler versions of adult Lesser Black-Backed Gulls. This hybrid also has to be ruled out before the extremely rare Yellow-Legged Gull can be identified. Like other hybrid combinations, this one is intermediate between parent species, with most birds appearing like Lesser Black-Backed Gulls, but a shade too light. Other apparent hybrids look more like Herring Gulls, but the mantle is a touch too dark and the legs have a yellowish hue. Because this combination was first recorded on Appledore Island, some have termed Herring × Lesser Black-Backed hybrids "Appledore" Gulls (Ayyash 2016). Regardless of what it is called, this hybrid adds an exciting new identification challenge for East Coast birders sorting through large gull flocks.

Extensive banding of Lesser Black-Backed Gulls in Europe has resulted in only two resightings in North America, which may indicate that the European population contributes little to the North American wintering population of Lesser Black-Backed Gulls. This leaves Greenland and Iceland as the major contributors to the North American wintering population, since the increase in Lesser Black-Backed Gulls in Greenland in recent decades corresponds to the increase in North America (Hallgrimsson et al. 2011). The breeding population of Lesser Black-Backed Gulls has increased dramatically in Greenland since they were first recorded breeding in 1990. They have bred as far north as 74 degrees north and have been observed at 81 degrees north (Boertmann 2008).

Lesser Black-Backed Gulls are a reminder of just how elastic bird populations can be. Whereas prior to 1980 many birders considered themselves fortunate to find one of these pretty gulls, now groups of several dozen can sometimes be found at East Coast beaches and landfills. With more Lesser Black-Backed Gulls being found in the summer and the increase in Lesser Black-Backed × Herring hybrids, it may be only a matter of time before breeding Lesser Black-Backed Gull pairs are documented in the United States.

Structures and Field Marks

Lesser Black-Backed Gulls have a slate-gray mantle, mustard-yellow legs, heavy streaking on the neck and head, and long primary extension. The mantle is medium dark gray, perhaps a shade or two darker than Laughing Gulls. When compared with Herring Gulls, Lesser Black-Backed Gulls appear more roundheaded, with a slightly smaller, more parallel-edged bill. The bill lacks the bulbous tip seen on Great Black-Backed Gulls and usually lacks the more pronounced gonydeal angle seen on Herring Gulls. On perched birds, the wings extend well past the tip of the tail, which, combined with the sleek build, makes Lesser Black-Backed Gulls appear slightly more attenuated toward the rear than most Herring Gulls. In flight, Lesser Black-Backed Gulls also have a more streamlined body and appear longer winged, owing more to the narrow wing base than the actual wingspan. These characteristics make them look similar to Laughing Gulls in flight.

First-Year Plumage

First-winter Lesser Black-Backed Gulls are dark brown with contrasting black primaries, tertials, and upper-wing greater coverts. They tend to be lighter on the underparts (breast and belly), having a white ground color with dark streaking rather than the mottled brown of Herring Gulls. This streaking is concentrated around the eye, giving the appearance of a subtle dark mask on an otherwise whitish head. However, this mark becomes less noticeable during the first year. The bill is all black, lacking the pink or diffuse base of most Herring Gulls. The mantle is darker and more contrasting than on similarly aged Herring Gulls, and the black tertials, dark greater coverts, and black primaries create a noticeable contrast between the darker upperparts and paler underparts. The primaries on the extended wing are uniformly dark in flight, compared to the pale area on the inner primaries of first-winter Herring Gulls. The white upper-tail coverts are barred with blackish brown, but the white base color contrasts strongly with the black distal band. Herring Gulls show much less contrast between the brown rump and upper-tail coverts and the mostly black tail.

Second-Year Plumage

Second-winter Lesser Black-Backed Gulls often begin to exhibit the slate-gray mantle that distinguishes them from similarly aged Herring Gulls. The dark upperparts contrast with the white head, throat, and breast. Similar to first-winter gulls, second-winter Lesser Black-Backed Gulls often retain some streaking around the eye. The upperparts tend to be a variegated mix of dark-brown feathers, some with pale edges. The upper-wing coverts are brown and finely marked, and the white tail retains a pronounced subterminal band. Many slow-developing individuals or early-season gulls may lack this feature, but other telltale markings are the smaller, more parallel-edge bill and longer primary extension. Even second-winter Lesser Black-Backed Gulls that have not begun to acquire the adultlike feathers on the mantle will appear darker brown above than Herring Gulls. By the second summer, the legs of Lesser Black-Backed Gulls have begun to acquire a yellowish hue.

Third-Year Plumage

Third-year Lesser Black-Backed Gulls retain some black in the bill, often present as a ring near the tip, while other birds have more extensive black on the bill. And, like other four-year gulls, third-winter Lesser Black-Backed Gulls have less white in the primary tips than adult birds. On gulls in flight, a more extensive, messy area of black on the wingtips is visible, compared to the confined pattern of adult birds. Frequently the black extends to the primary coverts. Third-winter gulls may also retain a trace of a tailband and have a brownish wash on the upper-wing coverts.

Adult Plumage

Adult Lesser Black-Backed Gulls stand out by virtue of the slate-gray mantle and yellow legs. Also of note is the heavy brownish or tan streaking on the head, nape, and sides of throat in winter, which is quite unlike the clean white, unstreaked head of winter adult Great Black-Backed Gulls. Lesser Black-Backed Gulls are slimmer than Herring Gulls and usually show a longer primary extension. In flight, the longer, narrow-based wings and slender body are evident, as is the extensive black in the wingtips and gray flight feathers on the underside of the wing.

The black on the primaries contrasts with the slate gray of the rest of the upper side of the wing, unlike adult Great Black-Backed Gulls, which appear more uniformly black above. The bill of adult birds is bright yellow and has a distinctive red spot, even in winter. Lesser Black-Backed Gulls regularly seen in North America (ssp. *graellsii*) have a medium-dark-gray mantle that is slightly darker above than adult Laughing Gulls, but noticeably paler than Great Black-Backed Gulls. In flight, adult Lesser Black-Backed Gulls have a small mirror on the outermost one or two primaries. The less common *intermedius* subspecies has a darker-black mantle with less contrast against the black wingtips.

Size

Lesser Black-Backed Gulls are slightly smaller than the average Herring Gull, with proportionally longer wings, more rounded head, and often a more parallel-edged bill.

Although Lesser Black-Backed Gulls are on average smaller in all measurements than Herring Gulls, overlap does exist. Lesser Black-Backed Gulls are 19.3 to 22.4 inches long and have a wingspan of 46.5 to 59.1 inches. Males weigh 1 pound, 11.1 ounces, to 2 pounds, 7 ounces, while females weigh 1 pound, 5.9 ounces, to 2 pounds.

This first-winter Lesser Black-Backed Gull is dark and heavily washed with brown on the head and nape. Note the whitish ground color to the upper-tail coverts, black primaries and tail, dark greater coverts, and small, all-black bill. Sandy Point State Park, Maryland, December 9, 2013.

Notice the blackish tertials and primaries on this first-winter Lesser Black-Backed Gull. The head is most heavily streaked around the eye. Salisbury Landfill, Maryland, March 4, 2020.

This first-winter Lesser Black-Backed Gull shows the slightly darker area around the eye, contrasting with the whiter nape, breast, and flanks. The upperparts are significantly darker brown than the underparts, which have a white ground color. Sugarloaf Key, Florida, January 2013.

The dark bill, heavily streaked head, dark greater coverts, and black primaries are still evident on this heavily worn Lesser Black-Backed Gull. The new scapular feathers look contrastingly dark and fresh against the faded wing coverts. Assateague State Park, Maryland, June 1, 2020.

The wing's evenly dark upper side (lacking a pale panel on the inner primaries) is evident on this first-winter Lesser Black-Backed Gull. Ocean City, Maryland, November 16, 2013.

A second-winter Lesser Black-Backed Gull's slate-gray feathers are just beginning to appear on the mantle and scapulars. Ocean City, Maryland, November 10, 2017.

These two photos show the same second-winter Lesser Black-Backed Gull. Note the all-dark primaries, lacking the pale panel on the inner primaries, and the dark tail contrasting with the white rump. The incoming gray feathers on the back can also be seen. Ocean City, Maryland, November 10, 2017.

This second-winter Lesser Black-Backed Gull looks similar to a first-winter gull, but note the dark gray coming in on the mantle. Ocean City, Maryland, February 26, 2020.

Second-winter Lesser Black-Backed Gull (*upper right*) with a second-winter Herring Gull. Note the finely marked lesser and greater coverts and extensive black tailband on the advanced second-winter Lesser Black-Backed Gull. Salisbury Landfill, Maryland, March 4, 2020.

This third-winter Lesser Black-Backed Gull retains extensive black on the bill and has a slight brownish wash to the wing coverts but otherwise looks much like an adult. Ocean City, Maryland, February 26, 2020.

This winter plumage adult Lesser Black-Backed Gull shows the dark flight feathers, limited white in the primary tips, and heavily streaked head. Indian River Inlet, Delaware, February 14, 2020.

A late-winter adult Lesser Black-Backed Gull retains little streaking on the head. It has a long primary extension and small bill. Salisbury Landfill, Maryland, March 4, 2020.

An adult nonbreeding-plumage Lesser Black-Backed Gull shows the slate-gray mantle, mustard-yellow legs, and streaking on the head and nape. Sandy Point State Park, Maryland, September 29, 2013.

An adult nonbreeding-plumage Lesser Black-Backed Gull stands on the ice of Schoolhouse Pond. Note the mustard-yellow legs, parallel-edged bill, and slate-gray mantle. Schoolhouse Pond, Maryland, January 22, 2019.

An adult Lesser Black-Backed Gull with an adult Great Black-Backed Gull. The difference in size and the shade of the mantle are clearly seen on birds in proximity. Sandy Point State Park, Maryland, September 29, 2013.

The adult breeding-plumage Lesser Black-Backed Gull has mustard-yellow legs and bill, a white head, and dark-gray wings contrasting with black wingtips. The clean white head is striking, and quite different from the heavily streaked head of nonbreeding birds. Also visible are the two small mirrors in the outermost primaries. Ocean City, Maryland, April 5, 2014.

Note the small amount of white in the primary tips, with small white mirrors on the two outermost primaries (P10 and P9) on this adult breeding-plumage Lesser Black-Backed Gull. Ocean City, Maryland, April 5, 2014.

WESTERN GULL

Background

Western Gulls are the dark-mantled gull of the West Coast and a fixture along Pacific Ocean beaches, where they serve as sentinels from seaside cliffs, rocky beaches, and offshore sea stacks. They breed on rocky islands and outcrops along the coast and seem to live their entire lives within view of the Pacific Ocean. These large birds are similar in size and structure to Glaucous-Winged Gulls, with which they hybridize freely where their breeding ranges overlap in the Pacific Northwest. Befitting their burly dimensions, Western Gulls are opportunistic foragers. At times they are so aggressive that they dominate feeding areas and coastal beaches, driving smaller gulls away. Western Gulls are adept at stealing food from other gulls, but they also associate readily with other waterbirds and gather in large numbers in mixed-species flocks.

A trip to a Pacific beach is rarely complete without a sighting of these gregarious birds. Arthur Cleveland Bent describes them as "a welcome visitor as a useful scavenger and a pretty feature in the seashore scenery." Perhaps more than any other species, Western Gulls are rarely seen even a few miles inland. Bent captures this relationship with the following description: "As we see these beautiful black and white birds sailing along the ocean cliffs they seem to reflect the clear freshness of the beach and sea and sky" (Bent 1921). Despite their affinity for the sea, Western Gulls do move into some of the larger estuaries such as Puget Sound and San Francisco Bay during the winter. They are also known to follow rivers inland for some distance during the salmon runs in the fall and winter, with some birds ending up in interior valleys in western Oregon (Pierotti and Annett 2020).

Western Gulls nest on offshore islands, rocky outcrops, and occasionally man-made structures, such as abandoned piers that are inaccessible to predators. The largest single colony is found on the Southeast Farallon Island, where an estimated 30 percent of the population breeds. Biologist William Finley conducted early research into the seabird colonies along the Oregon coast in 1905. His research was published by *The Condor* (a journal of western ornithology) in 1905 and provides a fascinating glimpse into lives of the birds that colonize the many rocky islands and sea stacks off the Oregon coast. Finley included this charming account of the parental attentiveness of Western Gulls at a colony in 1905:

They teach their young to keep hidden and to lie close. I have seen more than one gull impress this upon her children. One day I was walking along a ledge and came abruptly to a place where I could look down the top slope. Below me a few yards I saw two half-grown gulls; one crouches beside a rock, but the other started to run down the ridge. He hadn't gone two yards before the mother dove at him with a blow that knocked him rolling. He got up dazed and struck off in a new direction, but she swooped again and rapped him on the head till he seemed glad enough to crawl in under the nearest weed. (Finley 1905)

While Finley praised them as "masters of the air" and said that flocks of gulls "filled the air like so many feathered snowflakes," he was less complimentary of their other behaviors:

But what is beauty, if it is only skin deep? A gull is not the white-winged angel that the poet sees. A gull, in its own country, will steal like a politician and murder like a pirate. They swarmed about us like vultures after a battle. The moment our approach drove a murre or cormorant from its nest, the saintly-looking scalawags swoop down to eat the eggs and young. The gulls are freebooters and robbers on the island, but it is only when the other birds are frightened from their nests that they have a chance to carry out their nefarious trade. (Finley 1905)

Other authors, too, have described Western Gulls as "marauders," "scandalous," and "arrant thieves," with the conclusion that "they must be cordially hated and seriously dreaded by the various species among which they nest" (Bent 1921). While all of the large white-headed gulls engage in this type of feeding behavior from time to time, Western Gulls are likely more successful at it than most and, like the Great Black-Backed Gulls along the East Coast, probably levy a heavy toll on the nests of terns, alcids, and shorebirds.

Like earlier naturalists, I have fallen under the spell of the Western Gull as a striking and iconic symbol of our wild and stunningly beautiful Pacific coast. Few birds are as closely tied to a specific habitat. I always enjoy seeing these birds in this spectacular natural setting, whether it be a lone gull atop a wave-wracked sea stack in Northern California, a group of gulls flying over Monterey Bay, or a massive flock resting on a beach along the Sonoma coast. Western Gulls are frequently the first bird we see upon visiting the California coast, and many memorable visits are enhanced by the presence of these attractive sentinels of the West Coast.

Structure and Field Marks

Western Gulls are one of the largest of the regularly occurring West Coast gulls. Adult males, in particular, have a massive, disproportionately thick bill and muscular body. The primary extension is fairly short and the head is large, usually with a flat crown and a sloping forehead. Identification of pure birds is usually straightforward, though their tendency to hybridize with Glaucous-Winged Gulls in the Pacific Northwest can present a challenge. Western Gulls comprise two subspecies. The paler subspecies, *occidentalis*, has a slate-gray mantle color. This subspecies breeds roughly in the San Francisco Bay area and northward. The darker, more southerly subspecies, *wymani*, breeds mostly south of the Channel Islands and has a darker mantle that contrasts less with the primary tips. Birds between these two locations are intermediate in appearance, and the differences in mantle color appear to be clinal, with birds becoming paler farther north (Howell and Dunn 2007).

First-Year Plumage

Juvenile Western Gulls are a dark chocolate brown; the black primaries and tail are the darkest parts of the plumage—a shade or two darker than Herring Gulls of the same age. The mantle and upper-wing covert feathers are edged with white, giving them a neat, scalloped appearance. The head is dusky brown with dark streaking on the nape and face, particularly around the eye and through the ear coverts.

Their bill is black, and the black primaries contrast markedly with the medium-brown tertials and body. The brown rump, the same shade as the mantle, contrasts with the brownish-black tail. Some juvenile and first-winter birds show a paler, whitish belly, but most are uniformly grayish brown beneath. As Western Gulls enter their first winter, they tend to become paler on the head, throat, and breast and lose the pale feather edges on the upperparts. First-winter Western Gulls appear "messy" and dark overall, lacking any distinct barring or patterns.

In flight, Western Gulls are dark brown with contrasting with black primaries and tail. From below, the brown underwing coverts are slightly darker than the gray flight feathers, and this two-tone appearance can be seen from a significant distance. Viewed from above, flying Western Gulls have a dark-brown appearance, with black primaries and tail and a heavily streaked brown rump. The extended wing includes dark inner primaries, with birds lacking the pale inner primaries seen on first-year Herring Gulls.

Second-Year Plumage

Western Gulls begin to acquire their slate-gray mantle during their second year. Some second-year birds retain a brownish aspect, with only a few gray feathers showing in the mantle. The amount of gray can range from a small amount of the mantle to the entire mantle, which then contrasts with the immature upper-wing coverts. At this age, the white upper-tail coverts and rump contrast markedly with the blackish tail. Also, most birds become whiter on the head and the underparts, with heavier streaking on the nape and the belly. The bill can vary from mostly dark to a yellowish orange with a dark tip.

Third-Year Plumage

Western Gulls closely resemble adult birds by their third year. Much or all of the mantle and wing coverts have turned slate gray. Key points of difference between adult and third-year birds include some remaining black in the bill (at the tip or in a ring near the tip), a black tailband, and less white in the primary tips. Some third-year Western Gulls retain a subtle brown wash on the upper-wing coverts.

Adult Plumage

Adults have slate-gray mantles, pink legs, and extensive black on the primaries. They have an all-white head, lacking the streaking seen on Slaty-Backed or Lesser Black-Backed Gulls in winter. Eyes can be dusky olive to dark, and the bill is banana yellow with a bright-red spot at the gonydeal angle. In contrast to the slate-gray mantle, birds have white scapular and tertial crescents, as well as large white tips to the outer primaries.

As noted earlier, southern populations (ssp. wymani) are a shade or two darker than more-northern Western Gulls (ssp. occidentalis). However, both subspecies appear a medium to dark slaty gray in the field. East Coast birders will notice that both subspecies of Western Gulls are significantly more slate gray on the upperparts than Great Black-Backed Gulls, which appear black. Western × Glaucous-Wing hybrids can be found all along the Pacific coast in winter and are sometimes referred to as Olympic Gulls or Puget Sound Gulls. Adult hybrids should be suspected if the mantle or primaries are a shade too light for a Western Gull. Also, the primaries of the folded wing appear blackish to slate gray, not black as on pure birds.

Size

Large and bulky, Western Gulls are 24.1 to 26.0 inches long and have a wingspan of 53.2 to 55.1 inches. Birds from the South Farallon Island are variable in weight, with males being significantly larger than females. The males from this region weigh 2 pounds, 6.4 ounces, to 2 pounds, 8.7 ounces, while females vary between 1 pound, 12.3 ounces, and 2 pounds, 1.8 ounces. The Western Gulls farther south are smaller.

First-winter Western Gull (ssp. *occidentalis*). Western Gulls can appear similar to Herring Gulls at this age but tend to be darker, with a bulkier build and thicker bill. Monterey, California, September 30, 2009.

A juvenile Western Gull (ssp. *wymani*) has a white belly and white-edged coverts and scapulars. Subspecies *wymani* is difficult to distinguish from ssp. *occidentalis* at this age but tends to be more contrasting, with darker upperparts and paler underparts. Torrey Pines State Reservation, California, August 27, 2006.

Juvenile Western Gull. San Francisco, October 1, 2009.

A first-winter Western Gull is shown with an adult. The immature bird is fairly dark and coarsely marked above. Ventura, California, February 14, 2016.

A first-winter Western Gull is seen from below over Monterey Bay. Note how the underwing coverts are slightly darker than the flight feathers. Monterey, California, October 3, 2009.

Another first-winter Western Gull is shown in flight. The dark underwing coverts contrast with the paler flight feathers. Monterey, California, October 3, 2009.

A second-winter Western Gull is beginning to acquire gray feathers on the mantle. Santa Cruz, California, September 29, 2009.

The bicolored bill and uniform wing coverts are evident on this second-winter Western Gull. Tomales Bay, California, February 7, 2011.

The dark-gray mantle and brown wing coverts contrast strongly on this second-winter Western Gull. Note the heavily streaked head and mostly black bill. Tomales Bay, California, February 7, 2011.

This third-winter Western Gull has a pale eye and extensive black toward the bill tip and retains some brown in the tertials. Marina Landfill, California, February 9, 2018.

A third-winter Western Gull has limited white in the folded primaries, extensive black markings on the bill, and some brown on the wing coverts. Seacliff State Beach, California, September 30, 2009.

A third-winter Western Gull in flight looks much like an adult, except for the black in the bill and tail, limited white in the primaries, and gray markings in the underwing coverts. Monterey, California, October 3, 2009.

An adult Western Gull perched above the windswept Pacific Ocean. Monterey, California, September 30, 2009.

An adult Western Gull spreads its wings, showing the pattern of the primaries. The large white mirror is apparent on the outermost primary, and small white tips are seen on the other outer primaries. Sonoma Coast State Beach, California, April 9, 2008.

Note the dusky eye, yellow orbital ring, and heavy bill on this adult Western Gull. Sonoma Coast State Beach, California, April 9, 2008.

The adult Western Gull has broad wings and a barrel-chested body. Monterey, California, September 30, 2009.

This gull shows the yellow-orange orbital ring, bulky size, massive bill, and unstreaked white head typical of adult Western Gulls. Monterey, California, February 9, 2018.

Western Gulls in adult and first-winter plumages. The adult gull has dark, contrasting flight feathers. Monterey Bay, California, October 3, 2009.

GLAUCOUS-WINGED GULL

Background

Glaucous-Winged Gulls are the large pale gull of the Pacific Northwest coast, where they are common along the beaches and rocky headlands. While Western Gulls predominate along the coast to the south and Glaucous Gulls are abundant to the north, Glaucous-Winged Gulls are the most numerous large gull along the Washington State and British Columbia coast. It is the only regularly occurring West Coast gull whose primaries are the same shade of gray as the rest of the upperparts. The distinctive gray primaries, medium-gray mantle, and large size make adult Glaucous-Winged Gulls a memorable sight. As Bent noted during a trip along the Alaskan coast in May 1911, "The grand and picturesque scenery of those inside passages was enlivened and made more attractive by the constant presence of these gulls following the ship, drifting northward to their breeding grounds, or merely wandering in search of food" (Bent 1921).

Male Glaucous-Winged Gulls can be even bulkier and heavier than Western Gulls, with only the rare Glaucous Gull exceeding them in wingspan and girth within their range. However, Glaucous-Winged Gulls are known to hybridize with other large white-headed gulls. Although Glaucous-Winged × Western hybrids (or "Olympic" Gulls) from Oregon and Washington State are the most widespread hybrid and perhaps the most well known, Glaucous-Winged Gulls also hybridize with Herring Gulls (a hybrid sometimes called the "Cook Inlet" Gull) and Glaucous Gulls in Alaska, producing a bewildering array of hybrid gulls showing confusingly intermediate plumage and structural features. Glaucous-Winged Gulls hybridize freely with Western Gulls where their breeding ranges overlap in the Pacific Northwest, with the hybrid zone extending from the Strait of Juan de Fuca, Washington, to Coos Bay, Oregon (Hayward and Verbeek 2020). In fact, some colonies in the Pacific Northwest comprise up to 70 percent hybrids (Olsen and Larsson 2004).

The flight of Glaucous-Winged Gulls is strong and purposeful, with slow, shallow wing-beats. Adults have broad-based wings that, in conjunction with the thick body and large, blocky head, combine to give the impression of a compact, burly, and imposing gull. Arthur Cleveland Bent summarizes the grace and strength of Glaucous-Winged Gulls in flight, although elements of this description are just as apt for many of the other gull species that frequent North America:

> The flight of the glaucous-winged gull is buoyant, graceful, and pleasing, and its plumage is always spotlessly clean and neat. A gull in flight is one of nature's most beautiful creatures and one of its triumphs in the mastery of the air. It was a never-ending source of delight to watch these graceful birds following the ship at full speed without the slightest effort, dropping astern to pick up some fallen morsel or forging ahead at will, as if merely playing with their powers of flight. (Bent 1921)

One feature that sets Glaucous-Winged Gulls of all ages apart from those species that would likely be confused with them is that the wingtips are roughly the same color as the rest of the upperparts (wings and mantle). Whereas young and adult Glaucous Gulls have wingtips paler than the rest of the upperparts, and other large white-headed gulls (such as Herring or Western Gulls) have wingtips darker than the rest of the upperparts, Glaucous-Winged Gulls have wingtips that are the same color and shade as the rest of the upperparts. This is true also for some Iceland Gulls (ssp. *kumlieni*). However, usually the much-smaller size, rounder head, and more petite bill is sufficient to separate the typical "Kumlien's" Gull from the much-larger and robust Glaucous-Winged Gull, and their ranges do not overlap.

I have always considered Glaucous-Winged Gulls to be one of the most appealing and alluring species of our Pacific Northwest coast. The silvery-gray primary tips nicely complement the gray mantle and gleaming white body of adults and make Glaucous-Winged Gulls a distinctive and beautiful gull at both rest and flight. And the fact that they spend the majority of their time along some of the country's most stunningly beautiful beaches and waterways only adds to the mystique of this striking gull. Whether one is walking the rugged coast of Olympic National Park, photographing offshore sea stacks along the Oregon coast, or viewing birds drifting lazily over the Pacific Ocean, Glaucous-Winged Gulls lend an attractive avian element to the visit and help ensure that our memories will include not only the breathtaking scenery, but also the rich diversity of life that graces these rocky shores.

Structure and Field Marks

Glaucous-Winged Gulls are one of the largest of the regularly occurring West Coast gulls. Adult males in particular can be massive, with a bulbous bill, thick body, and large, blocky head. The eyes are small and high set, a look some have described as beady-eyed or having a primitive appearance (Ebels et al. 2001). Pete Dunne says it gives first-winter birds the impression of being "dull or dazed (in other words, not too bright)" (Dunne 2006). This feature distinguishes it from Iceland Gulls, whose eyes appear much larger within a small, rounded head. In flight, the wings appear broad and more rounded than many other large gull species.

First-Year Plumage

First-winter Glaucous-Winged Gulls have a uniform gray-brown plumage, lacking the fine barring and checkering seen on other first-winter gulls. The plumage is pale and a colder gray than Glaucous Gulls, resembling dull pewter with a tannish wash. They can also bleach to a striking white by late winter, although rarely as pale as on first-year Glaucous Gulls. The bill is heavy and all black. The primaries are consistently similar in shade and color with the rest of the upperparts, being neither darker (like Iceland Gulls, ssp. *thayeri*) nor lighter (like Glaucous Gulls). In flight, they lack a contrasting pale rump or darker secondary bar.

Second-Year Plumage

Second-winter Glaucous-Winged Gulls can appear similar to first-winter gulls, differing only in their more uniform wing coverts and tertials and pale bill base. They often lack paler marbling on the upperparts and thus retain the unpatterned appearance. Some gray may be coming in on the mantle (at least in late winter), lending a paler but still low-contrast appearance.

Third-Year Plumage

Third-year Glaucous-Winged Gulls can be similar in appearance to adults. Most third-winter Glaucous-Winged Gulls sport the pale-gray upperparts of an adult, while others retain a brown wash on the upper-wing coverts. Third-year Glaucous-Winged Gulls have the pale-gray primaries of an adult but lack the white in the primary tips. Most third-year Glaucous-Winged Gulls retain some dusky markings toward the tip of the bill, although there is much variation. The tail may retain some grayish-brown barring or spots, which form a broken tailband.

Adult Plumage

Adult Glaucous-Winged Gulls' imposing presence makes an icon at coastal locations. Perhaps most noticeable, the primaries are the same attractive silver gray as the rest of the upperparts. They lack the contrasting dark primary tips of most white-headed gulls. The eye is dark, the legs are pink, and the bill is heavy, dull to medium yellow with a red spot and a moderate to large gonydeal angle. Breeding-plumage adults have a clean white head, while nonbreeding adults have dusky mottling on the head, neck, and upper breast, giving them a dingier appearance. The pattern on the head and nape is unique to Glaucous-Winged Gulls (and some of its hybrid combinations). While other winter white-headed adult gulls have heavy, well-defined streaking in these areas, the pattern on Glaucous-Winged Gulls is much more diffuse, appearing as "smudges" or "thumb prints" as opposed to contrasting longitudinal streaks (Ebels et al. 2001).

In flight, adult Glaucous-Winged Gulls are distinguishable by their all-gray upper wing and all-white underwing. From below, they appear very pale in flight, with a clean white underwing showing pale flight feathers that almost blend with the rest of the underparts. The upper surface of the wing is a pale silvery gray, with the gray extending all the way to the primary tips, although the middle and outer primaries include distinct white tips and mirrors.

Size

These large birds are 23.6 to 26.0 inches long, with a wingspan of 53.9 to 59.1 inches. Males weigh between 2.6 and 3.7 pounds, while females are 1.8 to 2.9 pounds.

Note the uniform plumage on this typical first-winter Glaucous-Winged Gull. Point Reyes National Seashore, California, February 6, 2011.

This first-year Glaucous-Winged Gull's uniform, pale flight feathers are obvious when viewed from below. Point Reyes National Seashore, California, February 6, 2011.

A first-winter Glaucous-Winged Gull shows the uniform plumage typical of the species at this age. The folded primaries are similar in color to the rest of the plumage. Marina Landfill, California, February 9, 2018.

Another first-winter Glaucous-Winged Gull demonstrating primaries that are the same color and shade as the rest of the upperparts. Ventura, California, February 14, 2016.

This Glaucous-Winged Gull is entering its second calendar year; the heavily worn and bleached juvenile feathers contrast with the fresher incoming feathers. Sekiu, Washington, August 3, 2016.

This bird is a typically plumaged second-year Glaucous-Winged Gull with some gray on the mantle and wing coverts. Note the immature primaries. Sonoma Coast State Beach, California, February 7, 2011.

This third-year Glaucous-Winged Gull looks much like an adult but retains a black ring toward the tip of a pinkish bill and has limited white in the primary tips. Marina Landfill, California, February 9, 2018.

A third-year Glaucous-Winged Gull features incoming adultlike primaries, mostly dark bill, and traces of brown remaining on the greater coverts. Sekiu, Washington, August 3, 2016.

A third-year Glaucous-Winged Gull shows the black marking on the bill, limited white in the primary tips, and brownish wash to the wing coverts. St. Paul Island, Alaska, May 23, 2017.

The same gull as in the photo above is shown with its wings extended. Limited white is shown on the tips of the outermost primaries, and a brownish wash on the primaries extends to the alula. St. Paul Island, Alaska, May 23, 2017.

The even gray upper wing is evident in this adult Glaucous-Winged Gull in flight. Port Angeles, Washington, July 31, 2016.

An adult Glaucous-Winged Gull has folded primaries the same shade of gray as the rest of the upperparts. The folded primaries are faded and worn on this late-summer gull Sekiu, Washington, August 3, 2016.

This adult Glaucous-Winged Gull has folded primaries that are very similar in color and shade to the mantle. Point Arena, California, February 7, 2011.

The adult Glaucous-winged Gull is notably larger and bulker than the adjacent California Gull. Seacliff State Beach, California, September 30, 2009.

YELLOW-FOOTED GULL

Background

While gulls are most common in cold, windswept locations, the Yellow-Footed Gull thrives in a hot, steamy climate. They do not migrate, and their movements are largely restricted to postbreeding dispersal, most notably to the Salton Sea, although birds occasionally turn up farther north or west.

In fact, the Salton Sea is the only US location where they can reliably be located. The species was first recorded there in August 1965, and their numbers have increased since then. The birds favor jetties, rock outcrops, and pebble- or barnacle-strewn beaches (Patten et al. 1997). The first postbreeding gulls turn up in May, with numbers building through summer. They reach their highest numbers in July and August, when hundreds can be seen. Small numbers have been recorded wintering in recent years.

Obsidian Butte at Salton Sea National Wildlife Refuge is a favored location for Yellow-Footed Gulls. The vast expanse of the sea, parched habitat, and overwhelming smell of fish and brine combine to make for a memorable setting for observing this spectacular gull. My first experience with Yellow-Footed Gulls at the wildlife refuge was on a hazy day in late August, when the temperature touched 119 degrees. Yellow-Footed Gulls stood on the distant mudflats, bills partially open to mitigate the intense heat. The birds were partially obscured by the humid air and heat shimmer, which only added to the surreal experience of seeing this spectacular gull. It's a memory I have treasured ever since.

Only a handful of gull species are larger than Yellow-Footed Gulls. In addition to their large wingspan and weight, Yellow-Footed Gulls have broad wings and thick bills, which add to their bulky impression and imposing countenance. They were formerly considered a subspecies of Western Gull (or the Yellow-Footed Western Gull), and some experts have suggested, on the basis of morphology and vocalizations, that the Yellow-Footed Gull is more closely related to the Kelp Gulls of South America than to the Western Gulls of the nearby California coast (Patten 2020). Yellow-Footed Gulls are unusual among large white-headed gulls in that they acquire their adult plumage in three years, not four. Because Yellow-Footed Gulls have a smaller population than any other North American gull (estimated at 20,000 breeding pairs) and because they nest within a limited area, the birds have been the focus of conservation efforts. Yellow-Footed Gulls remain one of our least understood gulls, and much remains to be learned about their breeding biology and life history.

Structure and Field Marks

None of the many species of gulls and terns that frequent the Salton Sea come close to the Yellow-Footed Gull's massive wingspan, size, and bulk. They appear powerful in flight, with strong, measured wingbeats, and their black-and-white plumage lends an eagle-like impression.

In comparison, Western Gulls are extremely rare at the Salton Sea and have dull, yellowish legs (often tinged pink at the joints). They never match the bright, vibrant yellow seen on Yellow-Footed Gulls, whose legs and matching yellow bill provide a vivid contrast to the black, dark-gray, and white plumage.

First-Year Plumage

Juvenile Yellow-Footed Gulls are a dark grayish brown with a white belly. The dark tail contrasts with the mostly white rump and upper-tail coverts. Yellow-Footed Gulls are unique among the large white-headed gulls of North America in that they take only three years to reach maturity. They begin to acquire a slate-gray mantle in their first winter, and in most birds this adultlike mantle is well developed by their first summer. As they approach their first summer, Yellow-Footed Gulls show both adultlike feathers on the mantle (slate gray) and juvenile feathers on the upper-wing coverts (brown or a worn tan), and their legs have a yellowish wash. As they progress into their first winter, they become progressively whiter on the head and underparts.

Second-Year Plumage

Second-year birds have mostly dark-gray upperparts, although they often retain some brown on the wing coverts and tertials. The wingtips are all black, and the bill retains a well-delineated black tip. At this age, Yellow-Footed Gulls most closely resemble third-year Western Gulls. However, by their second year the yellow legs are usually obvious with good views. Another telling field mark at this age is the white, mostly unmarked rump and upper-tail coverts, which contrast strongly with the black tail. By their second summer, most birds look like adults but retain some black on the bill tip and variable amounts of black on the white tail.

Adult Plumage

Adult Yellow-Footed Gulls are a straightforward identification within their limited range. It is the only large white-headed gull with a dark-gray mantle that occurs regularly at the Salton Sea, with the yellow legs clinching the identification. Yellow-Footed Gulls also have a bright-yellow bill with a prominent red gonydeal spot, yellow eyes, and the previously mentioned bright-yellow legs. Much has been written about the bulbous-tipped bill, which ranges from subtle to prominent. In addition to the pronounced gonydeal expansion, the culmen is frequently enlarged toward the bill tip, enhancing its swollen appearance. Their red gonydeal spot is larger than on similarly aged Western Gulls (Howell and Dunn 2007).

Size

Yellow-Footed Gulls are 21.7 to 28.4 inches long and have a wingspan of 59.1 to 61 inches. They weigh between 2 pounds, 9.4 ounces, and 3 pounds, 8.5 ounces.

A juvenile/first-winter Yellow-Footed Gull retains a mostly dark bill and a dark-brownish wash overall. Salton Sea, California, October 9, 2011. *Photo by Bill Hubick*

An adult Yellow-Footed Gull keeps company with a Black-Necked Stilt near Obsidian Butte at the Salton Sea. The bright-yellow legs and slaty-gray mantle are evident. Salton Sea National Wildlife Refuge, California, September 14, 2015.

A group of adult Yellow-Footed Gulls brave 119°F temperatures at the Salton Sea. Salton Sea, California, August 28, 2006.

An adult Yellow-Footed Gull hangs out with a California Gull. The bright-yellow orbital ring and bulbous-tipped bill are apparent. Salton Sea National Wildlife Refuge, California, September 14, 2015.

Note the Yellow-Footed Gull's broad white border along the trailing edge of the wing and white mirror on the outermost primary (P10). Salton Sea National Wildlife Refuge, California, September 14, 2015.

Adult Yellow-Footed Gull in flight. Salton Sea National Wildlife Refuge, California, September 14, 2015.

The adult Yellow-Footed Gull is aptly named. Salton Sea, California, October 9, 2011. *Photo by Bill Hubick*

The adult Yellow-Footed Gull is distinguished by its thick bill, bulky body, and short primary extension. Salton Sea National Wildlife Refuge, California, September 14, 2015.

GLAUCOUS GULL

Background

Glaucous Gulls are the common large, white-winged species of the Far North, at home in their icy haunts along Arctic shores. In North America, they breed along the northern edge of Canada and Alaska, from Labrador to the West Coast of northern Alaska along the Bering Sea. Pale in all plumages, young birds are a striking whitish to creamy tan, while older birds obtain a light-silver-to-gray mantle with white wingtips. Imposing in size, commanding in demeanor, and striking in plumage, Glaucous Gulls are a great find and domineering presence among winter gull flocks. At many Arctic locations, they are the most abundant species, and they make their presence known as they fly powerfully above windswept seas, gather in large groups on frigid Arctic shores, and squabble noisily over food. Glaucous Gulls were formerly called Burgomaster Gulls, which is appropriate because burgomaster is a term used for the mayor or chief magistrate of some northern European towns. The role seems tailor-made for these burly birds, which take center stage on whatever harbor, lake, town, or inlet where they appear.

In *Birds of America*, Audubon described them as "notoriously greedy and voracious, preying not only on fish and small birds, but on carrion of every kind." Audubon goes on to report that on one of Captain Ross's expeditions, a Glaucous Gull "disgorged an auk when it was struck, and proved, on dissection, to have another in its stomach" (Audubon 1844).

The most colorful and passionate description of Glaucous Gulls, and perhaps the one that best captures their character, was written by Arthur Cleveland Bent in his classic *Life Histories of North American Gulls and Terns*:

The name burgomaster is a fitting name for this chief magistrate of the feathered tribes of the Arctic seas, where it reigns supreme over all the lesser water fowl, levying its toll of food from their eggs and defenseless young. Well they know its strength and dread its power, as it sails majestically aloft over the somber, rocky cliffs of the Greenland coast, where, with myriads of sea fowl, it makes its summer home; and useless is it for them to resist the onslaught of its heavy beak when it swoops down to rob them of their callow young. Only the Great Skua, the fighting airship of the north, dares to give it battle and to drive the tyrant burgomaster from its chosen crag. Its only rival in size and power among the gulls is the great black-backed gull, and where these two meet on the Labrador coast they treat each other with dignified respect. (Bent 1921)

Glaucous Gulls are adept at taking advantage of whatever food source is available, and their diet varies greatly depending on the season and where they happen to find themselves. While they can be seen scavenging for food at landfills and near human settlements, they also forage over tidal waters and beaches, preying on small mammals, as well as the eggs and young of other birds, and even in the pelagic zone searching for fish or other prey near the ocean's surface.

Glaucous Gulls breed in the High Arctic and winter in small numbers south to the mid-Atlantic region and central California coast, although they have been spotted farther south. Small numbers can also be found in the Great Lakes region in winter. They are medium-distance migrants, with immature birds found in the southern portion of their winter range and over the open ocean in the pelagic zone.

Glaucous Gulls have long been my favorite bird. My first sighting was a huge first-winter gull on the ice of Schoolhouse Pond many winters ago. The strikingly white Glaucous Gull towered over the surrounding Ring-Billed Gulls, its snow-white plumage in stark contrast to the mottled-brown immature Herring Gulls nearby. I continue to be thrilled every time I view these stunning gulls on the rare occasions that they have turned up near my Maryland home. But these sightings pale in comparison to my experiences along the shores of the Arctic Ocean, the heart of their homeland. Dozens of immature and adult gulls soared in graceful and determined flight over the windswept ocean. Close views were easy to come by; the birds rested on the beach or frequented the small ponds in and around the town of Barrow, Alaska. But the main show was along the lonely beach near Point Barrow, where thousands of birds of all ages were loafing on the beach, flying over the storm-tossed surf, and bickering over food scraps, with the flocks occasionally obscured by snow squalls. They exemplified the resourceful fortitude necessary to thrive in such an unforgiving environment.

Structure and Field Marks

One of the largest gull species in the world, Glaucous Gulls have massive bodies including a barrel chest, thick neck, and blocky head. The bill is thick and long but parallel edged, lacking the pronounced gonydeal angle of many other large gull species. The males, in particular, have a fierce appearance. Smaller females have more rounded heads but rarely approach the delicate appearance of an Iceland Gull. Glaucous Gulls have a short primary extension; this can be helpful in separating small Glaucous Gulls from Iceland Gulls, which have a longer primary extension. The large size and bulky body of male Glaucous Gulls are especially obvious among a flock of similarly sized or slightly smaller Herring Gulls, which lack the barrel chest and, with the longer primary extension, appear more elongated and streamlined. Due to their broad wings and massive body, flying Glaucous Gull are sturdy and imposing birds of powerful proportions.

First-Year Plumage

Glaucous Gulls have distinctive plumage during their first year. Birds in fresh juvenile plumage are tan overall, with neat, light-brown barring or markings on the upperparts. The primaries are the palest part of the plumage. Because Glaucous Gulls retain most of their juvenile plumage through spring, they get progressively more faded, worn, and pale as the season wears on. By mid- to late winter, most Glaucous Gulls have a more uniform, pale plumage lacking the fine barring and markings seen earlier in the season. Some birds bleach strikingly white by late winter and into their first summer. In flight, first-winter Glaucous Gulls appear extremely pale, like a "ghost" of a Great Black-Backed or Herring Gull. Whether perched or in flight, first-winter Glaucous Gulls are frequently identified by their pale plumage and massive size alone. At this age their bubblegum-pink bill with black tip is another mark of identification.

Second-Year Plumage

Second-winter Glaucous Gulls can be even more strikingly white than first-winter birds, particularly late in the season. They lack the neat barring and checkering that are especially notable on juvenile and early first-winter birds. Early in their second year, many Glaucous Gulls have dark, newly molted feathers, often appearing as sooty patches on the scapulars, which contrast sharply with the bleached older feathers retained from the first-year/juvenile plumage. However, they attain a uniform ghostly-white appearance by late winter or spring. Many second-year Glaucous Gulls have acquired a dusky or pale eye and have a small pale tip on the black distal end of the bill.

Third-Year Plumage

Third-winter Glaucous Gulls resemble adults. The most noticeable difference is the retention of some black on the bill, frequently seen as a ring near the tip of the yellow bill. In some birds, the bill can "regress" and retain a pinkish tinge and significant black throughout. Birds at this age can also retain some tan feathers in the upper-wing coverts and some darker, immature feathers in the tail. They may also show some brown mottling on the underparts, in contrast to the clean white body of adult Glaucous Gulls.

Adult Plumage

At this age, the pale-gray upperparts contrast only slightly with the white primary tips. Glaucous Gulls have slightly paler-gray upperparts than other large gulls. The white wingtips can be surprisingly hard to notice on perched gulls, depending on the angle of the bird or the positioning of other birds in a large flock. As with other ages of this gull, the bill is heavy and parallel edged, and a paler lemon yellow than other large gulls. The bright-pink legs and pale eyes are striking. In flight, birds appear all white from below. From above, the wing looks all gray with a white trailing edge; this white margin becomes slightly wider and extends around the primary tips. In winter, adult Glaucous Gulls have dark-brown spots and smudges on the head, nape, and upper breast. In summer, they have a clean white head, which nicely complements the pale-gray upperparts and snow-white primaries.

Size

Consistent with modern ornithologists, Captain Sabine found most Glaucous Gull specimens to be smaller than Great Black-Backed Gulls. However, the largest gull of any species that he encountered was a Glaucous Gull with a length of 32 inches, a wingspan of 65 inches, and a weight of 4.25 pounds (Audubon 1844)! It is interesting to note that the heaviest individual gull referenced by Olsen and Larsson in the *Gulls of North America, Europe, and Asia* was a third-year male Glaucous Gull that weighed an exceptional 5.8 pounds. This weight exceeds even the largest range given for Great Black-Backed Gulls elsewhere in the book. And, according to Birds of North America Online, the local population of gulls that has the largest mass in North America is the Glaucous Gulls found on the Chukot Peninsula and Wrangell Island, where males average between 4.4 and 5.95 pounds (Weiser and Gilchrist 2020)! Pete Dunne quite aptly describes Glaucous Gulls as the "Great White Gull" (Dunne 2006).

Glaucous Gulls are larger in wingspan and weight than any other gull species except the Great Black-Backed Gull. Like many other gull species, they are extremely variable in size, with males larger than females, sometimes significantly so. The largest males can approach or even match the size of the largest Great Black-Backed Gulls, while smaller females can be smaller than Herring Gulls. Glaucous Gulls are 24.4 to 27.6 inches long and have an average wingspan of 55.1 to 63 inches. They weigh more than 3 pounds.

This first-year Glaucous Gull is still in its brownish, juvenal plumage. But note the frosty wingtips and sharply demarcated, bicolored bill. Even on dark, fresh-plumage juvenile birds, the primaries are the palest part of the plumage. Barrow, Alaska, October 2, 2015.

First-winter Glaucous Gull in flight over a turbulent Arctic Ocean. Barrow, Alaska, October 1, 2015.

A typical first-winter Glaucous Gull becomes increasingly pale and bleached white in late winter. Marina Landfill, California, February 9, 2018.

A first-winter Glaucous Gull towers above Laughing and Ring-Billed Gulls. Brownsville, Texas, March 19, 2011. *Photo by Jeff Shenot*

Note the subtle size and color variations between these first-winter Glaucous Gulls. Barrow, Alaska, October 2, 2015.

The first-winter Glaucous Gull has a ghostly appearance; the palest part of the plumage is the flight feathers. Barrow, Alaska, October 2, 2015.

This first-winter Glaucous Gull shows the broad wings and powerful body typical of the species. Barrow, Alaska, October 2, 2015.

Another powerfully built first-winter bird in flight. Note the subtle streaking and barring on the body, undertail coverts, and tail. Barrow, Alaska, October 2, 2015.

Notice the blotchy plumage of many Glaucous Gulls entering their second-year, when incoming feathers contrast with older, worn feathers. This results in a "patchwork" of extremely pale areas that contrast with darker-brown or tan areas. Barrow, Alaska, October 1, 2015.

This early second-winter Glaucous Gull has a pale iris. Barrow, Alaska, October 4, 2015.

Second-winter Glaucous Gulls can bleach to strikingly white by late winter, appearing almost pure white at a distance. Note the pale bill tip, pale eye, and bleached plumage. Salisbury Landfill, Maryland, January 17, 2009.

A second-winter Glaucous Gull (*facing right*) and an adult Glaucous Gull (*facing left*). Glaucous Gulls are distinctive at all ages. Barrow, Alaska, October 2, 2015.

This third-year Glaucous Gull looks much like an adult but retains some pale-tan feathers in the wing coverts and has some faint dark markings on the bill tip. Barrow, Alaska, October 4, 2015.

This third-winter Glaucous Gull looks much like an adult but retains a pronounced ring on the bill. Barrow, Alaska, October 1, 2015.

Adult Glaucous Gulls are beautiful birds, with gleaming white plumage and folded primaries that contrast nicely with the pale-gray mantle and wing coverts. Barrow, Alaska, October 4, 2015.

Adult Glaucous Gulls can appear completely white in some light, with the pale-gray mantle and upper wings contrasting little with the bright-white body and lower wing surface. Barrow, Alaska, October 1, 2015.

Notice the smudging that occurs on the head and nape of winter plumage adult Glaucous Gulls (*front center*), while the adult (*back left*) retains an unstreaked white head characteristic of the breeding season. Barrow, Alaska, October 4, 2015.

Like other gull species, Glaucous Gulls often fight over the most marginal scrap of food even when an endless quantity is available. The bright-white underwing is seen on both adult birds, making adult birds appear almost pure white when seen from below in flight. Barrow, Alaska, October 4, 2015.

BLACK-HEADED GULL (NB)

BLACK-HEADED GULL (B)

FRANKLIN'S GULL (NB)

FRANKLIN'S GULL (B)

SABINE'S GULL (NB)

SABINE'S GULL (B)

NB=NONBREEDING B=BREEDING

HERRING GULL

GREAT BLACK-BACKED GULL

GLAUCOUS-WINGED GULL

GLAUCOUS GULL

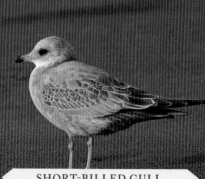

SHORT-BILLED GULL

RING-BILLED GULL

LESSER BLACK-BACKED GULL

WESTERN GULL

ICELAND GULL (KUMLIEN'S)

ICELAND GULL (THAYER'S)

CALIFORNIA GULL

HEERMANN'S GULL

BONAPARTE'S GULL (NB)

BONAPARTE'S GULL (B)

LITTLE GULL (NB)

LITTLE GULL (B)

LAUGHING GULL (NB)

LAUGHING GULL (B)

LAUGHING GULL

HEERMANN'S GULL

HERRING GULL

CALIFORNIA GULL

GLAUCOUS GULL

GREAT BLACK-BACKED GULL

GLAUCOUS-WINGED GULL

ICELAND GULL (SUBSPECIES *THAYERI*)

HERRING GULL

GREAT BLACK-BACKED GULL

GLAUCOUS-WINGED GULL

GLAUCOUS GULL

SHORT-BILLED GULL

RING-BILLED GULL

LESSER BLACK-BACKED GULL

WESTERN GULL

ICELAND GULL (KUMLIEN'S)

ICELAND GULL (THAYER'S)

CALIFORNIA GULL

HEERMANN'S GULL

BLACK-HEADED GULL

BONAPARTE'S GULL

LITTLE GULL

BLACK-LEGGED KITTIWAKE

LESSER BLACK-BACKED GULL

WESTERN GULL

FRANKLIN'S GULL

RING-BILLED GULL

SHORT-BILLED GULL

Iceland Gull

Background

Iceland Gulls breed on remote seaside cliffs in the northernmost reaches of North America, including the islands of the Canadian Arctic and Greenland. Because of their isolation, there is still much to learn about them. Iceland Gulls are always a nice winter find when they occur in mixed gull flocks, standing out from the more common Ring-Billed, Herring, and other large white-headed gulls with their pale plumage and distinctive wingtips.

Iceland Gulls in the East (ssp. *kumlieni*) are notably paler than any of the regularly occurring gulls, with immature birds having pale-tan primaries similar in shade to the rest of the plumage. Adults have gray to dark-gray/blackish tips to the outermost primaries. Along the West Coast, Iceland Gulls (ssp. *thayeri*) are slightly smaller than the average Herring Gull, with a rounder head and more delicate build. The folded primaries are brown or brownish black and pale edged in immature birds, blackish in adults (as opposed to darker jet black in most Herring Gulls). They are a subtler, dark-eyed counterpoint to the burly gulls that dominate Pacific beaches.

Noted Canadian Arctic ornithologist Dewey Soper aptly captured the beauty of Iceland Gulls in this description of a breeding colony on coastal Baffin Island:

On June 7, 1931, a small breeding colony was found on an island in Soper Lake, when many of the nests contained fresh eggs. Large numbers of Kumlien's Gulls were discovered at various places along the coast from Lake Harbour to Icy Cove. A particularly notable nesting colony of about three hundred individuals was observed in mid-July at the northern extremity of Itivirk Bay. It was quite impossible to reach these nests, but they were seen to hold immatures still being tended by the adults. The latter afforded a memorable sight as in a restless cloud they wheeled hysterically in dexterous evolutions against the bleak facade of the great promontory. (Soper 1946)

In Audubon's day, Iceland Gulls (ssp. *kumlieni*) were referred to as White-Winged Silvery Gulls (Audubon 1844), which seems appropriate for the pale eastern birds. Some pale adult *kumlieni* can resemble a miniature Glaucous Gull with white primary tips, while darker adults with blackish markings in the primaries more closely resemble ssp. *thayeri*. The taxonomy of Iceland Gulls remains muddled; until recently, *kumlieni* and *thayeri* were treated as separate species. However, the two were merged under Iceland Gull in 2017, largely on the basis of their inter-breeding on Baffin Island, eastern Southhampton Island, and Digges

Sound (Snell et al. 2020).

Three subspecies are now included under Iceland Gull: *kumlieni* (which winters in small numbers in the East), *thayeri* (which winters along the Pacific coast), and *glaucoides* (which winters in northwestern Europe). Because North American birders see only *kumlieni* and *thayeri*, this discussion is restricted to those two subspecies, which can usually be separated by the pattern and shade of the primaries and the color of the mantle, as well as their separate wintering ranges. However, strays of each subspecies have ended up on the "wrong" coast, and birds in the Midwest can be confusingly intermediate, so it pays to note the pattern of the primaries, shade of the mantle, eye color, and other marks to be certain which subspecies you are looking at. Also, much variation exists within both *thayeri* and *kumlieni*, and some gulls cannot be definitively assigned to subspecies.

Identifying the subspecies *thayeri* and distinguishing first-winter *thayeri* from faded first-winter Herring Gulls and West Coast hybrid combinations is particularly vexing and remains one of the most challenging aspects of gull identification. Adding to the conundrum, the subspecies *kumlieni* is notoriously variable, and some overlap exists between *thayeri* and *kumlieni*. However, as a general rule, *thayeri* have more-extensive and darker primary tip markings (dark brown in immatures and blackish or slaty gray in adults) and slightly darker mantles than *kumlieni*. With the recent merging of Kumlien's Gulls and Thayer's Gulls as one species, some have suggested that a new, more inclusive name be used; some of my favorites are Arctic Gull, Baffin Gull, or Silver-Winged Gull (Retter 2017).

Iceland Gulls are a rare treat wherever they occur. I have always enjoyed studying their nuanced plumage and debating with friends whether a particular bird is a "Kumlien's" or a "Thayer's" Gull. Both subspecies have shown up at Schoolhouse Pond, and finding one on my lunch break provided an optimistic "anything can happen" lens with which to view the rest of the day. I've always been fascinated by Arctic gulls, birds that breed in remote and inaccessible locations, and identification challenges, and Iceland Gulls have all these characteristics and more.

Structure and Field Marks

Iceland Gulls can be difficult to characterize at all ages owing to variation within the species and between the subspecies. Pale *kumlieni* can have wingtips as pale as Glaucous Gulls, while dark *thayeri* can have almost as much black in the wingtips as some Herring Gulls. Iceland Gulls are slightly smaller than Herring Gulls and display a slightly shorter, narrower, and daintier bill and a more rounded, dovelike head. However, male Iceland Gulls may overlap in size and structure with female Herring Gulls.

The *thayeri* subspecies has been called the "in-between gull" because they can resemble other species (Garner and Mactavish 2001). In many ways, for example, ssp. *thayeri* is intermediate in plumage, size, and structure between ssp. *kumlieni* and Herring Gulls. Thus, a suite of field marks need to be considered—for example, structure (head and bill shape, size) and plumage (wingtip shade and pattern, color of the upperparts and bare parts)—for identification.

First-Year Plumage

While variable in plumage, Iceland Gulls at this age tend to be paler and more neatly patterned than first-year Herring Gulls. Whereas immature Herring Gulls appear a messy, mottled mix of dark brown, tan, and black, Iceland Gulls are a pale creamy white or tan with a neat checkered pattern of tan-and-white markings. Subspecies *kumlieni* has primary tips that are whitish to light tan, similar to the rest of the upperparts. Also, the tertials are similar in color to the rest of the plumage, and the birds lack a dark secondary bar (or trailing edge of the extended inner wing) in flight. The tail is a medium brown that offers little contrast to the tan rump.

Subspecies *thayeri* is darker than *kumlieni* in all respects, although still paler than the vast majority of Herring Gulls, particularly on the folded primaries, tertials, and underwing. The tertials are medium brown, the primaries are dark brown with pale edges, and the rest of the upperparts is checkered with white or tan markings. The body is the palest part of the plumage, with the tertials darker and the wingtips and tail darkest—this gradation is lacking on similarly aged Herring Gulls or subspecies *kumlieni*. Also, the stepped gradation is usually muted on the hybrid combinations that look superficially similar to subspecies *thayeri*. If *thayeri* can be described as having a coffee-and-cream plumage, subspecies *kumlieni* is a shade or two paler, particularly on the tertials and primaries, much like coffee with too much cream.

Second-Year Plumage

At this age, many gulls acquire a pink bill with a well-defined black tip and some gray on the mantle. The mantle of eastern Iceland Gulls (subspecies *kumlieni*) is pale gray, while western Iceland Gulls (subspecies *thayeri*) have a slightly darker or medium-gray mantle. Many eastern Iceland Gulls attain a pale eye in their second year, while most western Iceland Gulls retain a dark eye. While second-winter *thayeri* can appear somewhat contrasting with blackish folded primaries, medium- or light-brown coverts, and medium-gray mantle, second-year *kumlieni* appear much more uniform, with a pale-gray mantle contrasting little with the pale-cream wing coverts and primaries.

Third-Year Plumage

Iceland Gulls in their third year look very much like adults. They have some dark feathers on the tail and a brownish wash to the wing coverts and retain some black toward the bill tip.

Adult Plumage

Western birds (*thayeri*) have black on the outer five or six primaries, interspersed with white tongues or white on the inner vanes, creating a "venetian blind" pattern of black and white stripes.

Eastern birds (*kumlieni*) are more variable; some adults have mostly or all-white folded primaries (much like subspecies *glaucoides* or a small Glaucous Gull), and others have extensive dark-gray markings on the primary tips (like *thayeri*). Most have dark-gray markings on the four or five outermost primaries and a large white tip on the outermost primary (Alderfer and Dunn 2014). In winter, the head and nape are washed with light-brown streaks and smudges, while breeding-plumage birds have a clean white head.

All adult Iceland Gulls acquire a red or reddish-purple orbital ring in breeding plumage that can be seen with close views and is useful in separating darker birds from adult Herring Gulls, which have a bright-yellow orbital ring. Western birds have dark eyes, while eastern birds have pale eyes. However, up to 20 percent of western birds have paler irises (Howell and Elliott 2001), while some eastern birds have dark eyes. So, although eye color is frequently mentioned as a field mark for *thayeri*, it is so variable that it is at best a supporting feature to be used with other field marks.

Size

Iceland Gulls are a medium to medium-large gull, about the same size as a small Herring Gull, but have a more rounded head and a thinner bill that lacks the pronounced gonydeal angle of many larger gulls. Western birds are slightly larger than eastern birds. Iceland Gulls average 20.5 to 23.6 inches long. Males weigh between 2 pounds, 1.2 ounces, and 2 pounds, 6.8 ounces. Females weigh between 1 pound, 12.9 ounces, and 1 pound, 15.7 ounces.

A typical late-first-winter Iceland Gull (ssp. *kumlieni*), showing a pale plumage overall, black bill, and subtly marked wing coverts and undertail coverts. Niagara Falls, New York, March 18, 2018.

A fairly dark juvenile/first-winter Iceland Gull (ssp. *kumlieni*). The primaries are concolorous with the rest of the upperparts. Cecil County Landfill, Maryland, January 7, 2017.

The extended wing and tail of this first-winter Iceland Gull (ssp. *thayeri*) are shown here. Note the pale-brown and tan pattern to the plumage, medium-brown tailband, and pale inner webs to the outermost primaries. Cecil County Landfill, Maryland, December 24, 2012. *Photo by Sean McCandless*

A resting juvenile/first-winter Iceland Gull (ssp. *thayeri*) shows the subtly marked "coffee and cream" plumage typical on West Coast birds. The feathers on the upperparts are edged with white. Barrow, Alaska, October 2, 2015.

The dark bill, large eye within a small head, and subtle plumage markings are evident on this first-winter Iceland Gull (ssp. *kumlieni*) in flight. Lewes, Delaware, December 2008.

A juvenile/first-winter West Coast Iceland Gull (ssp. *thayeri*) with a juvenile Glaucous Gull (*front bird*). The Iceland Gull has its wings spread, clearly showing the pale flight feather in contrast with the darker body and wing coverts. Barrow, Alaska, October 2, 2015.

A juvenile/first-year Iceland Gull (ssp. *thayeri*) with two first-year Glaucous Gulls. Barrow, Alaska, October 2, 2015.

A first-winter Iceland Gull (ssp. *kumlieni*) has pale plumage, including the tertials and primaries. Niagara Falls, New York, March 18, 2018.

The tertials and primaries of this first-winter Iceland Gull (ssp. *thayeri*) are darker than the rest of the plumage, and the brownish-black primaries have pale edges. Marina Landfill, California, February 9, 2018.

This second-summer Iceland Gull (ssp. *kumlieni*) displays a full gray mantle that contrasts with the pale, bleached body; wing coverts; and primaries. Assateague State Park, Maryland, May 21, 2020.

This second-winter Iceland Gull was identified as ssp. *thayeri* on the basis of range, but the plumage (particularly the tertials and folded primaries) approach the paleness seen on ssp. *kumlieni*. North Salmon Creek, California, February 6, 2011.

A second-winter Iceland Gull (ssp. *kumlieni*) in flight. Cecil County Landfill, Maryland, March 7, 2015. *Photo by Sean McCandless*

A second-winter Iceland Gull (ssp. *kumlieni*) in flight. Note the gray mantle, pale-brown tailband, and pale plumage. Cecil County Landfill, Maryland, March 7, 2015. *Photo by Sean McCandless*

A second-winter Iceland Gull (ssp *thayeri*). The medium-brown primaries separate it from ssp. *kumlieni*. Another identifier, the tertials, are a shade or two darker brown than the wing coverts. Cecil County Landfill, Maryland, December 24, 2012. *Photo by Sean McCandless*

An adult Iceland Gull (ssp. *thayeri*) has a large amount of white in the folded primaries and a dark eye. Cecil County Landfill, Maryland, March 19, 2015. *Photo by Sean McCandless*

Two adult Iceland Gulls (ssp. *thayeri*) feature a dark eye, bright-pink legs, and parallel-edged bill. San Francisco, January 28, 2016. *Photo by Sean McCandless*

An adult Iceland Gull (ssp. *thayeri*) in flight displays an alternating black-and-gray pattern on the spread primary tips. Cecil County Landfill, Maryland, March 19, 2015. *Photo by Sean McCandless*

This flying adult Iceland Gull (ssp. *kumlieni*) shows the restricted dark (slate-gray) markings on the extended primaries. Compare the color of the primaries with ssp. *thayeri*. Massachusetts, in February. *Photo by A. & J. Binns / VIREO*

Seen from below, this adult Iceland Gull (ssp. *thayeri*) is fairly pale, with only a narrow black border to the tips of the outermost primaries visible on the lower side of the wing. Cecil County Landfill, Maryland, March 19, 2015. *Photo by Sean McCandless*

This adult Iceland Gull (ssp. *thayeri*) shows significantly less black in the primaries of the extended wing than most Herring Gulls. Notice the "venetian blind" pattern of alternating black and gray/white in the wingtips. San Francisco, January 28, 2016. *Photo by Sean McCandless*

An adult Iceland Gull (*left*; ssp. *kumlieni*) is shown next to a Herring Gull. The blackish primaries with extensive white in the folded wing are evident, as are the slightly rounder head, smaller size, and smaller, more yellow-tinged bill compared to the Herring Gull. Niagara Falls, New York, March 17, 2018.

This adult Iceland Gull (ssp. *thayeri*) has a paler eye than most West Coast Iceland Gulls. Half Moon Bay, California, January 28, 2016. *Photo by Sean McCandless*

An adult Iceland Gull (ssp. *kumlieni*) with pale primaries showing extensive white and pale gray on the folded wings. Wells, Maine, in January. *Photo G. McElroy / VIREO*

This adult Iceland Gull (ssp. *kumlieni*) shows darker gray on the folded primaries than the gull in the preceding photo. St. John's, Newfoundland, in February. *Photo by J. Poklen / VIREO*

Chapter 3. Medium-Sized White-Headed Gulls

CALIFORNIA GULL

Background

Many visitors to the American West are surprised to see gulls in such a barren landscape. But California Gulls favor the saline lakes of the arid interior mountain West, frequently surrounded by vast expanses of dry habitat. They breed on islands in large lakes that offer predator-free areas for nesting. David Winkler summarized this apparent contradiction in *Birds of North America*:

Many summer visitors to the interior of western North America are puzzled when, hiking along the shore of a salt lake, a prairie slough, or an alpine tarn, they hear above them the sound of the sea. Looking up, they may be further surprised when they see a gull soaring, its white underparts gleaming from the reflected light of the water or salt flat below. This gull, far from the ocean, is likely breeding on islands in a nearby lake, for the California Gull is a breeding bird of inland seas. (Winkler 2020)

Highly adaptable, California Gulls are found with other gulls both in natural and man-made habitats. They sometimes run along the edge of saline lakes or nearby salt flats with their head down and bill open, scooping up brine flies as they go. They are opportunistic enough to get food for their young not just from the lakes on which they nest, but also from the surrounding habitat. They can even be seen flying over parched sagebrush flats if there are small bodies of water nearby. The largest breeding colonies include the Great Salt Lake in Utah and Mono Lake in California. While most California Gulls breed inland, they winter along the West Coast or at large interior lakes such as Lake Tahoe, the Great Salt Lake, Mono Lake, and Pyramid Lake. Small numbers of California Gulls are year-round residents along the Front Range of Colorado.

California Gulls are famous as the "seagull" that came to the aid of Mormon settlers in Utah during an insect plague in 1848. Vast numbers of "Mormon crickets" arrived in May of that year and rapidly began devouring the spring crops. All attempts by the settlers to end the infestation, including fire, water-filled trenches, and reportedly bludgeoning the insects with brooms, clubs, and other makeshift weapons, were unsuccessful (Smith 1922). California Gulls came to the rescue, descending in large numbers to devour the crickets. This event was dubbed the "miracle of the gulls" and is documented as follows:

When all seemed lost, and the Saints were giving up in despair, the heavens became clouded with gulls, which hovered over the fields, uttering their plaintive scream. Was this a new evil come upon them? Such were the thoughts of some who expected that what the crickets left the gulls would destroy; but not so, the gulls in countless battalions descended and began to devour the crickets, waging a battle for the preservation of the crops. They ate, they gorged upon the pest, and then flying to the streams would drink and vomit and again return to the battle front. This took place day by day until the crickets were destroyed. The people gave thanks, for this was to them a miracle. Surely the Lord was merciful and had sent the gulls as angels of mercy for their salvation. (Smith 1922)

In June 1848, Latter-day Saints president Brigham Young was told, "Sea gulls have come in large flocks from the lake and sweep the crickets as they go" (Sadler 1992). The *St. Louis Republican* reported on July 16, 1849, that "hundreds and thousands of gulls made their appearance early in the spring, and as soon as the crickets appeared, the gulls made war on them, and they have swept them clean, so that there is scarce a cricket to be found in the valley." Although other factors likely contributed to the crickets' demise, the California Gull's place in Utah lore was ensured.

California Gulls have been increasing across much of the West and are becoming more frequent in the East. They are now annual in the mid-Atlantic region and are increasing in the Great Lakes region and the Midwest. Therefore, it is important that birders in the East look for this western visitor among flocks of more-common Ring-Billed and Herring Gulls.

There are two subspecies of California Gull. The nominate *californicus* breeds in interior British Columbia, eastern Washington and Oregon, the Great Basin region, and Colorado. Ssp. *albertaensis* breeds from the northern plains to the Northwest Territories. The distribution of subspecies during nonbreeding season is not fully understood, but both subspecies appear to intermingle along the Pacific coast from southeast Alaska to northwest Mexico. Ssp. *californicus* is slightly smaller and has a darker mantle than *albertaensis*. While these differences are subtle, they are apparent on birds seen side by side.

California Gulls are an adaptable, widespread, and captivating species that can take advantage of harsh habitats seemingly unsuitable for "sea" gulls. Whether you are hiking along a saline lake in the arid West, scanning the birds of a small pond in the high plains, or searching through waterfowl at a wetland along the Front Range of Colorado, seeing a California Gull is a refreshing sight, a friendly reminder of the sea and the birdlife usually associated with it. The dark eye set in a white face, the long pencil-shaped bill, and yellow legs readily distinguish adults from the species with which they associate. The legs of many immatures are a strikingly brilliant shade of blue rarely matched by other species. Widespread in the West, rare and unexpected in the East, California Gulls are a welcome addition to any gull flock that they grace.

Structure and Field Marks

California Gulls are intermediate in size between Herring Gulls and Ring-Billed Gulls. Put simply, they are smaller and thinner billed and have a longer primary extension than any of the large white-headed gulls (Herring, Western, and Glaucous-Winged) with which they associate. In comparison, California Gulls have a longer wingspan and a heavier bill than either Ring-Billed or Short-Billed Gulls. The long wings are evident both at rest and in flight. And the trim, long, and attenuated body is evident on most birds, particularly in comparison to larger and bulkier Herring Gulls. In flight, California Gulls have noticeably longer wings than Ring-Billed Gulls. These wings may appear even longer in the field due to their narrowness, particularly at the base of the wing. In comparison, Herring Gulls have a much-broader wing at the base, making it appear shorter winged even though the wingspan is greater than in California Gulls. Last, California Gulls have a long, tubular bill, lending it in almost "pencillike" appearance. It is longer than the bill of a Ring-Billed Gull, while lacking the gonydeal expansion of most Herring Gulls.

First-Year Plumage

First-winter California Gulls, like most four-year gulls, are extremely variable in plumage. At this age, the species is easily confused with first-winter Herring Gulls. However, they are structurally different in the ways mentioned previously. The bill is bubblegum pink with a well-defined black tip. Herring Gulls can also have this pattern, but usually the black covers the entire bill or stretches from the tip to the gape. California Gulls tend to have more uniformly dark primaries on the extended wing, while first-winter Herring Gulls have a pale area on the inner primaries of the extended wing.

In other distinctions, California Gulls have a pale face, throat, and upper breast. The dark streaking on the nape and sides of the neck makes these white areas stand out. Although Herring Gulls often develop a paler head, particularly toward late winter, they almost always are more uniformly brownish or heavily streaked on the throat and upper breast. The mantle and scapulars of first-winter California Gulls frequently include a few gray feathers that are mixed in with the otherwise mottled brownish/tan upperparts. The dark greater coverts contrast with paler median and lesser coverts on resting California Gulls. This field mark is often visible from a great distance and is muted or absent on similarly aged Herring Gulls.

Second-Year Plumage

The medium-gray mantle is evident at this age and on older birds, and it is several shades darker than on the Herring Gull or first-winter Ring-Billed Gull. The dark greater coverts are also still evident at this age and contrast with the pale median and upper-wing coverts. Second-summer California Gulls can become bleached and worn, but the same field marks are visible. Both second- and third-year California Gulls can have a distinctly bluish cast to their legs and base of the bill, which is unique among North American gulls. Second-winter Ring-Billed Gulls can have a bluish-green tint to the legs, but this is much less consistently seen and tends to be paler, lacking the deep-bluish-gray tones of California Gulls.

Third-Year Plumage

Compared to adults, the gulls have more-extensive dark markings on the bill, duller bare parts, and sometimes the previously mentioned bluish legs. Like other four-year gulls, third-winter California Gulls often retain dark markings in the tertials and tail. Like adults, third-year California Gulls have dark eyes that contrast strongly with the white face.

Adult Plumage

Adult California Gulls are attractive birds with several distinctive field marks. The upper-parts are several shades darker than either Ring-Billed or Herring Gulls. This feature alone is usually enough to identify them. The long and tubular bill includes both black and red marks toward the tip, although the black mark may be missing or faint on some breeding adults. The red-and-black bill markings, in conjunction with the structure of the bill (long and parallel edged, lacking a pronounced gonydeal angle), make the bill distinctive. The dark eye is a particularly good mark to look for on an out-of-place California Gull in the East. Adult Iceland Gulls (subspecies *thayeri*) have dark eyes too, but their pink leg color separates them from California Gulls. Adult Short-Billed Gulls also have dark eyes but are significantly more petite than California Gulls and lack red markings on the bill.

Leg color in adult California Gulls can vary from dull yellow with a greenish tinge to mustard yellow. Another useful mark is the black in the outermost primaries, which reaches all the way to the primary coverts. The black in the wingtips contrasts strongly with the rest of the wing from above and below. This field mark can be seen from a long distance on flying gulls.

Size

California Gulls are medium to large, intermediate in size between Ring-Billed Gulls and Herring Gulls. They seem proportionally more long winged and streamlined than any of the large, white-headed gulls such as Herring and Western. Males are larger than females both in weight and wingspan, and *albertaensis* is larger than *californicus*, although there is overlap in both categories. Ssp. *californicus* weighs between 15.2 ounces and 1 pound, 15.2 ounces, while *albertaensis* weigh between 1 pound, 4 ounces, and 2 pounds, 4.9 ounces. California Gulls are 17.5 to 20.1 inches long and have a wingspan ranging from 48.0 to 55.1 inches.

Note the dark greater coverts and bicolored bill on this first-winter California Gull. Also note the variegated pattern of the upperparts, with a few adultlike gray feathers mixed into the mantle, which other first-year four-year gulls usually lack. Virginia Lake, Reno, Nevada, March 7, 2007.

This first-winter California Gull has a white throat and streaking on the side of the neck, as well as a gray speckled mantle and long primary extension. Virginia Lake, Reno, Nevada, March 7, 2007.

Note the white neck and breast of this first-winter California Gull. Similarly aged Herring Gulls are more heavily streaked in these areas. Ventura, California, February 19, 2016.

An adult California Gull (*above*) and a first-winter California Gull. Note the extensive black in the primary tips of the adult, and the lack of a pale panel on the inner primaries of the first-winter bird. Ventura, California, February 19, 2016.

Note the dark-brown primaries and secondaries, as well as the lack of a pale window in the inner primaries on this first-winter California Gull in flight. The barred rump contrasts with dark tailband. Monterey, California, October 3, 2009.

The first-winter California Gull has a pale forehead and throat, darker greater coverts, and variably patterned mantle. Ventura, California, February 19, 2016.

Although this first-summer California Gull is heavily worn, the dark greater coverts contrast with the pale median and lesser coverts, and its gray mantle feathers are coming in. Port Angeles, Washington, August 7, 2016.

A second-winter California Gull exhibits the bright-blue bill and legs some-times seen at this age. Ventura, California, February 19, 2016.

The dark gray mantle on this second-winter California Gull simplifies the identification. They have a significantly darker mantle than Ring-Billed and Herring Gulls. Virginia Lake, Reno, Nevada, March 7, 2007.

This second-winter California Gull has bluish legs; a black-tipped, parallel-edged bill; and incoming adultlike feathers on the mantle, wing coverts, and tertials. Point Reyes National Seashore, California, February 6, 2011.

Note the bluish tint to the legs and bill on this second-winter California Gull. Ventura, California, February 19, 2016.

This third-winter California Gull is aged by the brown in the wing coverts, extensive black on the tip of the bill, and bluish leg color. Pebble Beach, California, February 4, 2018.

The black ring on the bill (lacking the red gonydeal spot) and the dark markings on the tertials distinguish this third-winter California Gull from an adult. Ventura, California, February 14, 2016.

These adult California Gulls show some variation in the color of the bare parts. Virginia Lake, Reno, Nevada, March 7, 2007.

Note the distinct bill markings, dark eye, and short-legged appearance of this adult California Gull. Virginia Lake, Reno, Nevada, March 7, 2007.

The extensive black in the extended wing can be seen on the adult birds on the upper and lower side of the primaries. The immature birds show more black and brown on the extended wing and lack white on the primary tips. Pebble Beach, California, February 4, 2018.

Adult California Gulls.
Note the dark eye and
narrow, parallel-edged bill
with both black and red
markings toward the tip.
Marina Landfill,
California, February 9,
2018.

Ssp. *californicus* (*left*) and ssp. *albertaensis*
(*right*). The difference in mantle shade
and size is clearly seen. Ssp. *albertaensis* is
both larger and lighter than ssp. *californicus. Smithsonian Institution Collection,
Washington DC*

The red orbital ring and gape can be seen on
this adult breeding-plumage California
Gull. Virginia Lake, Reno, Nevada, March
7, 2007.

RING-BILLED GULL

Background

This common three-year gull is the most widespread North American gull and the most numerous in many areas. Ring-Billed Gulls have taken human adaptation to the highest level, not only living in proximity to people but interacting with them daily in parking lots and urban parks. Even in highly developed areas, it is common to see them flying overhead, resting on a light pole, or eyeing a fast-food dumpster. In areas where few other bird species can be found, Ring-Billed Gulls lend an avian presence, particularly when the opportunity for a free handout presents itself.

In Audubon's day, Ring-Billed Gulls were known as the "common American gull." Gregarious and feisty, winter flocks can number in the thousands at landfills; on sandy beaches, mudflats along estuaries, and frozen ponds; and in open fields, where they forage for insects and worms.

Although it is part of the white-headed gull complex, Ring-Billed Gulls have been known to hybridize with hooded gulls such as Laughing Gulls and Black-Headed Gulls. These hybrids can display a bewildering array of field marks, usually intermediate between the parent species, but some hybrids cannot be definitively identified. Leucistic and albino Ring-Billed Gulls also occur. Pure albino Ring-Billed Gulls are striking gulls displaying pure-white plumage with pinkish-orange bare parts, with a darker maroon ring around the bill.

I've often thought of this species as "the friendly neighborhood gull," and the reality of this was driven home by a fascinating study compiled by Ken MacKenzie of the Massachusetts Department of Conservation and Recreation (DCR). In "The Life and Travels of Ring-Billed Gulls," DCR tracked the movement of Ring-Billed Gulls to figure out how to discourage them from congregating around crucial intake structures of the Wachusett Reservoir, which supplies the drinking water for the Greater Boston area. Gulls were banded and wing-tagged; some were also fitted with satellite transmitters, which supplied the most-detailed information on their movements. Ring-Billed Gulls banded and tagged in Massachusetts turned up in a remarkable variety of far-flung locations.

One gull identified as 87428 visited multiple states, took advantage of a variety of food sources, and showed an affinity for areas with lots of people. Gull 87428 was located primarily in parking lots during the late fall and winter, often fed on worms in fields in early spring, and also frequented wastewater treatment plants, landfills, and parks for food. It visited metropolitan areas in the Northeast, with stops in Philadelphia, New York, Boston, Buffalo, Toronto, and Montreal, making a smaller number of visits to more natural locations near towns or bodies of water (I imagine a few stops at rest areas along I-95 as well). Gull 87428 roosted at a variety of freshwater and saltwater locations and used Wachusett Reservoir from October to December of each year. Another Ring-Billed Gull (A161) was recorded up and down the East Coast between New Jersey and Newfoundland. Others were sighted in Bermuda and Manitoba (MacKenzie 2013).

Ring-Billed Gulls nest in the interior of North America in the northern United States and across much of southern Canada. Nest sites are colonial and usually near a pond, lake, or river. In eastern North America, Ring-Billed Gulls breed in proximity with Herring Gulls, in the Great Lakes region they nest with Common and Caspian Terns, and in the West they nest near California Gulls. Ring-Billed Gulls winter along both coasts and across much of the south-central United States. Wintering populations can also be found at large interior bodies of water such as the Great Lakes, Lake Tahoe, and the Great Salt Lake.

These approachable, often-overlooked birds should be heralded for their adaptability to habitat altered by development. They epitomize the intelligence and flexibility that characterize gulls and make them so successful as a group.

Structure and Field Marks

Ring-Billed Gulls are medium sized, significantly smaller in wingspan and weight than Herring Gulls but slightly larger than Laughing Gulls. Structurally, they resemble a small Herring Gull, and in flight they appear larger and sturdier than Laughing Gulls. Of the white-headed gulls, only the Short-Billed Gull is smaller than the Ring-Billed. Short-Billed Gulls are decidedly more roundheaded and petite, with a slimmer and more delicate bill. And California Gulls are noticeably larger than Ring-Billed Gulls, with a distinctly longer bill. In flight, Ring-Billed Gulls are more buoyant and maneuverable than the larger white-headed gulls, with quicker wingbeats.

First-Year Plumage

As three-year gulls, Ring-Billed Gulls hold on to their juvenile plumage only briefly, molting into their first-winter plumage by early or mid-fall of their first year, when they acquire gray mantle feathers. Juveniles can be variable in appearance, with many birds light to medium brown and heavily washed with brown below, while others are paler with a grayish-white base color and fewer markings or mottling below (Ayyash 2013). The juvenile bill is mostly dark with a diffuse base.

The grayish-brown markings and tan wash fade throughout the winter, with the underparts becoming a more uniform white. The greater coverts are a plain grayish brown, while the lesser and median coverts are darker brown (brown feather centers with paler edges), becoming progressively more faded. The bill is bicolored: pink with a black tip. In flight, the body appears white, as does the underside of the wings, except for some dark-brown or gray markings along the trailing edge, the outermost primaries, and underwing coverts.

Second-Year Plumage

Second-winter Ring-Billed Gulls can closely resemble adults, but several features separate this age group from adults. Many have acquired the lighter eye of an adult, but some retain a dark or dusky iris into the second winter. They also have more extensive black in the wingtips, with limited or no white on the primary tips. They may have some black in the tertials. The color of the bare parts, while yellow, can also be a slightly duller tone than shown on adults. In rare instances, second-winter birds may have a greenish or blue-gray hue on the legs or bill. Some birds have a slightly broader ring on the bill; it covers more of the tip than is typical on adults. In flight, the more extensive and "messy" black in the wingtips is evident. Many birds also retain a trace of a black tailband that is visible in flight.

Adult Plumage

Adults are identified by the yellow legs, pale-gray mantle, pale-yellow eyes, and ring around the yellow bill. Most birds have a moderate to long primary extension. The black is extensive in the primaries of adults and is clearly demarcated on both the upper and lower wing. Small white mirrors are visible toward the tips of the two outermost primaries, appearing as a small white area contained within the black wingtips on flying birds. Seen from below, the black contrasts with the pale flight feathers. One other feature to look for on distant, flying Ring-Billed Gulls is that the upper side of the middle and inner primaries is slightly paler gray than the upper-wing coverts and mantle. This causes the wing to appear progressively paler until it reaches the black primary tips. Other similar species (California and Herring Gulls) have a consistent shade of gray on the mantle and wings, lacking the change in tone shown on Ring-Billed Gulls.

Size

Ring-Billed Gulls are medium sized, significantly smaller than most Herring Gulls, and slightly larger and bulkier than Laughing Gulls. Ring-Billed Gulls average 16.1 to 19.3 inches long and have a wingspan of 45.3 to 53.1 inches (Olsen and Larsson 2004). Adult males weight from 1 pound, 1 ounce, to 1 pound, 7 ounces; females average 13 ounces to 1 pound, 5 ounces.

This brownish Ring-Billed Gull shows close to the maximum amount of brown for a juvenile Ring-Billed Gull. Sandy Point State Park, Maryland, October 6, 2013.

This first-winter Ring-Billed Gull retains many aspects of juvenile plumage into late winter, including the mostly dark bill, brown coverts, brown streaking on the breast and belly, and limited gray on the upperparts. Schoolhouse Pond, Maryland, February 4, 2009.

Note the grayish tone to the greater coverts, which stands out on the pale-brown plumage of this juvenile Ring-Billed Gull. Sandy Point State Park, Maryland, October 19, 2013.

This juvenile/first-fall Ring-Billed Gull has not begun to acquire its gray mantle in late October. It also retains a mostly dark bill. Sandy Point State Park, Maryland, October 20, 2013.

This juvenile Ring-Billed Gull shows the white-and-brown underwing and brown bars and chevrons on the body. The bill is bicolored like typical first-winter Ring-Billed Gulls. Eagle Harbor, Maryland, July 21, 2009.

Note the tan wing coverts, incoming gray mantle, dark-brown primaries, black-tipped pink bill, and dark eye of these first-winter Ring-Billed Gulls. Schoolhouse Pond, Maryland, February 1, 2018.

The fresh mantle and scapulars contrast with the worn wing coverts on this first-winter Ring-Billed Gull. Schoolhouse Pond, Maryland, April 19, 2011.

A first-winter Ring-Billed Gull in flight displays the well-defined tailband and the mixture of gray, black, and brown feathers on the upper wing. Sandy Point State Park, Maryland, September 22, 2012.

This first-winter Ring-Billed Gull shows a gray mantle and worn brown tertials and primaries. It is fairly pale with a limited brown wash beneath. Schoolhouse Pond, Maryland, January 5, 2017.

Note the bluish-gray tinge to the bare parts and the lack of white on the folded primaries on this second-winter Ring-Billed Gull. Sandy Point State Park, Maryland, October 18, 2009.

This second-winter Ring-Billed Gull looks much like an adult, except for the all-dark primary tips and barring on the body. Schoolhouse Pond, Maryland, February 7, 2013.

This second-winter Ring-Billed Gull retains dark markings in the tertials and some brown in the wing coverts and lacks white in the primaries. Schoolhouse Pond, Maryland, November 27, 2008.

This second-winter Ring-Billed Gull displays a bluish tinge to the base of the bill and limited white in the primary tips. Schoolhouse Pond, Maryland, September 16, 2011.

These adult Ring-Billed Gulls are typical of the species in winter, with their lightly streaked heads and trademark black ring around the yellow bill. Schoolhouse Pond, Maryland, February 1, 2018.

This adult Ring-Billed Gull has the clean white head and reddish-orange orbital ring and gape typical of breeding-plumage Ring-Billed Gulls. Chalk Point, Maryland, July 1, 2010.

An adult Ring-Billed Gull shows the extensive and well-demarcated black in the outermost primaries. Assateague National Seashore, Maryland, November 11, 2017.

An adult Ring-Billed Gull has black on the underside of the primaries, contrasting strongly with the white underwing. Assateague National Seashore, Maryland, November 11, 2017.

An adult Ring-Billed in flight, with a first-winter Iceland Gull perched below. Notice how the black is extensive and strongly contrasting both on the upper and lower sides of the primaries. Schoolhouse Pond, Maryland, December 17, 2014.

Adult Ring-Billed Gull.
Sandy Point State Park,
Maryland, September 22,
2021.

This Ring-Billed Gull has
a lightly streaked head and
bold white spots on the
primaries, typical of adults
at this time of year.
Schoolhouse Pond,
Maryland, February 1,
2018.

This breeding-plumage
adult Ring-Billed Gull has
a clean white head,
reddish-orange orbital
ring, and reddish gape.
Chalk Point, Maryland,
July 1, 2010.

A leucistic/partial-albino Ring-Billed Gull. This bird has mostly snow-white plumage, with brown feathers only on the tertials and primaries, and some streaking on the head. Schoolhouse Pond, Maryland, February 26, 2015.

An albino adult Ring-Billed Gull is seen with second-winter Ring-Billed Gulls. The albino had a pure-white plumage, and the bare parts were a pinkish orange in color. The ring on the bill was a deeper reddish tone. Schoolhouse Pond, Maryland on March 27, 2002.

A leucistic adult gull with upperparts heavily marked with white. Schoolhouse Pond, Maryland, February 9, 2010.

SHORT-BILLED GULL

Background

Short-Billed Gulls are the smallest white-headed gull in North America. They were formerly known as Mew Gulls for their high-pitched, shrill call. They are flexible and adaptable, feeding and nesting both in saltwater and freshwater habitats. Short-Billed Gulls are the only white-headed gull that regularly nests in trees, although they also construct more-conventional nests on the ground. In breeding season, Short-Billed Gulls can be found in tundra, marshes, stream valleys, lakes, and seaside cliffs. During the nonbreeding season they are largely coastal birds, visiting beaches, estuaries, and ponds. Along the coast they feed on small fish and can be seen foraging for insects and grains in flooded fields. They are common at wastewater treatment plants but rarely visit offshore waters or the landfills where larger and more-aggressive species dominate.

Short-Billed Gulls are readily differentiated from other gulls by their proportions alone. Their small, rounded head; extremely thin, short, tapered bill; and dark eye give the gull a gentle, delicate, and confiding appearance. W. L. Dawson offered the following colorful description from his observations in Washington State in 1909:

A certain childish innocence and simplicity appear to distinguish these birds from the more sophisticated herrings and glaucous-wings. They are the small fry of the great gull companies which throng our borders in winter, allowed to share, indeed, when Petro dumps a rich load of restaurant waste, but expected to take a grumbling back seat when the supply of food is more limited. One may see at a glance that they are not fitted for competition. Their bills are not only shorter, but much more delicately proportioned than those of the other gulls; while their gabbling, duck-like notes oppose a mild alto to the screams and high trumpetings of their larger congeners. (Bent 1921).

Short-Billed Gulls bob buoyantly on the water's surface, sometimes spinning in a circle, phalarope-like, in search of food. In flight, they are equally agile and maneuverable, swooping down to the water or fluttering mothlike above it in search of food. In these behaviors, Short-Billed Gulls are more like Bonaparte's Gulls than the other larger and more-ponderous white-headed gulls. Their abbreviated call has been described as high and squealing, sharp and querulous, or a shrill mewing (by Sibley, Bent, and Alderfer and Dunn, respectively). Dr. Joseph Grinnell went so far as to say that their call notes "remind one of the bark of a terrier" (Bent 1921). To me, the call sounds like a squeaky honk, vaguely reminiscent of a small goose. It stands out in strong contrast to the vocalizations of the larger, more-bellicose gulls with which it is sometimes found: Short-Billed Gulls are the pip-squeak of any West Coast gull gathering. Closely tied to the Pacific coast, Short-Billed Gulls are a fantastic find whenever they occur farther East.

Structure and Field Marks

Short-Billed Gulls have a rounded head, dark eye, and short, thin bill that narrows at the tip. They are dwarfed by their companion Western and Glaucous-Winged Gulls.

First-Year Plumage

Juvenile Short-Billed Gulls are a uniform grayish brown above and below. The upperparts are pale brown, and feathers on the upperparts have pale edges, giving the birds a scalloped or scaled appearance. This brownish wash, combined with dark-brownish primaries with white edges, gives them an almost Thayer's-like appearance, although Short-Billed Gulls are significantly more petite. The brownish wash of juvenile and many first-winter Short-Billed Gulls includes the wing coverts, breast, belly, and tertials. By midwinter, some gray has come in on the mantle. However, because the wing coverts retain the warm brownish tint, there is often little contrast between the gray of the mantle and the rest of the upperparts. The eye is dark and appears large within the head. The bill is a dull flesh color with a black tip. The base of the tail and the rump has a brownish-tan base color with dense brown streaking, showing little contrast with the dark-brown or blackish tailband. Undertail coverts are also washed with tan. The underwing is dusky tan and mostly unpatterned.

Unlike Ring-Billed Gulls, first-winter Short-Billed Gulls retain a tan or gray wash to the underparts (flank and belly). By summer, many birds bleach significantly on the wing coverts and underparts and often appear pale and worn, their bleached wing coverts contrasting with the fresher gray mantle.

Second-Year Plumage

Second-year Short-Billed Gulls look similar to adult gulls but have more black in the primary tips, black toward the tip of the bill, and a trace of a black tailband. The legs can have a greenish hue. The tertials on some birds retain dark centers.

Adult Plumage

Adult Short-Billed Gulls are extremely attractive in breeding plumage. The upperparts are medium gray, a shade or two darker than Ring-Billed or Herring Gulls. Adult Short-Billed Gulls also have dark eyes that contrast strongly with the white face. The bill ranges from yellow to greenish yellow in winter, becoming brighter yellow in breeding plumage. Birds in nonbreeding plumage can have faint marks or a trace of a ring toward the bill tip. The yellow legs match the bill on many adult Short-Billed Gulls. Adult birds have bold white wingtips, with white tongues and white tips to the middle primaries (P5–P8), and large white mirrors on the two outermost primaries (Howell and Dunn 2007). Some adult Short-Billed Gulls (presumably older adults) have more white than black on the folded primaries. Birds in breeding plumage have an white, unstreaked head, which further accentuates the dark eye. In nonbreeding plumage, Short-Billed Gulls have extensive brown streaking on the nape and back of the head.

Size

Short-Billed Gulls are the smallest of the white-headed gulls, although there is much variation among the subspecies groups. They range from 16.1 to 18.1 inches long and have a wingspan of 39.4 to 47.2 inches. Males weigh 13.3 ounces to 1 pound, 1.4 ounces, while females range from 11.5 to 13.9 ounces.

Taxonomy

Short-Billed Gull (*L. brachyrhynchus*) was formerly considered a subspecies of Mew Gull. The American Ornithological Society revised the Checklist of North American Birds in 2021 to treat *L. brachyrhynchus* as a full species (Short-Billed Gull). The Old World subspecies of Mew Gull (*L. canus* and *L. kamtschatschensis*) are now included under the species now known as Common Gull.

A first-winter Short-Billed Gull forages along a muddy shore. Note the brownish-gray plumage with some gray coming into the mantle. The small, bicolored bill is also evident, as is the petite size and rounded head. Tomales Bay, California, February 6, 2011.

This Short-Billed Gull shows the soft tan upper-parts and pale-edged dark folded primaries similar to a first-winter Iceland Gull (ssp. *thayeri*). Note the long primary extension, thin bill, and rounded head. MacKenzie, British Columbia, September. *Photo by J. Jantunen / VIREO*

First-winter Short-Billed Gulls bear a superficial resemblance to first-winter Iceland Gulls (ssp. *thayeri*), with their light-tan body and wing coverts, medium-brown tertials, and brownish-black, pale-tipped primaries. Tomales Bay, California, February 5, 2011.

Note the light-tan plumage overall, darker-brown tertials, and medium-brown primaries with paler edges on this first-winter Short-Billed Gull. Ventura, California, February 15, 2016.

This standing Short-Billed Gull shows the delicate features (rounded head, thin bill) typical of the species. The incoming gray mantle is evident on this first-winter gull. Sonoma County, California, November. *Photo by T. Grey / VIREO*

A first-winter Short-Billed Gull in flight displays its brownish-black tail and heavily barred rump and upper-tail coverts. Metchosin, British Columbia, in October. *Photo by J. Jantunen / VIREO*

Note the thinner bill and smaller, more rounded head of the first-winter Short-Billed Gull (*top center*) relative to the adjacent Ring-Billed Gull. The dark eye appears large in the small head of the Short-Billed Gull. Ventura, California, February 20, 2016.

This second-winter Short-Billed Gull has some brown feathers on the wing coverts, lacks any white on the folded primaries, and retains a dark bill tip. Pebble Beach, California, February 4, 2018.

Note the black in the tertials, the dark bill tip, and the lack of white on the folded primaries on this second-winter Short-Billed Gull. Tomales Bay, California, February 6, 2011.

This adult Short-Billed Gull shows the pattern of black, gray, and white in the primaries. The amount of black is significantly less extensive than of adult Ring-Billed Gulls. Nome, Alaska, in June. *Photo by Doug Wechsler / VIREO*

A breeding adult Short-Billed Gull has extensive white on the folded primaries. The specimen was collected on May 9, 1936, from Anchorage, Alaska. *Smithsonian Institution Collection, Washington, DC*

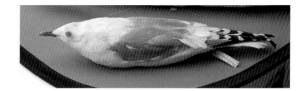

This beautiful adult Short-Billed Gull shows the dark eye, thin yellow bill, and white primary tips typical of the species at this age. Pebble Beach, California, February 4, 2018.

Those accustomed to finding gulls at the beach and songbirds in the treetops can be shocked by their first sighting of a Short-Billed Gull in a tree. They are the only white-headed gull that regularly nests in trees, as well as in more-conventional ground locations. Anchorage, Alaska, May 20, 2017.

These adult Short-Billed Gulls show the slender mustard-yellow bill and dark eye within a small, rounded head. Ventura, California, February 17, 2016.

This adult Short-Billed Gull shows the small, rounded head; dark eye; and thin yellow bill typical of the species at this age. The extensive white in the primaries and the long primary extension is also evident. Monterey, California, February 7, 2018.

Note the large white mirrors on the two outermost primaries and how the lower surface of the wing is a muted mirror image of the darker upper side on this adult Short-Billed Gull. An adult breeding-plumage Heermann's Gulls is in the background. Ventura, California, February 14, 2016.

Chapter 4. White-Hooded Gull

HEERMANN'S GULL

Background

Heermann's Gulls are arguably the most attractive of the North American gulls. They are distinctive at all ages but are at their most striking as breeding adults. Named after nineteenth-century naturalist Adolphus Lewis Heermann, they are sometimes called White-Headed Gulls, a term that applies most readily to breeding adults, whose slate-gray body, red bill, and snow-white head are truly stunning and set these birds apart from others. Even juvenile or first-winter birds are distinctive, and a much-darker sooty or chocolate brown than their counterparts.

They are more aggressive than similarly sized gulls, pirating food from pelicans or pursuing terns in jaeger-like flight. (In fact, young Heermann's Gulls can resemble immature jaegers with their brownish-gray plumage. An extremely small proportion of adult Heermann's Gulls have a variable white patch on the primary coverts, which is also reminiscent of jaegers.) While they pirate food both from birds and marine mammals, one of their favorite targets are Brown Pelicans. Like Laughing Gulls, Heermann's Gulls will even try to steal fish directly out of the pouch of Brown Pelicans! Arthur Cleveland Bent's *Life Histories of North American Gulls and Terns* provides insight on this behavior in a quote from A. W. Anthony:

Heermann's Gull is by far the most active and successful in catching small fish from the surface; but as a rule will seldom attempt to catch his own dinner if there are any pelicans among the delegates to the convention. I remember a very amusing incident of this nature I once witnessed on the coast of Lower California. The pelican, after securing a herring, "hacked water" until it was supposed to be far enough from its parasite to venture swallowing it, but as the huge bill was tipped up and opened the gull plunged forward and thrust its entire head and neck into the pouch; the pelican, somewhat quicker than most of its kind, closed down with a snap and caught the intruder, which in turn had caught the fish; neither would yield any advantages gained, and for perhaps half a minute the pelican towed the gull about by the head, amid most violent protest from a hundred or more gulls assembled, while other pelicans sat like solemn Judges, perhaps offering to arbitrate the question. At last a more violent twist than usual on the part of the gull freed him from limbo, minus a few feathers, but in no manner daunted, for a moment later it was following closely in the wake of the same pelican, waiting for it to plunge for another fish, and I never did learn which really swallowed the one in controversy. (Bent 1921)

They also follow fishing boats to score chum or other handouts. They forage over the ocean shoreline, dipping down to find prey or plunge-diving for small fish. At other times they feed in offshore kelp beds. Only at the landlocked Salton Sea are they found inland with any regularity.

Heermann's Gulls are the only North American gull that migrates south to breed and north for the nonbreeding and winter months, although some nonbreeding birds stay along the California coast year-round. They nest on desert islands in the upper portion of the Gulf of California, east of the Baja California peninsula. Due to tidal upwelling, this region is one of the most productive marine environments in the world, with small pelagic fish such as Pacific sardines and northern anchovies comprising the bulk of the gulls' diet (Islam and Velarde 2020).

Isla Raza (translated Flat Island) is the largest breeding ground for these gulls; an estimated 300,000 were counted during the 1990s (Islam and Velarde 2020). Their numbers have been increasing since it was declared a National Reserve and Refuge for Migratory Birds in 1964, thus protecting breeding colonies from egg collectors and other disturbances. Massive numbers of the gulls arrive at dusk and depart at dawn from their breeding colonies from mid-February to mid-March (Verlarde 1999). In summer and early fall they head north into coastal California and Washington and Vancouver Island. Their movement coincides with the postbreeding dispersal of Brown Pelicans. As noted earlier, Heermann's Gulls take advantage of this timing by following the pelicans and snatching fish from their bills when the larger birds emerge from the water.

They are one of only three North American gulls that breed in subtropical latitudes—Yellow-Footed Gulls and Western Gulls (subspecies *wymani*) are the others. Heermann's Gulls are closely related to Gray Gulls of South America. They share a distinctive white head and dark body, and both nest in desert habitat close to the sea. These two species are referred to collectively as white-hooded gulls of subgenus *Xema* (Howell and Dunn 2007).

Structure and Field Marks

Heermann's Gulls are distinctive in that young birds are dark brown as juveniles, becoming progressively grayer in their second and third years, while breeding adults are like a "photo negative" of a hooded gull—instead of a white body and black head, they have a white head and dark-gray body (Alderfer and Dunn 2014). While they are about the same size as Ring-Billed Gulls, they have a stouter bill, broader wings, and fuller chest. A short tail adds to this sturdy impression in flight.

First-Year Plumage

Juvenile Heermann's Gulls are a dark chocolate brown with lighter-brown feather edges on the upperparts. The mantle, scapulars, and upper-wing coverts have pale feather edges, lending a scalloped appearance. Legs are black and the bill is dull pink with a variable dusky tip. The tail and wingtips are black and contrast slightly with the dark-brown plumage. As Heermann's Gulls go into their first winter, the mantle and scapulars take on a grayer tint and contrast with the faded brown wing coverts. In flight, first-year gulls appear dark brown, with slightly darker flight feathers and tail. The wings are entirely dark, lacking any lighter areas above or below. The brown rump and upper-tail coverts contrast only slightly with the darker tail, unlike more-mature birds, which have a contrasting pale-gray rump.

Second-Year Plumage

Some birds are brownish gray, while others obtain a more advanced gray cast. The bill is pinkish orange to orange, decidedly brighter than on first-year birds. Second-year birds start to show small tertial and scapular crescents. In flight, second-year gulls lack the narrow white trailing edge to the secondaries and tail that is seen on third-year and adult gulls.

Third-Year Plumage

Third-year Heermann's Gulls look similar to nonbreeding adults, with adultlike plumage and a heavily streaked head and neck. However, several field marks can be used to reliably identify third-year birds. At this age they often retain a pale base to the lower mandible, which can be seen at close range. This yellowish or greenish area contrasts with the red color of the rest of the bill. Other points of distinction include a more evenly gray (or densely streaked) head, even during breeding season, and a brownish tinge to the upper-wing coverts. In flight, third-year gulls may show a narrower white trailing edge to the upper side of the wing compared to adult birds. The white extends only to the inner primaries of the open wing, not to the outer primaries as with adult birds (Howell and Dunn 2007).

Adult Plumage

Their dark-gray plumage above and below, snow-white head, and bright-red bill make the sight of a breeding adult Heermann's Gull unforgettable. Although the entire body is dark gray, the upperparts are a shade or two darker than the underparts. The black outer primaries, white-tipped black tail, and large tertial and scapular crescents provide additional contrast. In nonbreeding plumage, adult Heermann's Gulls have dense gray streaking on the head, which reduces the contrast between the white head and the dark-gray body. In flight, adult

Heermann's Gulls display a pale to medium-gray rump that contrasts strongly with the black tail. The upper wing and body appear evenly slate gray, with a slightly darker secondary bar and outer primaries. The lower side of the wing is a shade or two paler gray, with slightly darker outer primaries and wing coverts. In breeding plumage, the bright-white head and contrasting dark-gray body and wings are noticeable even on distant flying gulls.

Size

Heermann's Gulls are medium sized, similar or slightly larger than Ring-Billed Gulls. Males are slightly larger than females, although there is overlap. Length averages between 18.1 and 20.5 inches, with the wingspan averaging between 50.4 and 52.0 inches. Heermann's Gulls weight between 13.1 ounces and 1 pound, 6.7 ounces.

A first-year Heermann's Gull (*right*) with a second-year Heermann's Gull (*left*). First-year birds are a deep chocolate brown with lighter-brown highlights on the wing coverts and body. Second-year birds are still brownish but have a grayish cast. Santa Cruz, California, September 29, 2009.

A first-year Heermann's Gull (*left*). Note the brownish color with tannish wing coverts. The bill is a dull pink with a dark tip. Santa Cruz, California, September 29, 2009.

An advanced second-year gull is similar in many ways to a third-year Heermann's Gull. However, note the extensive black on the bill and the small tertial crescent indicative of a second-year gull. Monterey, California, October 2, 2009.

A second-year Heermann's Gull has uniform brownish plumage overall, with the darkest brown on the head. This bird has developed small scapular and tertial crescents. Santa Cruz, California, September 29, 2009.

Note the brownish wash to the head and nape, dull pinkish/orange bill, and brownish upperparts, including the scapulars and mantle, of this second-year Heermann's Gull. Monterey, California, October 3, 2009.

Many third-year Heermann's Gulls are indistinguishable from adults. This bird is aged by the pale base on its lower mandible and more uniform grayish head. Half Moon Bay, California, September 29, 2009.

This third-winter Heermann's Gull is aged by the faint brown wash to the wing coverts and the pale base to the lower mandible. Ventura, California, February 15, 2016.

This third-year Heermann's Gull looks much like an adult but has extremely heavy head streaking and a pale base on the lower mandible at a time of year when adults have a clean white head. Ventura, California, February 15, 2016.

Two adult Heermann's Gulls with a first-winter Western Gull (*top-rear gull*). The wing coverts and outer primaries are slightly darker than the flight feathers when seen from below. Monterey, California, October 3, 2009.

A group of flying Heermann's Gulls follow a boat on Monterey Bay. Monterey, California, October 3, 2009.

An adult Heermann's Gull and a Pigeon Guillemot. Monterey, California, October 3, 2009.

A worn adult Heermann's Gull. This fellow is missing some primaries. Torrey Pines State Reservation, California, August 27, 2006.

An adult Heermann's Gull has gray underparts, a white trailing edge to the secondaries and inner primaries, and a white-tipped, dark tail. Monterey, California, October 3, 2009.

Breeding-plumage adult Heermann's Gull. The gleaming white head contrasts with the sooty-gray body. Ventura, California, February 14, 2016.

A worn adult Heermann's Gull in nonbreeding plumage along a California beach. Torrey Pines State Reservation, California, August 27, 2006.

A breeding adult Heermann's Gull with the dark-gray body, white head, and red orbital ring. Point Mugo, California, February 17, 2016.

The bright-white head contrasts with the gray body on this breeding-plumage adult Heermann's Gull. The contrast between the white head and gray body can be seen from great distances on flying birds. Ventura, California, February 17, 2016.

A small percentage of Heermann's Gulls show a white patch on the primary coverts that is visible from great distances on flying gulls. Ventura, California, February 19, 2016.

Notice the white primary coverts of this otherwise typical adult Heermann's Gull. Ventura, California, February 14, 2016.

Breeding-plumage adult Heermann's Gulls are among the most stunning of gulls. The gleaming white head contrasting with the dark-gray body is unique among North American gulls. Ventura, California, February 17, 2016.

Chapter 5. Arctic Species, Pelagic Species & Vagrants

IVORY GULL

Background

Ivory Gulls range farther north than any other North American bird, sometimes even approaching the North Pole. Their adult plumage is a stunning white, appearing even whiter than the surrounding snow and ice. They are one of the most sought-after, enigmatic bird species in the world, rarely venturing south of their remote Arctic home. Arthur Cleveland Bent noted that "the names 'ice-partridge' and 'snow bird' are appropriately applied to this species, for the bird lives almost constantly in the vicinity of ice and snow, where its spotless plumage matches its surroundings" (Bent 1921).

Indeed, adult birds appear as a gracefully sculpted shard of ice that has sprouted dark legs, eyes, and a bill. Wintering birds rarely occur south of the pack ice, but those that do re usually young and approachable, allowing for close and extended views. However, the remarkable influx of Ivory Gulls into southern Labrador, Newfoundland, Prince Edward Island, and New England in January 2009 included many adult birds. My first sighting of an adult Ivory Gull in Plymouth, Massachusetts, remains one of the most memorable highlights in over thirty years of birdwatching. The gull was at the center of an icy parking lot, surrounded by camera- and binocular-wielding birders and apparently indifferent to the attention. Later that year, I was blessed to spot an Ivory Gull in Cape May, New Jersey, this one with an equally large group of admirers. It perched obligingly on the mudflats below the pier, peering up curiously at the horde of birders jockeying for position.

Although Ivory Gulls eat small fish and other marine life, they are drawn to carrion, often feeding on the remains of polar bears or their scat. Bent observes, "The feeding habits of the ivory gull are hardly becoming a bird of such pure and spotless plumage. It is a greedy and voracious feeder and is none too particular about the quality of its food or how it obtains it" (Bent 1921). Although they generally avoid large groups of gulls, they can be aggressive around food, even chasing off larger gulls.

The vast majority of Ivory Gulls breed north of 70 degrees, with the primary nesting areas between 75 and 83 degrees north (Blomqvist and Elander 1981). In North America they breed on islands in the Canadian Arctic and in northern Greenland. In Canada they nest in the crevices of nunataks, rocky outcrops on glaciers or ice fields. They have also been documented nesting on remote, flat plateaus with access to nearby ponds or other open water, and even on glacial ice floes (Mallory et al. 2020).

In his classic birding adventure *Kingbird Highway*, Kenn Kaufman describes Ivory Gulls as "phantoms of the shifting ice." His account of seeing his first Ivory Gull on the shores of Gambell, Alaska, is perhaps my favorite passage, describing it as "a bird the color of deep snow, the color of distant icebergs, a bird of shocking white" (Kaufman 1997).

Even their scientific name, the genus *Pagophila*, means "ice loving." Like many owl species, Ivory Gulls cast up pellets of indigestible matter consisting of fur or bones.

Structure and Field Marks

Ivory Gulls have a bulky, compact body with comparatively short wings, short legs, and a pencil-shaped, parallel-edged bill. Although they weigh more than Ring-Billed Gulls, their wingspan is about 10 inches shorter, a unique structure for a North American gull. In fact, when an Ivory Gull is walking on ice, it is more likely to be confused with a pigeon than another gull species due to its shape and stiff gait. However, their white plumage sets them apart. Ivory Gulls have an especially well-developed rear toe, which functions as a hind claw for traction on snow and ice.

First-Year Plumage

Juvenile and first-winter Ivory Gulls are mostly white, with varying amounts of black or dusky markings on the wing coverts and primaries and around the face. Some birds also have dark markings on the underparts, although these tend to be sparse and less noticeable. As with adults, the legs are black. The bill can be similar to an adult but is a duskier gray with a less distinct yellow tip, and some birds' bills have a greenish-blue tinge at the base. A dark orbital ring surrounds each eye. Regardless of whether the bird is heavily or lightly marked, the base color is the ivory seen on adults. Birds molt directly from juvenile to adult plumage. Some first-summer birds retain a few black markings on the primary tips and wing coverts or around the face.

Adult Plumage

Adult Ivory Gulls have a snow-white plumage, sometimes with a slightly creamy tinge. The white plumage, black legs, and grayish-green bill with a yellow tip set adult Ivory Gulls apart from other birds, including albino gulls. Adult Ivory Gulls are a uniform white both at rest and in flight. Some faded and bleached first- and second-winter Glaucous and Iceland Gulls can appear entirely white, but the larger size, the different structure, and the color of the bare parts separate them from Ivory Gulls.

Size

Ivory Gulls have a medium-sized gull body with a small wingspan. They weigh more than Ring-Billed Gulls but have a wingspan more comparable with a Franklin's or Black-Headed Gull. They range from 15.8 to 16.9 inches long and have a wingspan of 42.5 to 47.3 inches. Adult males weigh between 1 pound, 1.6 ounces, and 1 pound, 8.2 ounces, while adult females weigh between 15.8 ounces and 1 pound, 4.6 ounces.

This close view of an immature Ivory Gull shows the dusky face markings and the black pattern on primaries, tail, and wing coverts. Cape May Harbor, New Jersey, November 28, 2009.

A first-summer Ivory Gull forages on the ice. This bird retains black markings only on the primary tips and around the bill. Gambell, St. Lawrence Island, Alaska, May 31, 2008. *Photo by Phil Davis*

Notice the narrow broken tailband on this immature Ivory Gull. Cape May Harbor, New Jersey, November 28, 2009.

The gleaming white plumage and translucent flight feathers are seen on this immature Ivory Gull. Cape May Harbor, New Jersey, November 28, 2009.

A first-summer Ivory Gull perches atop an ice formation. The bird retains some dusky markings on the face and a few black marks on the primary tips but has otherwise begun to acquire the snow-white plumage of an adult. Gambell, St. Lawrence Island, Alaska, May 31, 2008. *Photo by Phil Davis*

Ivory Gulls in their natural snowy and icy environment are truly a beautiful sight. A first-summer bird is shown here. Gambell, St. Lawrence Island, Alaska, May 31, 2008. *Photo by Phil Davis*

The stunning plumage of this adult Ivory Gull is a cleaner, brighter white than the snow and ice around it. The pencil-shaped bill, short legs, and stout body are evident. Cape Ann, Massachusetts, January 18, 2009. *Photo by Bill Hubick*

An adult Ivory Gull. Belying their pure, snowy appearance, Ivory Gulls frequently scavenge for food. Plymouth, Massachusetts, January 24, 2009.

An adult Ivory Gull with a first-winter Herring Gull. Cape Ann, Massachusetts, January 18, 2009. *Photo by Bill Hubick*

An adult Ivory Gull inspects a meal. Plymouth, Massachusetts, January 24, 2009.

With its pristine white plumage, this adult Ivory Gull looks like a sculpted piece of ice or porcelain as it glides by. Cape Ann, Massachusetts, January 18, 2009. *Photo by Bill Hubick*

ROSS'S GULL

Background

Picture yourself on a blustery, snow-dusted beach with the Arctic Ocean extending as far as the eye can see, whipped into a tumultuous fury of white caps and swells by strong westerly winds. Point Barrow lies in front of you, with a massive flock of Glaucous Gulls scattered along the beach. Intermittent snow squalls obscure the ocean from view, adding to the "edge of the world" feeling. Offshore you can see flocks of migrating Ross's Gulls, formerly called Rosy Gulls. They are as graceful as they are beautiful, some far enough from land that a spotting scope is needed for good views, while others pass by so close that the brilliant-pink wash to the belly, wedge-shaped tail, and delicate black bill can be seen. You are witnessing the migration of one of North America's rarest and most beautiful birds. Tantalizingly elusive, they regularly appear only in North America off Point Barrow, Alaska, in the fall. Breeding adult Ross's Gulls are perhaps the most beautiful of all the world's gulls, with their pearly-gray upperparts, dapper black collar, and pinkish blush below. As Arctic and sub-Arctic breeders, Ross's Gulls seldom venture to more-temperate climates. They were documented breeding in Churchill, Manitoba, in the late 1970s and '80s; however, they have not been recorded at that location regularly in recent years.

Arctic explores and ornithologists began to piece together the distribution and movements of this elusive gull in the late 1800s. The first description of a Ross's Gull was provided by James C. Ross during the 1823 expedition organized by William E. Parry to find the Northwest Passage. In 1879, Lieutenant Commander George W. De Long led the Jeannette Arctic Expedition on the search for a route to the North Pole via the Bering Strait. While trapped in the ice on the East Siberian Sea, the explorers saw flocks of Ross's Gulls in numbers far greater than anything previously recorded. In 1881, the ship was crushed by the shifting ice, and many of the crew perished trying to reach the Siberian mainland, including De Long. A survivor, biologist Raymond Lee Newcomb, preserved the skins of three Ross's Gulls by carrying them under his clothing during the long, brutal journey back to civilization (Blomqvist and Elander 1981).

Dr. E. W. Nelson took a specimen of an immature Ross's Gull near St. Michael, Alaska, on October 10, 1879. Additional specimens were obtained on the International Polar Expeditions to Point Barrow of 1881, 1882, and 1883. An expedition report included the following summary of the birds' migration past Point Barrow:

In 1881, from September 28 to October 22, there were days when they were exceedingly abundant in small flocks, generally moving toward the northeast, either flying over the sea or making short excursions inshore. Not a single one was seen during the spring migration or in the summer, but one or two stragglers were noticed early in September—a few out among the loose pack ice; and on September 21, 1882 they were again abundant, apparently almost all young birds. They appeared in large, loose flocks, coming in from the sea and from the southwest, all apparently traveling to the northeast. Most of the flocks whirled in at the mouth of our lagoon and circled around the station with a peculiarly graceful, wavering flight, and many were shot close to the house. A cold easterly wind was blowing at the time. They continued plentiful for several days, while the east wind blew, all following the same track, moving up the shore, and making excursions inland at each of all beach lagoons. After September 28 they disappeared until October 6 when for several days there was a large flight. On October 9, in particular, there was a continuous stream of them all day long moving up the shore a short distance from the beach, and occasionally swinging in over land. None were seen to return. (Bent 1921)

Ross's Gulls continue to be recorded in the fall off Point Barrow, with trips organized annually to witness the migration. Although totals vary year by year, they are usually seen in good numbers. Perhaps the most thorough documentation of this annual movement was in the interagency report *Fall Migration of Ross' Gull (*Rhodostethia rosea*) in Alaskan Chukchi and Beaufort Sea*, by George J. Divoky of the Institute of Arctic Biology and Gerald A. Sanger, Scott A. Hatch, and J. Christopher Haney of the US Fish and Wildlife Service and Alaska Fish and Wildlife Research Center. Between 1970 and 1986, Divoky and his coworkers observed Ross's Gulls in late summer and early fall during nineteen cruises on the Chukchi and Beaufort Seas. Divoky also conducted aerial surveys and made land-based observations from Point Barrow during 1976, 1984, and 1986. Additional observations were collected from Point Barrow in 1987 through work sponsored by the Fish and Wildlife Service and Mineral Management Service. During this period, it was estimated that the number of Ross's Gulls migrating past Point Barrow ranged from 4,500 to 16,000 birds, with most of the eastbound migration occurring in late September and early October (Divoky et al. 1988).

More recently, the High Arctic Research Group has gathered groundbreaking data on the breeding, migration, and wintering habits of Ross's Gulls in the Canadian High Arctic, capturing stunning photographs of a small colony on Nasaruvaalik Island. This colony was discovered by Canadian Wildlife Service seabird biologists while they were doing aerial surveys over the Queen's Channel in 2005. The island contained hundreds of Arctic Terns, Sabine's Gulls, and Common Eiders, as well as five pairs of Ross's Gulls. Ross's Gulls have a strong association with Arctic Terns, frequently nesting near or among the much more numerous tern species. The researchers' ongoing monitoring with geolocators confirmed that the northern Labrador Sea serves as a wintering ground for at least some Ross's Gulls, the first solid evidence of where this elusive and little-known species spends the dark, cold months (Maftei et al. 2015). The biologists also documented the fall migration of Ross's Gulls past Point Barrow in 2011. Over the course of thirty-nine days between September 20 and October 28, they tallied 27,428 Ross's Gulls, with a peak count of 7,116 gulls during a three-hour period on October 16 (Maftei et al. 2014)!

Polar explorer Fridtjof Nansen expressed his excitement at finding his first Ross's Gull in 1894:

A remarkable occurrence took place: we were visited by the Arctic ross-gull – today my longing has been satisfied—This rare mysterious inhabitant of the unknown north, which is only occasionally seen, and of which no one knows whence it cometh or whither it goeth, which belongs exclusively to the world to which the imagination aspires, is what, from the first moment I saw these tracts, I had always hoped to discover as my eyes roamed over the lonely plains of ice. (Maftei 2012)

I was fortunate to witness the fall migration of Ross's Gulls on a recent October trip to Barrow (now known as Utqiagvik), Alaska. Although the large flocks of Glaucous Gulls and the scattered sightings of Spectacled Eiders, Hoary Redpolls, and Snowy Owls were memorable, the Ross's Gulls were the uncontested stars as they passed offshore over a turbulent sea. Some gulls flew tantalizingly close to our position on the beach, allowing views of the beautiful, pink-washed underparts that are part of their allure.

Structure and Field Marks

Ross's Gulls resemble Little Gulls in plumage, though they have longer and pointier wings, a cigar-shaped body, and a longer, wedge-shaped tail that give them a tern-like appearance. Their short bills seem inordinately tiny, even relative to their small size and round head.

Breeding adults have a thin, dapper black collar. Adults are heavily washed with pink below, although some younger birds can share this feature. Although other gulls (particularly small hooded gulls) can have a pink wash below in breeding season, Ross's Gulls have taken this trait to a brilliant extreme.

First-Year Plumage

The juvenile plumage of Ross's Gulls is briefly held and rarely seen. Juveniles are heavily washed with brown on the crown, hind neck, and top of the breast. The back is a darker sooty brown with buff feather edges, giving young birds a scaly appearance. The gray back is acquired in early fall as birds molt into first-winter plumage. Like many small hooded gulls, first-winter Ross's Gulls have a dark M pattern on the upper wings. This is most evident in flight but also visible on perched birds in the form of black wing coverts, tertials, and some black on the folded primaries. First-winter Ross's Gulls have a faint ear spot and dark markings around the eye, which make the eye appear larger in the small head (Olsen 2018). The dark tips on the long central tail feathers look like an extended black "tab" on the white tail of flying birds. As Ross's Gulls enter their first summer, many acquire the thin black collar and all-white tail.

Adult Plumage

Adults in breeding plumage are beautiful and distinctive, with their narrow black collar and wedge-shaped tail. The underwings are a medium, smoky gray, lacking the blackish tones of adult Little Gulls, but still the same shade or slightly darker than the upper wing. The upper wing looks similar to that of adult Little Gulls—an even pearly gray above with a narrow white border around the trailing edge. This white margin widens slightly on the inner primaries. Like many of the hooded gulls, Ross's Gulls can achieve a diet-related rosy wash to the underparts. However, it's particularly noticeable on this species, earning them the moniker "pink seagull." In nonbreeding plumage, some gulls retain a trace of the dark collar, but most show only a thin ear patch in winter. While brightest during the breeding season, the pinkish wash is also significant on some nonbreeding birds in the fall. Second-year birds can sometimes be identified by the retention of dark feathers in the wing coverts or tertials, and paler-red legs.

Size

Ross's Gulls are one of the smallest gulls, similar to Bonaparte's Gulls and only slightly larger than Little Gulls. They are 11.4 to 12.2 inches long and have a wingspan between 35.4 and 39.4 inches. Their weight ranges from 7.1 to 8.8 ounces.

Ross's Gulls are known for their epic migration past Point Barrow, Alaska, each fall. This photo shows the distinctive pinkish wash of adult Ross's Gulls along with the bold markings of a first-fall bird. Point Barrow, Alaska, October 6, 2015. *Photo by Peter Relson*

In flight, adult Ross's Gulls show an all-gray upper wing with a broad white trailing edge on the secondaries and inner primaries. The medium gray underwing is seen on the bird on the right. Point Barrow, Alaska, October 3, 2015.

This adult Ross's Gull shows the thin, black collar and pinkish underparts typical of breeding adults. The wedge-shaped tail is also evident on this flying gull. Kolyma, Siberia, July. *Photo by H. & J. Eriksen / VIREO*

This bird shows the deep-pinkish hue that birders long to see on this species. Point Barrow, Alaska, October 6, 2015. *Photo by Peter Relson*

Adult Ross's Gulls are beautiful birds in flight with their even gray upperparts, gray underwings, pale-pinkish wash on the body, and petite bill. Point Barrow, Alaska, October 6, 2015. *Photo by Peter Relson*

The wedge-shaped tail is evident on this adult Ross's Gull. Point Barrow, Alaska, October 6, 2015. *Photo by Peter Relson*

A perched winter adult Ross's Gull displays a small, rounded head and tiny, stubby bill. Half Moon Bay, California, January 13, 2017. *Photo by Jeff Shenot*

The Ross's Gull forages on a tidal mudflat. Half Moon Bay, California, January 13, 2017. *Photo by Jeff Shenot*

The compact, plump body, small head, and tiny bill are evident on this adult Ross's Gull. Half Moon Bay, California, January 13, 2017. *Photo by Jeff Shenot*

Seeing one of these gorgeous gulls up close, it is difficult to imagine a more beautiful bird. Note the even gray primaries, rounded head, and tiny bill. Half Moon Bay, California, January 13, 2017. *Photo by Jeff Shenot*

The medium-gray underwing is noticeable as this Ross's Gull flies gracefully over the water. Half Moon Bay, California, January 13, 2017. *Photo by Jeff Shenot*

Adult Ross's Gulls are one of the most beautiful gulls in nature, with their trim black collar, bluish-silver upperparts, and pink wash below. Churchill, Manitoba. *Photo by A. Morris / VIREO*

RED-LEGGED KITTIWAKE

Background

Red-Legged Kittiwakes are an Alaskan specialty, a jewel of the Bering Sea, They breed on only a few remote islands in the Bering Sea and along the Aleutian Islands, on inaccessible cliffs up to 900 feet above the water. Over 75 percent of the population nests on St. George Island, part of the Pribilof Island group. They are pelagic most of the year, feeding along the continental shelf or over deeper waters during the breeding season. Their winter range is less well known, but most sightings are from the Gulf of Alaska, along the edge of the ice pack on the Bering Sea, and presumably farther out into the North Pacific Ocean.

Red-Legged Kittiwakes form large, active groups (or "melees") with Black-Legged Kittiwakes as they search for prey near the surface of open water. Like their black-legged cousins, Red-Legged Kittiwakes are well adapted to a life over the harsh ocean environment, and they use the wind to their advantage as they forage over the sea. Their flight is similar to that of Black-Legged Kittiwakes, though more erratic and with quicker, snappier wing-beats. Their large eyes help them locate prey in the churning sea and allow them to hunt for food day or night, sometimes feeding on lampfish and squid after dark (Byrd and Williams 2020).

Most birders get their first look at Red-Legged Kittiwakes on the Pribilof Islands, isolated deep in the Bering Sea, and seeing this species on the remote island cliffs is an unforgettable experience. In 1899 William Parker provided this eloquent description of the species from the Pribilof Islands:

To my mind this is the most beautiful species on the islands. Always graceful, whether on the cliffs or flying, its beautiful form and delicate snow-white plumage, with its vermilion feet, adds much to the avifaunal wonders of these islands. Unlike its cousin, which carries its feet extended when flying, this species nearly always buries them in the feathers of its under body, as if fearful of showing their beauty except when absolutely necessary. (Bent 1921)

Red-Legged Kittiwakes continue to be a major attraction on the Pribilof Islands, although there has been stiff competition in the many alcids and Asian vagrants there. Experiencing kittiwakes in the company of a wide variety of puffins, murres, auklets, and other cliff-nesting seabirds only adds to the allure of observing Red-Legged Kittiwakes in their habitat. When birding on the islands during migration, one often has the feeling that anything can happen, and often it does, whether it is close views of the incredibly cute Least Auklet or a fleeting glimpse of a rare White-Tailed Eagle. Red-Legged Kittiwakes are a big part of what made the islands so irresistible to me, and I was not disappointed with the views of these pretty gulls in flight over the Bering Sea, resting in large numbers on a tidal mudflat, and foraging over the roughest seas in the world.

Structure and Field Marks

Although similar to their black-legged kin, Red-Legged Kittiwakes have several structural features that make them distinctive from the much more common Black-Legged Kittiwakes. While they have a larger head relative to their body, Red-Legged Kittiwakes also have a larger eye, placed centrally within their face. The large size of the head, steep forehead, and large eye serve to accentuate the short, stubby bill, which almost looks "pushed in" to the flat face; hence Pete Dunne's nickname for the species: the Pug-Faced Kittiwake (Dunne 2006). While Red-Legged Kittiwakes are slightly smaller than Black-Legged Kittiwakes, they also appear more compact and stocky (or pigeon-like). Adding to this stocky appearance are the unusually short legs—an adaptation to nesting on precarious ledges on steep cliffs—which give the species an awkward, shuffling gait. Audubon characterized it best: "The Kittiwake is on land the most awkward of its tribe; and, although it walks often on the rocks, its gait manifests a waddling gaucherie" (Audubon 1844).

However, Audubon goes on to conclude that although kittiwakes seem awkward on land, in flight "few birds surpass it in buoyancy, grace, and ease of motion." With their deft maneuvering in strong winds, quick turns, and snappy wingbeats, they are in their element over the open ocean. Flying Red-Legged Kittiwakes demonstrate narrower wings and a more compact, stout body in comparison to Black-Legged Kittiwakes. Their build is reminiscent of the sturdy Ivory Gull. Although birders often look to the leg color for separating the two species of kittiwake, for distant birds the darker upperparts and dusky-gray underwing are more easily seen field marks. The upperparts of Black-Legged Kittiwakes are several shades paler, and the underwing is a clean white. The difference in the shade of the mantle between the two kittiwake species is striking when the birds are seen in proximity.

First-Year Plumage

Red-Legged Kittiwakes are subtly marked in their first year, lacking the bold markings of similarly aged Black-Legged Kittiwakes or Sabine's Gulls. Juveniles are distinctive in that they acquire mostly gray, adultlike upperparts, unlike the browns and tans seen on most juvenile gulls. And Red-Legged Kittiwakes have a white tail in their first year, lacking a tailband or any other dark markings. They lack the bold dark markings (M pattern) on the upperparts of first-year Black-Legged Kittiwakes. However, the outermost primaries and primary coverts contain an extensive amount of black. The inner primaries and the trailing edge of the wing are white, contrasting with the dark gray of the upper-wing coverts and mantle. The black, white, and gray pattern on first-winter Red-Legged Kittiwakes is reminiscent of Sabine's Gulls, but more muted overall. The mantle is medium dark gray, several shades darker than on Black-Legged Kittiwakes and lacking the black markings on the wing coverts. Even at this age, Red-Legged Kittiwakes have bright-orangish-red legs, which give the species its name, although they are paler and more orange in color than on adults. They also have a dusky-gray hind collar, which is a washed-out, pale version of the much more prominent black hind collar seen on Black-Legged Kittiwakes.

Second-Year Plumage

At this age, Red-Legged Kittiwakes look similar to adults. Features that indicate a Red-Legged Kittiwake in its second year include more extensive black in the outermost primaries, black extending down to the primary coverts or alula, and the retention of a black tip to the yellow bill.

Adult Plumage

The dark-gray mantle, bright-red legs, and short, stubby bill all are noticeable on adult Red-Legged Kittiwakes. The black wingtips on Red-Legged Kittiwakes contrast little with the rest of the dark-gray wing. Although the legs are usually tucked and out of view when the bird is in flight, the stubby bill and darker upperparts separate adult Red-Legged Kittiwakes from Black-Legged Kittiwakes. Also, Red-Legged Kittiwakes have a grayish cast to the flight feathers on the underside of the wing, lacking the bright-white underwing seen on adult Black-Legged Kittiwakes. The upper wing of Red-Legged Kittiwakes is also uniform in shade for its entire length. By comparison, Black-Legged Kittiwakes have a paler outer wing, which contrasts with the slightly darker inner wing and mantle.

Size

Red-Legged Kittiwakes are small but sturdily built. They are smaller than Black-Legged Kittiwakes, although some overlap exists in most measurements. Red-Legged Kittiwakes weigh from 10.4 ounces to 1 pound, 1.3 ounces. They average 13.9 to 15.4 inches long and have a wingspan of 33.1 to 36.2 inches.

A first-year Red-Legged Kittiwake (*front center*). Note the grayish wash to the nape, dark markings on the bill, pale-orange legs, and immature wing coverts. St. Paul Island, Alaska, May 22, 2017.

A first-year Red-Legged Kittiwake with wings partially extended. Note the black leading edge to the upper side of the extended wing, and the pale-white triangle along the trailing edge. St. Paul Island, Alaska, May 22, 2017.

A first-year Red-Legged Kittiwake (*center*). This bird is less heavily marked than some of the other birds shown, particularly on the nape. The orangish-red legs are a recognizable field feature. St. Paul Island, Alaska, May 22, 2017.

The darker upper wing of the Red-Legged Kittiwake (*on right*) is clearly seen in comparison with a Black-Legged Kittiwake. St. Paul Island, Alaska, May 23, 2017.

The dark underwing is visible on a flying adult Red-Legged Kittiwake. Similarly aged Black-Legged Kittiwakes have a clean white underwing. St. Paul Island, Alaska, May 21, 2017.

The short, stout bill; flat face; compact body; and short but brilliant red legs are seen on the standing Red-Legged Kittiwakes. St. Paul Island, Alaska, May 22, 2017.

Red-Legged Kittiwakes nest on impossibly narrow ledges. St. Paul Island, Pribilof Islands, Alaska, May 25, 2008. *Photo by Phil Davis*

The stunningly bright-crimson legs of adult Red-Legged Kittiwakes stand in stark contrast to their gray-and-white plumage and gray sand. St. Paul Island, Alaska, May 22, 2017.

Note how the wing of the Red-Legged Kittiwake (*rear center*) looks significantly darker than the surrounding Black-Legged Kittiwakes from both above and below. St. Paul Island, Alaska, May 23, 2017.

BLACK-LEGGED KITTIWAKE

Background

A small but hardy three-year gull, Black-Legged Kittiwakes live up to the moniker of "seagull" by spending a large portion of their lives over the open ocean. Although they nest on coastal cliffs in the far north, they spend much of the nonbreeding season ranging far and wide over the open ocean, out of view from land. As one of the few truly pelagic species of gulls, kittiwakes are usually seen only far from shore and are in the company of birds such as Northern Fulmar, Manx Shearwater, and a variety of alcids above and on cold winter seas, rather than with other species of gulls, which usually stay closer to land.

Black-Legged Kittiwakes are adept and distinctive fliers, well suited to life above rough, windswept waters. Although graceful and nimble in flight, they can be very strong fliers in heavy winds and at times appear almost shearwater-like as they glide up and down with stiff wings over the choppy, wind-tossed waves. At other times, they assume an almost nighthawk-like shape as they fly with their long and narrow wings bent and gently angled back at the wrist. When the long wings are held back like this, they assume an curved shape resembling a boomerang. In calm winds, they fly with quick, abbreviated wingbeats yet still appear buoyant and maneuverable, always ready to turn, stop, or change course when needed.

Bent notes that Black-Legged Kittiwakes were formerly referred to as the "winter gull" or the "frost gull" in New England, since the arrival of kittiwakes along the New England coast heralded the beginning of hard frosts and harsh winter weather (Bent 1921). And, consistent with this, most North American birders will see kittiwakes only during the cold winter months. It is truly a treat to see one of these graceful birds from the deck of a boat during a winter pelagic and watch them pick food nimbly from the surface of the water or "shearwater" strongly over the rolling sea. Luckier still are those who have one of these birds follow their boat for an extended period of time, when kittiwakes are more than capable of holding their own against larger birds as they fight for "chum" heaved overboard. Audubon described the kittiwake's manner of flight by saying, "Few birds surpass it in buoyancy, grace, and ease of motion." He went on to observe:

Bearing up against the heaviest gale, it passes from one trough of the sea to another as if anxious to rest for an instant under the lee of the billows; yet as these are seen to rear their curly crests, the gull is already several feet above them and preparing to plunge into the next hollow. While in our harbor, and during fine weather, they seem to play with their companions of other species. Now with a spiral curve they descend towards the water, support themselves by beats of their wings, decline their heads, and pick up a young herring or some bit of garbage, when away they fly, chased perhaps by several others anxious to rob them of their prize. (Audubon 1844)

Other writers have attempted to capture the beauty and unique manner of kittiwakes in flight, with Dr. E. W. Nelson paying tribute to "the graceful motions and powers of flight possessed by this handsome gull" by saying this:

Its buoyancy during the worst gales we met was fully equal to that possessed by the Rodger's fulmar, with which it frequently associated at these times. These birds were continually gliding back and forth in graceful curves, now passing directly into the face of the gale, then darting off to one side on a long circuit, always moving steadily, with only an occasional stroke of the wings for long periods if there was a strong wind. (Bent 1921)

Anyone who has seen kittiwakes negotiating strong winds on a winter pelagic will surely agree with this assessment of the bird's ability to handle rough conditions over a stormy, white-capped sea with the utmost blend of daring, grace, and beauty. Kittiwakes are also very buoyant, maneuverable, and efficient in flight, using the wind to its best advantage as they make tight turns, banking from side to side and changing direction as needed at moment's notice. Dr. Charles W. Townsend poignantly described the spectacle of a flock of several thousand kittiwakes off the coast of Labrador with the following description:

At Hamilton Inlet thousands of kittiwakes covered the water, and as we steamed on they rose in bodies of 500 or more and whirled about like gusts of snow driven by the wind, their pure white plumage lit up by the rays of the setting sun. (Bent 1921)

Although rarely seen from land during the nonbreeding season, occasionally these birds appear in coastal harbors and inlets, as well as bays and interior lakes. When seen at interior locations away from their usual winter habitat at sea, they can appear particularly confiding and approachable, showing little trepidation around nearby birders or photographers. And, as at sea, these sturdy birds more than hold their own when jousting for position or fighting for scraps with the larger, more common coastal or land gulls. Kittiwakes spend the majority of their lives in a vast watery world far removed from land, and they are well adapted to thriving in the harsh pelagic environment. It is a thrill to see one of these birds on a winter boat trip along the Pacific or Atlantic coast, as they navigate strong winds and ocean swells with the utmost skill and grace. Seeing a group of breeding kittiwakes on seaside cliffs is equally memorable, with birds resting in nests high above the ocean on astoundingly narrow ledges, periodically swooping down from their perch to forage over the open ocean. Kittiwakes are masters of the air, and they are at their finest when navigating their pelagic environment. Whether at a cliffside nesting colony in the Bering Sea or over a rough Atlantic Ocean off the coast of New England in winter, those fortunate enough to see these "seagulls" will not soon forget the experience.

Structures and Field Marks
Black-Legged Kittiwakes are small in size, but with a thick body and long, narrow wings. Their tails are subtly clefted or forked, although this is not always noticeable under field conditions. The wings are gently curved or bowed back in flight, unlike the sharper angles seen in other species such as Bonaparte's Gulls, which also have a heavier body.

First-Year Plumage
First-winter Black-Legged Kittiwakes are distinctive, with a bold black bar on the upper-wing coverts, a narrow black band on the tail, and an all-black bill. Perhaps most noticeable, their thick black hind collar is unique to first-winter Black-Legged Kittiwakes, reminiscent of the smudged eyeblack that athletes use to reduce glare. In flight, first-winter Black-Legged Kittiwakes show a bold, black M pattern on the upper side of the wings that is formed by the black outer primaries and black ulnar bar across the inner wing coverts. This pattern is visible even on distant flying kittiwakes.

Second-Year Plumage
Second-winter Black-Legged Kittiwakes show more extensive black in the outermost primaries and often retain a dusky or dark-tipped bill.

Adult Plumage
Black-Legged Kittiwakes are attractive in adult plumage, unlikely to be confused with other species if well seen. Field guides usually note that the wingtips look as if they have been dipped in black ink; this is accentuated by the wings' pale-white undersides. Birds in winter have a greenish-yellow, unmarked bill that sets it apart from most other species. Short-Billed Gulls have a similarly plain yellow/green bill, but it is thinner and more delicate, particularly toward the tip. Adult Short-Billed Gulls also have extensive white in the folded primaries and brown streaking (not a grayish wash) to the head and nape in the winter.

Perhaps most noticeable on flying Black-Legged Kittiwakes is the three-toned pattern of the extended upper wing: medium gray on the inner wing, paler gray on the primary coverts and base of the primaries, and the jet-black wingtips. Unlike adults of other species, adult Black-Legged Kittiwakes have no white mirrors, tongues, or edges in the black of the primary tips. Adult Black-Legged Kittiwakes also attain a black ear spot and a gray wash to the nape in winter. This gray wash is quite different from the brown streaking seen on nonbreeding white-headed gulls. During the breeding season, adult kittiwakes have a clean white head (lacking the ear spot and gray wash to the nape), which further accentuates the dark eye. Also, the bill tends to be a brighter yellow, lacking the greenish tones seen in many nonbreeding-plumage adult birds. The small, unmarked greenish-yellow bill and dark eyes set within a clean white head give adult kittiwakes a gentle, confiding expression.

Size

Black-Legged Kittiwakes are small, but long winged and sturdy, well suited to a life spent in harsh ocean conditions. They are 14.9 to 16.2 inches long, with a wingspan between 36.5 and 47.3 inches. On average they weigh 14 ounces, although birds from the Pacific Ocean are typically heavier.

Geographic Variation

Kittiwakes from the Pacific Ocean or "Pacific" Kittiwakes (*Rissa tridactyla pollicaris*) are slightly larger, longer billed, and darker above than Atlantic birds (*R. t. tridactyla*). Pacific birds also have a significantly longer life span than Atlantic birds, while kittiwakes from the Atlantic have a much-higher reproductive rate (Hatch et al. 2020). More research is needed to determine the factors causing these apparent differences, and this additional work may shed additional light on what further distinguishes these two populations.

This first-winter Black-Legged Kittiwake displays the distinctive bold M pattern on the upper wings, black hind collar, and black bill typical of first-winter birds. The narrow tailband and medium-gray mantle are also apparent. Sandy Point State Park, Maryland, November 25, 2014.

The distinctive upper-wing pattern of first-winter Black-Legged Kittiwakes is visible from a great distance at sea. Offshore from Ocean City, Maryland, November 19, 2011.

A first-winter Black-Legged Kittiwake at close range. Sandy Point State Park, Maryland, November 30, 2014.

Even from an angle, the dark-black hind collar and ear spot are visible on first-winter Black-Legged Kittiwakes. Offshore from Ocean City, Maryland, February 1, 2014.

Note the narrow tailband, long and gently curved wings, and thick body. Sandy Point State Park, Maryland, November 25, 2014.

It is a rare treat to see a first-winter Black-Legged Kittiwake at close range, when its field marks can be appreciated in detail. Sandy Point State Park, Maryland, November 25, 2014.

Adult and first-winter (*on right*) Black-Legged Kittiwakes over the Bering Sea. Even from an angle, the bold upper-wing pattern is obvious on the immature gull. St. Paul Island, Alaska, May 23, 2017.

The thick, black hind collar is evident on this perched first-winter Black-Legged Kittiwake. Sandy Point State Park, Maryland, November 25, 2014.

Note the subtle beauty of a first-winter Black-Legged Kittiwake's gray, black, and white plumage. Sandy Point State Park, Maryland, November 30, 2014.

Black-Legged Kittiwakes over the Bering Sea. The pale underwing and black wingtips are easy to see. St. Paul Island, Alaska, May 23, 2017.

This adult Black-Legged Kittiwake shows the clean white underparts and clearly demarcated black wingtips (as if "dipped in ink"). St. Paul Island, Alaska, May 23, 2017.

Note the contrasting black wingtips of an adult Black-Legged Kittiwake and the outer wing that is slightly paler than the inner wing and mantle. St. Paul, Alaska, May 23, 2017.

The sturdy body, yellow-green bill, and black ear spot are evident on an adult Black-Legged Kittiwake. Offshore from Ocean City, Maryland, February 1, 2014.

An adult Black-Legged Kittiwake captures prey over the Bering Sea with graceful, wind-assisted flight. St. Paul Island, Alaska, May 23, 2017.

Note the sharp demarcation between the black wingtips and the white underwing of an adult Black-Legged Kittiwake. Offshore from Ocean City, Maryland, February 1, 2014.

Flying Black-Legged Kittiwakes have a boomerang shape. Offshore from Ocean City, Maryland, February 1, 2014.

An adult Black-Legged Kittiwake with a Herring Gull. The black-tipped wings are clearly seen from above and below. Offshore from Ocean City, Maryland, February 1, 2014.

This "Pacific" Black-Legged Kittiwake demonstrates the longer bill of the western population, compared to Black-Legged Kittiwakes found over the Atlantic Ocean. Gambell, St. Lawrence Island, Alaska, June 1, 2008. *Photo by Phil Davis*

An adult Black-Legged Kittiwake deftly uses the winds to its advantage as it forages for food over the Bering Sea. St. Paul, Alaska, May 23, 2017.

GRAY-HOODED GULL

Background

This spectacular stray has been documented in North America only twice; its unique gray hood and distinctive wing pattern set it apart from all regularly occurring North American gulls. They are found in the Southern Hemisphere, with separate populations in South America (subspecies *cirrocephalus*) and Africa (subspecies *poiocephalus*). Differences in subspecies are slight and may not always be discernible in the field. However, the larger ssp. *cirrocephalus* has larger mirrors on the two outermost primaries and slightly paler-gray upperparts (Olsen and Larsson 2004).

Gray-Hooded Gulls breed along subtropical coasts, estuaries, lakes, and rivers. The first documented sighting in North America was of an adult bird seen and photographed at St. Vincent National Wildlife Refuge in Apalachicola, Florida, on December 26, 1998. It was seen for only one day and was associated with Laughing and Ring-Billed Gulls as it foraged on scallop shells along the waterfront near the refuge headquarters (McNair 1999).

The second North American record was from Coney Island, New York, from late July through early August 2011. This bird was seen and photographed by many observers at a popular beach near the amusement park, often in the company of Laughing Gulls. The gull attracted throngs of bird watchers. eBird declared it "the avian sensation of the summer." It was covered in a *New York Times* article, which stated that hordes of birders from across the country descended on the beach, lugging cameras, telephoto lenses, tripods, and binoculars, making for "an unusual scene, even for Coney Island" (Stelloh 2011). The Wonder Wheel and other amusement park rides served as a backdrop for this rare avian guest. I was one of those visitors who saw it in flight over the beach, perched atop beach volleyball posts, and walking on the sand near camera-wielding birders and beachgoers. While the birders talked excitedly among themselves and snapped photos at a furious pace, the local sunbathers looked on quizzically, puzzled about the source of the ruckus.

While remarkable, these two sightings fit the recent pattern of South American gulls occurring casually in North America, as reflected by records of Kelp Gulls, Belcher's Gulls, and Swallow-Tailed Gulls north of Mexico. As they would in their native South America, here too the Coney Island gull loosely associated with Laughing Gulls on the beach. One can only hope that more visits from this beautiful vagrant will occur in the future.

Structure and Field Marks

Gray-Hooded Gulls are medium-sized, hooded gulls similar in size and structure to the familiar (to North American birders) Laughing Gull, with a comparable wingspan; long, attenuated shape (perhaps accentuated by the long primary projection); and a long bill. The upperparts are lighter than those of a Laughing Gull, and intermediate between that species and the Ring-Billed Gull.

First-Year Plumage:

First-winter Gray-Hooded Gulls have a dull-pink bill with a dark tip, an ear spot, brown smudging on the head, and extensive brown on the wing coverts. In flight, they have a more muted pattern on the upper wings than do adults, having much more extensive black and brown on the upper wings, including a black secondary bar. The white tail has a narrow black subterminal band.

Adult Plumage

The bright-red bill and legs and attractive gray hood set Gray-Hooded Gulls apart from all other North American gulls. The hood is pale gray with a darker-gray border. Gray-Hooded Gulls have pale yellow to whitish eyes, which stand out prominently in the gray head. The pattern of the extended wings is equally unique. Look for a uniformly gray underwing and a black-and-white pattern on the upper wing. The base of the primaries and the primary coverts are white, which creates a large white wedge on the upper wing. The primaries have extensive black, with large white mirrors on the two outermost primaries. In nonbreeding plumage, the head is white; some birds have a pale hood or a faint ear spot.

Size

Gray-Hooded Gulls are medium-sized gulls, proportionally similar to Laughing Gulls. They have an average wingspan of 15.4 to 16.5 inches and are 39.4 to 45.3 inches long. They weigh from 7.4 to 13.5 ounces.

The second North American record of a Gray-Hooded Gull occurred on Coney Island. Coney Island, New York, August 2, 2011.

The distinctive pattern of extended primaries and the gray underwing is typical breeding plumage on adult Gray-Hooded Gulls. Western Division, Gambia, in March. *Photo by Robin Chittenden / VIREO*

Note the bright-red legs and bill and the diagnostic gray hood of this adult Gray-Hooded Gull. Coney Island, New York, August 2, 2011.

Close view of a Gray-Hooded Gull. The hood and mantle color are similar. Coney Island, New York, August 2, 2011.

Notice the size and structural similarities between Gray-Hooded and Laughing Gulls. Coney Island, New York, August 2, 2011.

This Gray-Hooded Gull has a pale, yellowish-white eye. The bold white eye crescents are visible above and below the eye, although the contrast is greater on gulls with darker hoods. Coney Island, New York, August 2, 2011.

A Gray-Hooded Gull glances toward a throng of birders and photographers on a popular beach. The gray hood and red bare parts are striking. Coney Island, New York, August 2, 2011.

KELP GULL

Background

A widespread resident of the Southern Hemisphere, Kelp Gulls are a recent addition to the birdlife of North America. They are normally found in coastal areas, with populations in South America, Africa, Australia, and Antarctica. In many ways, Kelp Gulls are the counterpart to the large, black-backed gulls of the Northern Hemisphere, such as Great Black-Backed and Western Gulls. It surprises many birders to learn that Kelp Gulls also have a population in Antarctica. While the Antarctic Kelp Gulls are migratory, they disperse only as far north as the edge of the pack ice or the extreme southern tip of South America, meaning that Kelp Gulls are hardy, cold-weather birds indeed. However, the majority of Kelp Gulls breed in more-temperate climates along the coasts of South America, Africa, and Australia, favoring rocky islands, coastal beaches, or lava fields.

Kelp Gulls have undergone a recent range expansion that has taken them farther north in small numbers, into the Caribbean and United States. The first Kelp Gull record for North America occurred in 1989 on the Chandeleur Islands off the coast of Louisiana, where a territorial pair was found. At the time of the July 8 sighting, the birds were tentatively identified as Lesser Black-Backed Gulls, since the probability of Kelp Gulls turning up in North America seemed beyond the realm of possibility (Dittmann and Cardiff 2005). However, they were later identified as Kelp Gulls on the basis of their dark-black mantle and large size. Kelp Gulls have been documented breeding on the island is subsequent years, both with other Kelp Gulls and with Herring Gulls. By 2004, only hybrid pairs remained, and the Chandeleur Islands were severely impacted by Hurricane Katrina in 2005. There are no records in Louisiana since that time, although Kelp × Herring hybrids (Chandeleur Gulls) are still found.

At about the same time Kelp Gulls were being observed in Louisiana, they were also recorded at several other locations, including Texas, Indiana, Colorado, and Maryland. The Kelp Gull in Maryland (nicknamed Shrimpie) became famous for his long stay—from 1998 until early 2005—and was perhaps the most observed individual bird in the history of North American birding. It frequented the pilings and piers behind a restaurant, where the gull got its nickname from the shrimp and other handouts from the employees. Shrimpie bordered on celebrity status, with a huge onslaught of observers after the initial identification and a steady stream of birders in subsequent years. An article in the *Baltimore Sun* stated, "With its snowy-white head and breast and black wings with white spots like pearl studs, the bird looks quite elegant on the [utility] pole, an old-school gentleman in a dress suit. Its bill, a yellow schnozzola worthy of W. C. Fields, undercuts the elegance a bit" (Schoettler 2004).

I saw the Kelp Gull in Maryland on three occasions, and the greenish-yellow legs clearly set it apart from the surrounding pink-legged Great Black-Backed Gulls. One visit was particularly memorable, since snow flurries were in the air and a strong wind whipped the sullen waters of the Patuxent River into a tumult of white caps. The Kelp Gull perched on a pier behind the restaurant with a handful of Great Black-Backed and Herring Gulls. I commented to a companion that it seemed ironic viewing a South American bird in such a cold, wintering setting. I treasured the opportunity to get that close to this rare vagrant. Since 2005, sightings in North America have been scattered and few, with records from California, Florida, the Ohio River valley, Ontario, and even St. John's, Newfoundland! So, this Southern Hemisphere species has the potential to turn up just about anywhere in North America.

Structure and Field Marks

Large, stocky, and long-legged, adult Kelp Gulls are darker above than Great Black-Backed Gulls and several shades darker than Yellow-Footed, Lesser Black-Backed, and Western Gulls. Smaller than Great Black-Backed Gulls, Kelp Gulls are comparable in size to Herring Gulls, but with a stockier build, thicker bill, and broader wings. Adults can usually be separated from Lesser Black-Backed Gulls by the much-darker mantle and heavier build. Overall, Lesser Black-Backed Gulls appear slimmer and more attenuated to the rear, due in large part to their longer wing projection. Kelp Gulls tend to have a thick-set, deep-chested appearance when perched that is rarely matched by Herring or Lesser Black-Backed Gulls.

First-Year Plumage

First-year Kelp Gulls are similar in plumage to Lesser Black-Backed Gulls of the same age, with a dark-brownish mantle and white base color on the heavily streaked head and underparts. However, the structure and pattern of the tail can be used to separate the two species: first-year Kelp Gulls have a thicker bill, a bulkier body, and an entirely dark tail, which can be seen in flight. The smaller and trimmer Lesser Black-Backed Gulls have a bright-white base to the tail, with a wide black distal band.

Second-Year Plumage

Second-year Kelp Gulls begin to acquire their black mantle, which, combined with the unpatterned dark-brown wing coverts, makes for a darkly plumaged bird overall. Compared to second-year Great Black-Backed Gulls with their marbled (with a white ground color) wing coverts, the medium-brown wings of a second-year Kelp Gull seem especially dark.

Third-year Plumage

Third-year Kelp Gulls are similar to adults but often retain some immature feathers on the upper-wing coverts and dark markings on the tail.

Adult Plumage

Adult Kelp Gulls are readily identified by the dark-black upperparts and greenish-yellow legs. Those legs separate adult Kelp Gulls from Great Black-Backed and Western Gulls. In winter, adult Kelp Gulls remain white headed, lacking the heavy streaking of adult Lesser Black-Backed Gulls. Kelp Gulls also have a thicker bill with a more pronounced gonydeal angle. While Yellow-Footed Gulls are unlikely to be seen away from the Salton Sea or Southern California, their mantle is grayish black compared to the pure black of Kelp Gulls, and Yellow-Footed Gulls have brighter-yellow legs.

In flight, adult Kelp Gulls show one small mirror (white spot) at the tip of the outermost primary, and a broad white border on the trailing edge of the wings. In comparison, Great Black-Backed Gulls have pink legs and mirrors on the two outermost primaries. In addition to being round and blunt tipped, the wings of Kelp Gulls are also broad, so that on adults the secondaries extend beyond the upper-wing greater coverts on the folded wing. The result is that the white secondary tips are visible beneath the black greater coverts, creating a white border or secondary "skirt" to the folded wing that is often not visible on gulls with narrower wings.

Size

Kelp Gulls are large gulls, similar in size to Herring Gulls but with bulkier proportions. Their wingspan ranges from 50.4 to 55.9 inches, and they are 21.3 to 25.6 inches long. Males weigh between 1 pound, 14.7 ounces, and 3 pounds, 1 ounce.

An adult Kelp Gull with Great Black-Backed Gulls in the background. Note the long, yellow-green legs. Sandgates, Maryland, August 31, 2002.

An adult Kelp Gull features dark flight feathers and a small white mirror on the outermost primary on the lower surface of the extended wing. Sandgates, Maryland, January 1, 2005. *Photo by Sean McCandless*

The Kelp Gull's dark-black mantle and yellow-green tint to the legs are clearly seen here. Sandgates, Maryland, January 1, 2005. *Photo by Sean McCandless*

The adult Kelp Gull has a characteristic large bill and orange orbital ring. Sandgates, Maryland, January 1, 2005. *Photo by Sean*

SWALLOW-TAILED GULL

Background

One of the world's most spectacular gulls, Swallow-Tailed Gulls breed primarily in the Galápagos Islands. They are highly pelagic the rest of the year and are found in the deep water off the northwest coast of South America. Swallow-Tailed Gulls have been recorded in North America four times—three times off the coast of California and once outside Seattle. The first record was an adult bird seen in Pacific Grove, California, on June 6 and 7, 1985, and at nearby Moss Landing Harbor the following day. The second record was also an adult gull, seen on March 3, 1996, on Southeast Farallon Island, California. The most-recent records were from the fall of 2017, when an adult gull was seen in Washington State from August 31 to September 10, allowing many birders unforgettable views. The gull was seen at multiple locations, ranging from Carkeek Park in northwestern Seattle to Everett, but most sightings were around the Edmonds waterfront along Puget Sound. Later that fall, a lone Swallow-Tailed Gull (possibly the same bird) was recorded at Bodega Bay, California. This bird was a one-day wonder, photographed on the rocks at the point on October 5.

Swallow-Tailed Gulls are inimitable in appearance, behavior, and biology, differing from other gulls in several significant ways. They are the only fully nocturnal gull; their exceptionally large eyes allow them to forage in the dark, when they feed on squid and small fish or glean marine organisms from the water's surface. They are even known to take prey heavier than they are. There may be several reasons why Swallow-Tailed Gulls find it advantageous to feed at night: squid may come closer to the surface after dark, they avoid harassment and kleptoparasitism from frigate birds, and they eliminate competition with Red-Billed Tropicbirds, which hunt for similar prey (Harris 1970). Whatever the reason, Swallow-Tailed Gulls fill a unique niche in the ecosystem. Even the grayish-white bill tip of adults is uniquely adapted to nocturnal habits, because it is visible at night to their young, just as a red gonydeal spot is a feeding stimulus during the day on many large white-headed species.

Unlike most gulls that nest on level terrain (ground-nesting species), Swallow-Tailed Gulls nest on broken cliffs or lava ledges, an adaptation they share with the kittiwakes. Nesting in such inaccessible locations may provide added protection from predators and provide ready access to their pelagic feeding habitat. Due to their tropical breeding location, they can lay eggs at all months of the year, and their reproductive cycle is nine to ten months. Breeding at less than an annual interval is also unusual for gulls.

Other behaviors resemble terns or shorebirds. Adult Swallow-Tailed Gulls have been observed doing a distraction display in which an adult flies close to a potential predator (such as a frigate bird or approaching person) and regurgitates foods, possibly in an attempt to distract the attacker from nearby young. This behavior is similar to the distraction display that the Killdeer use in defense of their young. Swallow-Tailed Gulls also have an "erect" display like that of terns, where the bill and head are pointed vertically upward.

One hopes that their future visits to North America will allow more birders to enjoy this uniquely adapted gull, a true gem of the Galápagos.

Structure and Field Marks

Swallow-Tailed Gulls are unique and unlikely to be confused with any of the regularly occurring North American gulls. Although the three-toned pattern on the extended wing is superficially similar to that of Sabine's Gulls, Swallow-Tailed Gulls are significantly larger and dark overall than that species. The three-toned wing pattern (black, white, and gray in adults; black, white, and dark brown in juveniles) is visible on flying Swallow-Tailed Gulls at considerable distances.

First-Year Plumage

Juvenile and first-winter birds have contrasting brown-and-white plumage. The head is whitish, but a black mask or "eye patch" is visible around each eye. The large eyes, combined with the eye patch, give juvenile birds a "goggle-eyed" appearance (Howell and Dunn 2007). The forked white tail has a dark distal band. The bill is all black, and the mantle, scapulars, and lesser coverts are dark brown with pale feather edges. The dark-brown upperparts contrast strongly with the white underparts and, combined with the black bill, make juvenile birds a study in contrasting dark brown and white. They also share the diagnostic three-tone wing pattern of adults, with immature dark-brown feathers on the mantle in place of the gray shown on adults.

Adult Plumage

Adult Swallow-Tailed Gulls are unlikely to be confused with any other species. In breeding season, the dark, sooty black hood; dark eye; fire-engine-red orbital ring; and mostly black bill make it unmistakable. Adults have a black bill that droops toward the grayish-white tip. The pattern of the extended wing is equally distinctive, with gray, black, and white triangles and wedges on the upper side of the wing. While it resembles that of Sabine's Gulls, Swallow-Tailed Gulls have more extensive white on the wing, with the "white wedge" including the greater wing coverts and more of the primaries. Also, the scapulars have a thin white border that appears as a narrow white line across the upperparts of resting birds, separating the scapulars from the wing coverts. The medium-gray mantle extends to the thin white border that appears as a narrow white line across the upperparts of resting birds, separating the scapulars from the wing coverts. The medium-gray mantle extends to the underparts as a grayish wash to the upper breast. Raspberry-pink legs add to the gaudy appearance of breeding adults.

In nonbreeding season, the black hood is lost, and the head becomes white with a black mask or eye patch, which accentuates the dark eye, making it appear even larger. The grayish wash to the nape and upper breast is retained, and a faint ear spot lends a dusky appearance to the head. The bold pattern of black, white, and gray on the extended wing is also retained and makes nonbreeding adults unmistakable in flight.

Size

Swallow-Tailed Gulls are medium sized, with an average wingspan of 39.4 to 47.2 inches and a length of 22 to 24 inches.

The black hood, dark-gray mantle, bold red eye ring, and white knob at the base of the black, gray-tipped bill are unmistakable on adult Swallow-Tailed Gulls. Edmonds, Washington, September 7, 2017. *Photo by Jeff Shenot*

Swallow-Tailed Gulls have a distinctive extended-wing pattern. Edmonds, Washington, September 7, 2017. *Photo by Jeff Shenot*

Note the diffuse wing pattern when viewed from below, and the black trailing edge to the middle and outermost primaries. The deeply forked tail is also visible on flying birds. Edmonds, Washington, September 7, 2017. *Photo by Jeff Shenot*

A gray-tipped black bill is characteristic of Swallow-Tailed Gulls. Edmonds, Washington, September 7, 2017. *Photo by Jeff Shenot*

SLATY-BACKED GULL

Background

Slaty-Backed Gulls are the dark-backed marine gull of northeastern Asia and are regular visitors to western Alaska. The only large, dark-backed gull within their range, Slaty-Backed Gulls have become annual along the Pacific coast south to California and have a prodigious history of vagrancies elsewhere in North America, with records coming from such far-flung locations as South Texas, South Florida, Newfoundland, Chicago, and Duluth, Minnesota. Given its propensity to wander, it is hoped for, though never expected, in winter gull flocks across North America.

These dark and heavily marked gulls contrast with the pale Glaucous and Glaucous-Winged Gulls that predominate in many areas. Farther south along the West Coast in winter, adults can be separated from Western Gulls by the pale eyes, parallel-edged bill, bright-pink legs, and heavily streaked head, face, and nape. Through 2019 there were seventy-two accepted records for Slaty-Backed Gulls in California. The first occurred in February 1995 at the Ventura Marina. And since 2005, at least one Slaty-Backed Gull has been recorded in California every year except 2010. This Asian rarity has become an annual visitor to the Pacific coast of the United States, and sightings are increasing elsewhere in the country.

Along with a handful of other gull species from Asia that have begun to turn up in North America with increased frequency, Slaty-Backed Gulls add an exciting dimension to gull watching in Alaska and along the Pacific coast. Even more thrilling is when one of these dark-backed Asian vagrants turns up in eastern North America. Their propensity to wander and turn up in unexpected places makes Slaty-Backed Gulls a tantalizing possibility for gull watchers. One of my favorite Slaty-Backed Gull sightings was of a second-year bird at the Marina Landfill outside Monterey, California. The gull stood out from the hordes of Western Gulls with its heavily streaked head, pale eyes, and bright-pink legs. The bill shape and developing slate-gray mantle clinched the identification.

Structure and Field Marks

Slaty-Backed Gulls are large gulls with a thick body and short legs. Similar in most dimensions to Herring Gulls, Slaty-Backed Gulls are bulkier, with a fuller chest, potbelly, and broader wings. These features makes them appear particularly low to the ground when standing and lumbering in flight. The bill is heavy but parallel edged, lacking the bulbous tip seen on many other large gull species.

First-Year Plumage

The identification of first-year Slaty-Backed Gulls is still being worked out, but much progress has been made in recent years. The best synthesis of known field marks for first-year Slaty-Backed Gulls appeared in the November/December 2014 issue of *Birding* magazine. It discusses both structural and plumage marks that distinguish first-year Slaty-Backed Gulls from similarly appearing gulls of the same age, including several hybrid combinations that bear superficial similarities. While these details are beyond the scope of this book, first-year Slaty-Backed Gulls are variable and hard to describe in general terms. However, they display the heavy but parallel-edged bill, short legs, and burly dimensions of older birds. The plumage is uniform. Darker birds are grayish brown, while paler birds are light tan. Some birds bleach to whitish by midwinter. The primaries, secondaries, and tail are dark brown to black and are the darkest part of the plumage. The upper-wing coverts are plain and mostly unmarked. The bill is all black and the legs are pink. They are similar to Glaucous-Winged Gulls in that much of their upperparts are pale and lack a distinctive pattern. In flight the underwing is pale with a narrow black trailing edge to the primaries, and the upper wing has a pale panel on the inner primaries.

Second- and Third-Year Plumage

Second- and third-year Slaty-Backed Gulls can also be identified by the dark mantle or upperparts, strikingly pale eye on heavily streaked head, bright-pink legs, and parallel-edged (not "blob-tipped") bill.

Adult Plumage

Adult Slaty-Backed Gulls are readily identified by their bulky size, dark-gray mantle, pale eye, and raspberry-pink legs. They are most likely to be confused with Western Gull on the West Coast and Great Black-Backed or Lesser Black-Backed Gulls in the East. However, adult Western and Great Black-Backed Gulls have a strikingly white or mostly white head during the winter or nonbreeding season. Conversely, adult Slaty-Backed Gulls have a heavily streaked head, causing it to appear messier than the clean black-and-white plumage of Great Black-Backed and Western Gulls. Adult Lesser Black-Backed Gulls share the heavily streaked head and nape in the winter but lack the Slaty-Backed Gull's hefty proportions, and their legs are mustard yellow. The Slaty-Backed Gull's bill lacks the pronounced gonydeal angle seen on Western or Great Black-Backed Gulls. Another unique field mark is the "string of pearls" pattern on the primaries of the extended wings. This pattern consists of white tongues or spots on the black feathers of the middle primaries: P4 or P5 through P8 (Alderfer and Dunn 2014).

Size

Slaty-Backed Gulls are thickset, with an average wingspan between 57.1 and 59.1 inches and length of 24.0 to 26.0 inches. They weigh about 2 pounds, 15.6 ounces.

A second-winter Slaty-Backed Gull is at the center of the photo, immediately behind the preening California Gull. Although viewed head on, the slaty-gray mantle feathers; plain, pale wing coverts; and pale eye can be seen. Marina Landfill, California, February 9, 2018.

The pale eye and parallel-edged bill are evident on this second-winter Slaty-Backed Gull. This species lacks the bulbous tip to the bill seen on many Western Gulls. Marina Landfill, California, February 9, 2018.

The dark, slate-gray mantle of the late second-year or early third-year Slaty-Backed Gull (*right*) and the dusky plumage of the immature Slaty-Backed Gull (*third from right*) stand out from the pale Glaucous Gulls. Nome, Alaska, June 3, 2008. *Photo by Phil Davis*

This perched adult Slaty-Backed Gull shows the heavily streaked head and heavy but parallel-edged bill typical of adults. Kamchatka, Russia, October. *Photo by Y. Artukhin / VIREO*

Flying adult Slaty-Backed Gulls show contrast between the slaty mantle and wings and black primary tips. The white spots within the black primary tips form the distinctive "string of pearls." Kamchatka, Russia, in June. *Photo by Rick and Nora Bowers / VIREO*

BLACK-TAILED GULL

Background

Black-Tailed Gulls are part of a small cadre of Asian gull species that rarely visit North America (the others are Slaty-Backed Gulls, "Kamchatka" Gulls—the Asian subspecies of Common Gulls—and Vega Gulls—the Asian subspecies of Herring Gull). In fact, given the increasing occurrence of Slaty-Backed Gulls in North America, the propensity of Black-Tailed Gulls to turn up just about anywhere in North America, and the recent records of "Kamchatka" Gulls in the Midwest and Northeast, some have referred to Asian gulls as the next great challenge in North American gull identification.

The widespread records of Black-Tailed Gulls across North American are truly remarkable, given their small breeding range along the coast of eastern Asia from northern Japan south to northeastern China, and limited postbreeding dispersal to the south. While Black-Tailed Gulls generally stay close to their small home range in East Asia, when they wander they sometimes take extremely long-distance trips and end up in unexpected places. While many North American sightings are from Alaska, there are records from up and down the West Coast, along the East Coast from Newfoundland to North Carolina, and in the Great Lakes region.

In California, the first record of a Black-Tailed Gull occurred in November 1954, when an adult female was found at the north end of San Diego Bay. That remained California's only record for several decades, but between 2008 and 2019 another six records were accepted in the state (Tietz and McCaskie 2018). And remarkable records exist from the Brownsville Landfill in Texas in 1999; Brantley Lake, New Mexico, in 2008; and Ashtabula, Ohio, in 2011. Truly, this Asian vagrant can turn up just about anywhere!

My sighting of this spectacular stray required a long wait outside the wastewater treatment plant in Ashtabula. I was among a large gathering of birders with scopes and cameras focused on a massive gull flock. The adult Black-Tailed Gull was perched within the tightly clustered flock, allowing only distant views as it slept. Eventually it stirred, and the full glory of the trademark black tailband was seen as it glided past a blue warehouse. The broad band extended unbroken across the tail, was cleanly demarcated, and contrasted markedly with the white rump and base of the tail. The long wait had been rewarded.

Structure and Field Marks

Black-Tailed Gulls most resemble California Gulls at all ages in plumage, size, and structure. Although slightly smaller than California Gulls, Black-Tailed Gulls share the same build, long primary extension, and long, parallel-edged, pencil-shaped bill. Other structural similarities include the short legs and long, narrow wings. The plumage also has some similarities: adults of both species have medium-dark mantles and red and black marks toward the bill's tip.

First-Year Plumage

First-winter Black-Tailed Gulls share similarities with California Gulls of the same age. In addition to the similar build and size, both are brown and have black-tipped, pink bills. However, Black-Tailed Gulls are darker brown overall, particularly on the underparts. First-winter Black-Tailed Gulls also have thin but contrasting white eye crescents that are lacking on similarly aged California Gulls. However, the easiest and most definitive mark for separating the species at this age is the Black-Tailed Gull's black tail and white rump. California Gulls have heavily barred, brown upper-tail coverts and rump, lacking the strong contrast with the dark-brown tail.

Adult Plumage

Adult Black-Tailed Gulls are identified by the bold black tailband (which is very noticeable in flight), pale eyes, medium-dark mantle, and yellow bill with a black subterminal band and red tip. The upperparts are a shade or two darker than on California Gulls, approaching the darkness of a Lesser Black-Backed Gull. Note that some third-year Lesser Black-Backed Gulls can appear similar to a third-year or adult Black-Tailed Gull, owing to the darkness of the upperparts and the retention of some black on the tail and bill. However, Lesser Black-Backed Gulls lack the well-defined band across the tail shown by Black-Tailed Gulls. They also lack the crisp black band and red tip on the end of the bill, although some third-year Lesser Black-Backed Gulls may have a black band toward the tip of the bill.

Size

Black-Tailed Gulls are medium sized, similar to California Gulls. Their wingspan averages 46.5 to 48.8 inches, and their length ranges from 18.1 to 18.9 inches. They weigh between 15.3 ounces and 1 pound, 6.6 ounces.

First-winter Black-Tailed Gulls are medium brown with a parallel-edged, black-tipped pink bill. Kurile Island, Russia, August. *Photo by Y. Artukhin / VIREO*

This perched adult Black-Tailed Gull has a parallel-edged, pencil-shaped bill; medium-gray mantle; and distinctive black ring / red tip to the bill. Nando Islet, South Korea, June. *Photo by P. O. Won / VIREO*

In flight, adult Black-Tailed Gulls show the diagnostic black tail. Charlotte, Vermont, in October. *Photo by G. Malosh / VIREO*

Appendix

CASE STUDY:
SCHOOLHOUSE POND, MARYLAND

It has been said that you can't identify a rare or out-of-place gull until you know your common gulls at all ages and in all seasons. This is true but not easy, since a flock of, say, twenty Ring-Billed Gulls all can look identifiably different. The best way to learn the variability within a gull species is to start locally. Find a place where gulls gather regularly in large numbers, and study them over an extended period of time. Taking a close look at the group will reveal how they vary in size (males are larger than females) and appearance from breeding to nonbreeding season, how wear and tear affects their looks, and how plumage varies among birds of the same species and age (such as the amount of streaking on the head, the amount of black in the wingtips, the color of the bare parts, and the size of the white tips on the primaries).

I learned much about my local gulls at Schoolhouse Pond in Upper Marlboro, Maryland. The pond is across the street from the office building where I worked for many years, so I was able to visit it before work, at lunchtime, and after work. Schoolhouse Pond is also about 2 miles (as the gull flies) from the Brown Station Road landfill. I often see hundreds of gulls flying over the pond toward the landfill in the morning, and sometimes they are resting on the pond or standing on the ice during my lunchtime walk. The numbers can be staggering, with well over 1,500 gulls present on some days. The sight of Laughing Gulls in the fall gives way to the predominance of Ring-Billed and Herring Gulls in winter. I particularly enjoy fall and spring mornings, when the call of the Laughing Gulls can be heard virtually nonstop overhead. On many mornings a steady stream of gulls fly overhead in small-to-medium-sized groups. It is possible to pick out rarities in flight, and I've seen several white-winged gulls pass overhead during my morning walks.

I've kept daily tallies of the gulls at Schoolhouse Pond since 2000 and noticed patterns. I learned that the largest groups of Laughing Gulls appear in late October or early to mid-November, that most Laughing Gulls depart before ice forms on the pond, that most Bonaparte's Gulls migrate during the last week of March and the first two or three weeks in April, and that the largest concentrations of gulls occur when the pond is frozen over during the coldest part of winter. I was thrilled on the days when I was able to find a white-winged gull mixed in with the Herring and Ring-Billed Gulls in winter, excited at the handful of times that a Black-Headed Gull turned up at the pond, and ecstatic when a first-fall Little Gull flew over the pond on Labor Day weekend 2009—the only time I have seen a Little Gull at the pond. I also enjoy the noisy flyover hordes of Laughing Gulls each spring and the sporadic, but usually annual, groups of flyover Bonaparte's Gulls each April. Perhaps my favorite sighting was on February 5, 2010, when I found an adult Black-Headed Gull standing on the ice as a blizzard swept in, the first of a two-part-punch "snowmageddon" that hit the East Coast. I'll also never forget my first sighting of a Glaucous Gull at the pond, a massive, bleached-white, first-winter bird with the distinctive black-tipped, bubblegum-pink bill. The Glaucous Gull dwarfed the surrounding Herring and Ring-Billed Gulls, and its ghostly white plumage and massive size made the bird an imposing presence.

But, for the sheer excitement, daily drama, and number of rarities, probably no month at Schoolhouse Pond can top December 2004. For a period of three weeks there were large number of gulls to sort through, and it seemed as if another rare (and at times extremely rare) gull was turning up each time I checked. I wrote an article summarizing the many gulls that occurred at Schoolhouse Pond during that month for *Maryland Birdlife*, the journal of the Maryland Ornithological Society, and a brief summary follows. In my thirty-plus years of walking around Schoolhouse Pond, December 2004 remains the single most exciting month of gull watching that I've ever experienced.

Early December of that year brought a large number of gulls to Schoolhouse Pond. Seasonably cool temperatures caused a layer of ice to form, which set the stage for the largest gull flocks at the pond. Despite the large numbers, through December 13 I had not spotted anything rarer than a few Lesser Black-Backed Gulls. However, on December 14, I found a first-year Iceland Gull during my lunchtime gull count. The gull's creamy-white plumage stood out in stark contrast to the surrounding Ring-Billed, Herring, and Laughing Gulls. Little did I know that the Iceland Gull was just the beginning of what would prove to be an impressive wave of rare gulls at the pond.

On December 16, I was trudging up the stairs at work when a coworker and fellow birder raced down the stairs in the opposite direction, binoculars in hand, exclaiming, "There's a Black-Headed Gull on the pond!" I grabbed my binoculars and bolted outside, where another local birder had the gull in his spotting scope—a beautiful adult male in winter plumage, complete with the red bill, red legs, pearly-gray mantle, and black ear spot. On December 18, both the Black-Headed Gull and a first-winter Glaucous Gull were seen.

On December 24, the birders spotted an adult winter Mew Gull. Mew Gulls (now called Short-Billed Gulls) are West Coast birds, a truly spectacular find in Maryland, and a first county record that would keep birders flocking to the pond over the coming week. Also seen on the pond that day was a first-winter Glaucous Gull, possibly the same bird reported the week before. So, on that particular day the small pond hosted not only a first-county-record West Coast gull, but a rare white-winged gull from the Arctic!

On December 26, four Lesser Black-Backed Gulls were seen, plus an adult gull that was intermediate between Lesser Black-Backed and Herring Gull in appearance. This bird was a possible hybrid between the two species, a rare but increasing occurrence along the East Coast in recent years. Even more unusual, there was a beautiful adult Glaucous Gull on the ice, distinguished by its massive size, pale-gray mantle, and snow-white wingtips. While immature Glaucous Gulls are rare at Schoolhouse Pond, an adult Glaucous Gull was unprecedented.

As our small group began to pack up in late afternoon, another unexpected bird flew in—an adult Iceland Gull (subspecies *kumlieni*)! This bird was distinguished from the adult Glaucous Gull by the smaller size, with a more rounded head and characteristic gray in the wingtips. We enjoyed watching this bird on the ice and then as it circled over the pond several times before flying off. The experience of viewing an adult Glaucous and Iceland Gull was practically unprecedented for the mid-Atlantic—a rare treat.

The rare gull sightings continued into the last week of December, with a first-winter Thayer's Gull (now classified as a subspecies *thayeri* of Iceland Gull) present on December

27. Birders enjoyed viewing its beautiful "coffee and cream" plumage and debating whether the bird was a better fit for a Thayer's or Iceland Gull identification. Lesser Black-Backed Gulls continued throughout the month, with multiple birds seen on several days. Although often overshadowed by the rarer species reported over the month, the sixteen Lesser Black-Backed Gulls seen at the pond during December 2004, including four on one day, were another memorable aspect of this unforgettable month.

A Black-Headed Gull (*center, bill pointed to the right*) braves a blizzard at Schoolhouse Pond in February 2010.

A partial albino Ring-Billed Gull was seen at Schoolhouse Pond in February 2015.

Table 1: Gulls at Schoolhouse Pond in December 2004

Species	Number	Notes
Ring-Billed Gull	10,378	
Laughing Gull	4,185	Numbers declined significantly over the month as temperatures dropped and ice formed on the pond.
Herring Gull	2,599	
Great Black-Backed Gull	52	
Lesser Black-Backed Gull	16	
Iceland Gull	2	
Glaucous Gull	2	1 adult and 1 first-winter. The first-winter gull was seen on December 18, 24, and 26.
Thayer's/Kumlien's Gull	1	first-winter gull
Black-Headed Gull	1	Winter plumage adult seen on December 16 and 18.
Mew Gull (now called Short-Billed Gull)	1	Winter plumage adult, subspecies *brachyrhynchus*. First Prince George's County record.
Possible Lesser Black-Backed × Herring hybrid	1	Adult. Intermediate in leg color and the shade of the mantle between Herring and Lesser Black-Backed Gulls
Total	17,238	

Fortunately, the gulls on Schoolhouse Pond are willing subjects for daily study and provide ample opportunities for learning. I've tried to keep track of the gulls that have occurred at or passed over the pond each day. Table 2 is a ten-year summary of the gulls seen at the pond each year. Although perhaps an arbitrary definition, I tend to think of the "gull season" as extending from late summer and early fall (when the first postbreeding birds and early migrants turn up there) through the winter (when huge flocks can gather on the ice of the pond) and into the spring migration (when the Laughing Gulls fly noisily overhead and the Bonaparte's Gulls pass through on migration). My observations included the flyover gulls in the morning (usually passing overhead on their way to the nearby landfill) and at times glorious lunchtime gull counts when I would sift through the gull flocks on the water or frozen surface of the pond.

Table 2 shows that the vast majority of my time was spent looking at the common Ring-Billed, Laughing, and Herring Gulls. This allowed me to learn the shape, structure, and variation within each of these species, and how they change over the course of a year. Great Black-Backed, Lesser Black-Backed, and Bonaparte's Gulls were seen less frequently and in smaller numbers. Other species were truly rare, occurring at the pond perhaps once or twice a season, or once every other year. The white-winged gulls fit this category. And still other species are rarer still, seen only once or a handful of times, such as the Short-Billed Gull, the first county record.

Table 2: Cumulative Schoolhouse Pond Gull Count:
A Ten-Year Snapshot

Species	2002-03	2003-04	2004-05	2005-06	2006-07	2007-08
Ring-Billed	30,968	26,051	27,594	14,557	28,492	12,764
Laughing	20,600	11,854	21,906	15,924	24,777	19,804
Herring	6,860	4,108	4,854	5,707	6,564	3,596
Bonaparte's	305	40	22	14	70	71
Great Black-Backed	136	89	108	29	75	38
Iceland (ssp. *kumlieni*)	3	1	3	0	2	3
Iceland (ssp. *thayeri*)	2	0	1	0	0	0
Glaucous	1	0	4	0	0	0
Black-Headed	0	0	1	0	0	1
Franklin's	0	0	0	1	0	0
Mew	0	0	1	0	0	0
Little	0	0	0	0	0	0
Herring × Glaucous	0	0	0	0	1	0
Lesser Black-Backed × Herring	0	0	1	0	1	1
Totals	58,911	42,178	54,516	36,249	60,001	36,296

2008-09	2009-10	2010-11	2011-12	Totals
15,196	33,971	19,247	12,283	**221,123**
12,777	18,675	10,489	15,047	**171,853**
5,134	5,617	2,727	2,848	**48,015**
142	15	27	65	**771**
70	77	15	18	**655**
2	3	2	0	**19**
3	2	0	0	**8**
2	1	0	0	**7**
1	1	0	1	**5**
0	1	0	1	**3**
0	0	0	0	**1**
0	0	1	0	**1**
0	2	0	1	**4**
0	0	0	0	**3**
32,793	58,630	32,492	30,271	**442,467**

My observations about these results are summarized below.

• Laughing Gull numbers at the pond peak in the mid- to late fall. Laughing Gulls are "warm weather" gulls, and numbers drop off dramatically at the pond when the weather gets cold and the pond begins to freeze over.

• White-headed gull numbers peak during the winter. Numbers seem highest at the pond when there is layer of ice on the water. And I've noticed time and again that the "best" gull-watching days at the pond (days with the biggest numbers and the appearance of rarities) tend to occur when the weather is at its worst (rain, snow, impending blizzard, sleet, cold, wind, etc.).

• Even when you think that only common gulls are present, it pays to check and double-check the flock. There have been times that I've found a rarity on my third time scanning through a sizeable flock of gulls at the pond. Individual gulls can be hidden behind a cluster of birds, and it can be easy to overlook something special in a large, closely clustered flock.

• Schoolhouse Pond sees a decent turnover of gulls at the pond during the course of a morning or afternoon. When flocks are gathered on the ice, gulls are constantly coming and going, either heading to the nearby landfill or toward Jug Bay Natural Area along the Patuxent River. So even though I might spend several hours sorting through the same flock of gulls, due to the turnover of birds I was usually finding new birds during that time.

• Bonaparte's Gulls are sometimes seen flying over the pond in late March and throughout April. They are seen flying overhead early in the morning in small-to-medium-sized groups as they migrate south in the spring. They are much rarer at the pond in the fall and through the winter.

• All the Black-Headed Gulls that were seen at the pond were with Ring-Billed Gull flocks.

• The noise of the Laughing Gulls as they fly over the pond in the spring can be impressive to behold. Even a lone Laughing Gull can generate a tremendous racket when giving its laughing-like cry while flying overhead.

• A pure albino Ring-Billed Gull was seen at the pond in March 2002. This bird appeared to be an adult and had an entirely pure-white plumage. The bare parts were pinkish/orange, with a darker-orange ring evident on the bill. Leucistic (partial albino) Ring-Billed Gulls were seen on several other occasions.

Although I considered Schoolhouse Pond to be special, there is nothing magical about the location. Birding "hotspots" can be found in and around any city or region. If you find your own local gathering point for gulls and visit it frequently, you will begin to understand their patterns of occurrence and behavior, how they change in appearance over the course of a year, and the variability within each species. You might even turn up a rare or unexpected gull or two!

Gulls of Schoolhouse Pond

Herring Gull

Ring-Billed Gull

Great Black-Backed Gull

Lesser Black-Backed Gull

Laughing Gull

Black-Headed Gull

Bonaparte's Gull

Glaucous Gull

Gull flocks at Schoolhouse Pond

Above: A winter flock gathers at Schoolhouse Pond during an ice storm.

A large group of Ring-Billed Gulls stand on the ice of Schoolhouse Pond.

Above: Iceland Gull

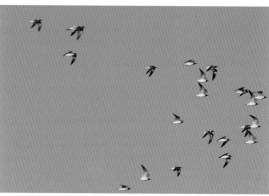

A flyover flock of Laughing Gulls (and one Ring-Billed Gull) pass over Schoolhouse Pond on a spring morning.

THE EPIC FRANKLIN'S GULL FALLOUT

Sometimes nature provides us with events that are so out of the ordinary as to defy easy explanation. The possibility of sighting a rare, vagrant bird can give every field trip an aura of discovery. One such event occurred on November 13, 2015. eBird News dubbed it the "Epic 2015 Franklin's Gull flight to the East Coast."

In a 1999 issue of *North American Birds*, Edward S. Brinkley described how tropical systems and strong weather fronts can displace large numbers of birds. In it, he described the "great storm" of November 9–11, 1998, which displaced large numbers of geese, Sandhill Cranes, Franklin's Gulls, and other late migrants throughout the Midwest and East Coast. The storm brought sustained winds of 50 to 70 mph, with gusts approaching 100 mph, and the lowest barometric pressure ever recorded in the Midwest. While most birders along the East Coast consider themselves fortunate if they see one Franklin Gull in a year, large numbers were recorded in eastern states, including eleven in South Carolina, sixteen to nineteen in New York, four in Maryland, and an incredible eighty-eight in New Jersey.

However, this event paled in comparison to what would take place in 2015, the result of a November 12 midwestern storm remarkably similar to the 1998 storm in intensity, scope, and track. The system precipitated a large movement of Cave Swallows to the mid-Atlantic region, and unprecedented numbers of Franklin's Gulls on the East Coast. The biggest flocks of Franklin's Gulls were reported in New Jersey: over sixty at Cape May, and a fourteen-bird block in Ocean City. The one-day total at Cape May on November 13 was at least 350 gulls, far exceeding the fallout from the 1998 storm (Reed 2017). Maryland also established a high count for the state, and Connecticut had as many as twelve Franklin's Gulls. This was the case from Virginia to Massachusetts, with birders finding lone Franklin's Gulls and small-to-medium-sized flocks along the coast (eBird News 2015).

Just using Maryland as an example, the 1998 storm left four Franklin's Gulls in the state, an impressive-enough total for the small mid-Atlantic state. However, the 2015 fallout included a group of four Franklin's Gulls in the parking lot of Ocean City inlet on the morning of November 13. After this initial group of birds departed, another lone first-winter Franklin's Gull was found late in the afternoon, again in the parking lot. However, the majority of the Franklin's Gull action was over the ocean and along the immediate coast in the late afternoon, with groups of birds being seen flying over the ocean and the inlet. A total of twenty-five were seen at the inlet, consisting of two lone birds, groups of three and six flying down the beach, and a kettle of fourteen over the mouth of the inlet. At the same time the Franklin's Gulls were being observed flying off Ocean City inlet, two adult Franklin's Gulls were also seen to the south at Public Landing. In addition to this bonanza of birds along the coast, lone gulls or small flocks were also recorded the same day at locations along or near the Chesapeake Bay, including Sandy Point State Park and Loch Raven Reservoir. Approximately ten days later, a lone Franklin's Gull was recorded near Sycamore Landing on the Potomac River.

As impressive as this fallout was in Maryland, it was dwarfed by the numbers seen in Cape May, New Jersey, on the same day. Although Franklin's Gulls were recorded all along Cape May on November 13, Tom Johnson was able to document some of the largest flocks that passed along the coast, noting groups of nine, twenty-two, and twenty-three that flew along the shore near the convention center. A group of sixty-two Franklin's Gulls that briefly rested on the rough, wind-tossed ocean off Cape May City represented perhaps the largest congregation of the species every recorded on the Atlantic Ocean (Reed 2017). Significant numbers of Franklin's Gulls were also reported from the Cape May hawk watch platform, Coral Avenue dune crossing, 2nd Street jetty, and Cape May Migratory Bird Refuge, just to name a few. With the one-day total at Cape May on November 13 being a minimum of 350 gulls (Reed 2017), it far exceeded the previous high noted after the 1998 storm, when Franklin's Gulls were reported from November 14 through the 16. This has led to comparisons between the two events, and whether the 2015 fallout was in fact bigger than the 1998 event, or if it simply reflected a more efficient and instantaneous dissemination of information, greater numbers of more-knowledgeable observers in the field, or some combination of factors. There are likely no easy answers to these questions. However, the 2015 event was exceptional, and undoubtedly the rapidness that the word was spread about the sightings maximized the number of birders in the field looking for additional Franklin's Gulls.

While the epicenter of the Franklin's Gull sightings centered on the mid-Atlantic region, birds were seen elsewhere along the East Coast, as documented by eBird. In Massachusetts, three Franklin's Gulls were seen in Plymouth and a lone Franklin's Gull was documented in Miller's Farm, Vermont. The following day, on November 14, Franklin's Gulls were reported in Lynn Beach, Massachusetts; in the parking lot of K-Mart in Queensbury, New York; and at Sunset Farm near Portsmouth, New Hampshire. Another one was spotted near Quebec City, Canada, on November 15—perhaps the most northerly report of the fallout. This epic event will not be forgotten by the birders who experienced the excitement, which highlighted what can happen when a strong weather front coincides with a migratory species and gulls' natural propensity to wander.

THE IVORY GULL INVASION OF 2009

One of the most remarkable invasions of Ivory Gulls in recent memory occurred in January 2009. Large numbers both of immature and adult birds were seen over a period of several weeks from Labrador to Newfoundland, Prince Edward Island, Nova Scotia, and Massachusetts. Some observers in Newfoundland tracked down as many as twelve on January 10. The most-southerly birds reported were adult gulls at Gloucester and Plymouth, Massachusetts. What follows are the highlights, gleaned from rare-bird postings and bird forums as well as personal observations and conversations.

The first bird reported was an Ivory Gull in North Rustico, Prince Edward Island, on December 26, 2008, the third documented sighting for Prince Edward Island. It stayed put through January 31, by all accounts the longest stay-over of the invasion, and was known to take handouts of eel guts from local fishermen.

Then on January 8, 2009, seventeen Ivory Gulls were spotted in southern Labrador. These tame and approachable birds fed on scraps of meat in the town of Pinware. Of the nine birds photographed, eight were immature. On January 9, Bruce Mactavish speculated that forecasted strong northwest winds along the Labrador coast would likely drive Ivory Gulls down into Newfoundland (Mactavish 2009; nf.birds). This was exactly what happened, as witnessed by multiple observers during the weekend of January 10 and 11.

John and Ivy Gibbons birded the Newfoundland coast on Saturday, January 10, the day of the most sightings that month. They surveyed the Northern Peninsula from Deadman's Cove to Eddies Cove East and found both adult and immature birds at various stops. Two adult Ivory Gulls were flying along the shoreline at Flowers Cove and were described as "whiter than the new snow they were flying over" (Gibbons 2009; nf.birds). Two more adults and one immature Ivory Gull were seen at Sandy Cove along the edge of a wharf with a group of Glaucous, Iceland, and Herring Gulls. Immature Ivory Gulls were also found at the north and south ends of Pine Cove. Another immature bird was found at Eddies Cove East, foraging on slushy ice.

On the return trip, four Ivory Gulls were seen at Sandy Cove. However, this time there were three immature birds and one adult! The Gibbonses confirmed that they saw eight different birds and as many as ten or twelve Ivory Gulls (Gibbons 2009; nf.birds). On Sunday, January 11, other observers saw an immature bird flying south at Seal Cove, and another immature bird flying north at Summer Side near the end of the causeway in Cow Head. Two individual adult birds were found on January 12 at Cape Spear, flying south along the rocky shoreline. That same day, an immature Ivory Gull was seen near the sewage outlet by Goodland Road at Conception Bay South. The gull flew back and forth along the shore, resting briefly on the water with a group of Iceland Gulls. Later in the afternoon, an Ivory Gull was reported on the ice of Quidi Vidi Lake, foraging on a gull carcass. This same gull was spotted the following day.

On January 16, another fortunate observer found both an adult and an immature Ivory Gull during a lunch break at Rocky Harbour. The next day, four were found in proximity at Trinity Bay. These gulls consisted of an adult bird at Islington Cove and two adults and an immature near Hearts Delight. At Hearts Delight, a strong wind was pushing ice up against the rocks along the shoreline, providing ideal foraging conditions for the ice-loving gulls.

January 17 was a fruitful day in New England too; an adult Ivory Gull appeared on the jetty at Eastern Point in Gloucester, Massachusetts. This bird foraged in flight over the harbor and perched atop the jetty, ideal for close views and photos. One birder recorded the thrill: "In the breathless cold clear air, in the sun shining down with an unimpeded chilling light, the Ivory Gull was a remarkable sight. It was so pure and so white; so brilliant that it seemed to glow in the midday light" (Chickering 2009; massbird). This remarkable bird, together with the Plymouth Ivory Gull that was found on January 20, would cause birders to flock to Massachusetts from across the country in search of these spectacular vagrants.

Back in Newfoundland, another attempt was made to survey Ivory Gulls at a variety of locations on January 18. The Gros Morne coast was birded from Rocky Harbour north. Three immature gulls and one adult were spotted dip-feeding over the slushy ice in the harbor near the fish plant. The search continued up the coast. Except for the Rocky Harbour birds, all the gulls were flying south along the coast. Additional birds were seen at other places. One immature showed up at Sally's Cove, three or four immature gulls and two adults were seen at Broom Point / St. Paul's Inlet, one immature was seen at Three-Mile Rock, and another immature at Parson's Pond. This was another remarkable day during the monthlong invasion.

Ivory Gull sightings continued the next week, though at a slower pace. An adult gull was seen on January 19 on the Lower Coast of Trespassey near Roseate Tern Rock. This gull was accosted by an aggressive Glaucous Gull. The larger gull grasped the Ivory Gull by the nape and swung it back and forth ruthlessly before pinning it to the ground. Although the Glaucous Gull eventually left, it was apparent that the Ivory Gull was injured. An adult Ivory Gull was seen at Lush's Bight, Long Island, on January 22. Continued searches in the Rocky Harbour area turned up no gulls during the early part of the week. However, on the 24th, the winds began to blow out of the east, and a single juvenile Ivory Gull was seen flying through the snow squalls at Norris Point. The bird vanished into the snow within seconds.

On January 22, an adult Ivory Gull was found in Sambro Harbour, Nova Scotia, remaining there for well over a week. On January 28, two adult Ivory Gulls were seen at Sambro Harbour, flying between the fishery buildings and piers and docks in the harbor. Although the second gull was apparently not seen again, a single Ivory Gull continued to be seen in the harbor until February 3. Rounding out the Nova Scotia sightings was an adult Ivory Gull photographed in Lower Prospect HRM (Halifax Regional Municipality) on January 31. No Ivory Gulls were reported in New Brunswick during the invasion period. However, they continued to be seen in Newfoundland, with an adult reported along the Northeast River in Trespassey. The bird fed on seal carcasses and was spotted the following day as well. Because the bird appeared to be injured, there was some speculation that this may have been the same gull that was attacked in Trespassey on January 19.

Meanwhile, in Massachusetts, the adult Ivory Gull was seen repeatedly in Gloucester. At times the gull was approachable and allowed prolonged views, while other times it flew tantalizingly from cove to cove, forcing birders to race from site to site on snow-clogged roads. The bird was seen on January 18, 19, and 20. Another adult Ivory Gull was found in Plymouth Harbor early in the afternoon of January 20, flying around the harbor and feeding on a pigeon carcass. Although the Gloucester Ivory Gull disappeared after January 22, the Plymouth gull lingered in the Plymouth Harbor area for more than a week longer, offering throngs of birders a close view as it fed on a chicken carcass left in the parking lot. It flew off after January 30, marking the end of the invasion in Massachusetts.

The sightings were winding down elsewhere as well; the birds disappeared as quickly and mysteriously as they arrived. The last Newfoundland and Price Edward sightings were on January 31, and the last Nova Scotia sighting was on the morning of February 3, by a forklift operator at Sambro Harbour. Although it is difficult to determine exact numbers, seventy-five different birds may have been present during this period. Of the birds that were aged, twenty-eight were adults and thirty-six were immature. By February 4, all of the Ivory Gulls had retreated to their more northerly habitat. Birders across the continent will remember January 2009 as the chance of a lifetime to view this elusive and magnificent bird.

Note: A variety of online sources were used to compile this summary. The majority of information was based on rare-bird listservs and blogs. These include the Nova Scotia Rare Bird Alert, the Massachusetts Birding List, Newfoundland Birds, PEEPS Online, Maine Birds, Nature New Brunswick, and Ontario Birds. Most of the original links are no longer available online.

Bibliography and Further Reading

A variety of sources were consulted in the development of this book. One of the joys of this project was exploring the vast body of literature related to birds in general and gulls in particular. I used not only recent, cutting-edge references but also classic books written at a time when much was still being discovered about North America's birds. These authors conveyed delight and a spirit of adventure and discovery. Included here are all the sources referenced in this book, along with a brief summary of each source (excluding some of the more technical references). I hope my all-too-brief summaries have done these great sources justice.

BOOKS AND PERIODICALS

"28th Report of the ABA Checklist Committee." *Birding* 49, no. 6 (2017): 28–35. This report includes the removal of Thayer's Gull from the ABA checklist and explains the placement of *thayeri* as a subspecies of Iceland Gull.

"Sixty-Second Supplement to the American Ornithological Society's Check-List of North American Birds." *Ornithology* 138 (2021): 1–18. This supplement splits *Larus brachyrhynchus* from the Old World breeding subspecies and elevates it to a full species called Short-Billed Gull (previously included as a subspecies under Mew Gull). All Old World breeding subspecies now fall under *L. canus* (Common Gull).

Adams, Mark T., and Matt Hafner. "Middle Atlantic (Regional Report)." *North American Birds* 63, no. 1 (2009): 55. This quarterly regional report includes documentation of the probable Black-Headed × Ring-Billed Gull hybrid seen over several days in Eagle Harbor, Maryland, in August 2008.

Adriaens, Peter. "Iceland and Kumlien's Gulls: Photo Guide." *Birdwatch* 238 (2012): 41–47. This article is a great resource for separating Kumlien's Gulls (ssp. *kumlieni*) from Iceland Gulls (ssp. *glaucoides*) in the field. It also includes a thoughtful discussion of the taxonomic situation within the Iceland Gull complex.

Alderfer, Jonathan, and Jon Dunn. *Complete Birds of North America*. 2nd ed. Washington, DC: National Geographic, 2014. This book provides a great summary of the distribution, identification, and occurrence of all the bird species that have been recorded in North America. It incorporates a tremendous amount of information on each species into one volume. In addition to the well-written species accounts, the book also includes information on identifying large white-headed gulls and separating first-winter California and Herring Gulls. Along with *Sibley Guide to Birds* and the various gull specialty guides, this is one of my first references to consult when I find a particularly hard-to-identify gull.

Aubry, Yves. "First Nests of the Common Black-Headed Gull in North America." *American Birds* 8, no. 3 (1984): 366–367. This article summarizes the discovery of the first nests of Black-Headed Gulls when multiple pairs of Black-Headed Gulls, fledged young, and flightless chicks were observed in the vicinity of empty nests on the Madeleine Islands in the Gulf of St. Lawrence in summer 1982.

Baldwin, William P. "Laughing Gull Robs Brown Pelican." *The Auk* Vol 63 (1946): 96–97. This article documents how Laughing Gulls steal food from Brown Pelicans by landing on their head. He writes, "A pelican has never been observed to show anything but stoic calm during this procedure."

Barnard, C. J., and D. B. A. Thompson. *Gulls and Plovers: The Ecology and Behaviour of Mixed-Species Feeding Groups*. New York: Columbia University Press, 1985. This book documents how plovers and gulls interact while feeding in mixed-species groups. Lapwings, golden plovers, and Black-Headed Gulls are the subjects of this book, which provides insight on the interactions of the three species as they feed in agricultural fields. Lapwings are exploited as food "scouts," while both the lapwings and golden plovers are exploited by the kleptoparasitic gulls.

Belant, Jerrold L., and Richard A. Dolbeer. "Migration and Dispersal of Laughing Gulls in the United States." *Journal of Field Ornithology* 64, no. 4 (1993): 557–665. Recovery records of banded Laughing Gulls were analyzed to determine the migration and dispersal patterns for Laughing Gulls from the Northeast and the Gulf coast. Differences between the two populations are noted.

Bell, Douglas A. "Genetic Differentiation, Geographic Variation and Hybridization in Gulls of the Larus Glaucescens-Occidentalis Complex." *The Condor* 98 (1995): 527–546.

Bent, Arthur Cleveland. *Life Histories of North American Gulls and Terns*. New York: Dover, 1921. This is by far my favorite reference on gull behavior and biology, written with an enthusiasm, charm, and personal touch that is frequently lost in today's more technically accurate but cold and impersonal writing. The book is a glimpse at a period when much was being discovered about North American birds, and Bent clearly reveled in the subject matter.

Blom, Eirik. "Identifying Gulls: Don't Panic!" *Birdwatcher's Digest* 23, no. 3 (2001): 33–38. This article explains a simplified approach to gull identification that all birdwatchers can use regardless of skill level.

Blomqvist, Sven, and Magnus Elander. "Sabine's Gull (*Xema sabini*), Ross's Gull (*Rhodostethia rosea*) and Ivory Gull (*Pagophila eburnean*): Gulls in the Arctic; A Review." *Arctic* 34, no. 2 (1981): 122–132. This delightful article summarizes what was learned about some of our northernmost gulls during the heroic era of exploration in the nineteenth century and the beginning of the twentieth century. Sightings of all three species are thrilling, and this article summarizes the expeditions and misadventures of early explorers and what they discovered regarding these three species at a time when very little was known. Anyone interested in this trio of stunning gulls and early explorations of the Far North should read this article.

Boertmann, David. "The Lesser Black-Backed Gull, *Larus fuscus*, in Greenland." *Arctic* 61, no. 2 (2008): 129–133. This article documents the growing breeding population of Lesser Black-Backed Gulls in Greenland and notes that breeding has been confirmed as far north as 74 degrees north.

Boswall, Jeffery, and Michael Barrett. "Notes on the Breeding Birds of Isla Raza, Baja California." *Western Birds* 9, no. 3 (1978): 93–108. Included in this comprehensive report is documentation on the largest breeding colony of Heermann's Gulls in the world. Breeding only on a small number of islands off Baja California, over 90 percent of the world's population of Heermann's Gulls nest on Isla Raza.

Brinkley, Edward S. "Changing Seasons: Low Pressure (Fall Migration: August through November)." *North American Birds* 53, no. 1 (1999): 12–19. This article documents the influx of Franklin's Gull into the eastern United States during November 1998. It also provides an example of the role that strong weather systems can have on bird displacement and movements.

Coulson, J. C., and E. White. "Observations on the Breeding of the Kittiwake." *Bird Study* 5 (1958): 74–83. This article documents the breeding biology of Black-Legged Kittiwakes. Much of the data comes from a colony on a warehouse in North Shields, Northumberland.

Daniels, Denver. "Vocal Behaviour in the Kittiwake Gull." *Lundy Field Society Annual Report* 34 (1983): 13–15. This article documents the function of the various vocalizations made by Black-Legged Kittiwakes and provides evidence that cliff-nesting kittiwakes have a larger vocal repertoire than ground-nesting kittiwakes.

Devillers, Pierre, Guy McCaskie, and Joseph R. Jehl. "The Distribution of Certain Large Gulls (*Larus*) in Southern California and Baja California." *California Birds* 2, no. 1 (1971): 11–26. This article provides a fascinating summary of the occurrence and distribution of gulls in Southern California, by some of the region's most knowledgeable experts. California is a great location to watch gulls, and this article explains where and when the different species can be found in this bird-rich state.

Dittmann, Donna L., and Steven W. Cardiff. "The 'Chandeleur' Gull: Origins and Identification of Kelp × Herring Gull Hybrids." *Birding* 37 (May/June 2005): 266–276. This article documents and describes the Kelp × Herring Gull hybrids (or "Chandeleur" Gulls) from the Chandeleur Islands off the coast of Louisiana. It also provides background on the initial discovery of a Kelp Gull on Curlew Island and the subsequent breeding of both Kelp Gull pairs and Kelp and Herring Gull pairs.

Divoky, George J., Gerald A. Sanger, Scott A. Hatch, and J. Christopher Haney. *Fall Migration of Ross' Gull (Rhodostethia rosea) in Alaskan Chukchi and Beaufort Seas.* Intra-Agency Agreement No. 14-12-0001-30391, Task E. Anchorage, AK: Alaska Fish and Wildlife Research Center, 1988. This comprehensive work compiles the data collected on Ross's Gulls in the 1970s and 1980s, with a focus the distribution, abundance, and movements of the species in the Alaskan Beaufort and Chukchi Seas in summer and fall. During this period, data was collected on cruises, by land, and with aerial surveys. By assembling data over an extended period of time, much is revealed about the habits, movements, and abundance of this little-known species.

Dunne, Pete. *Pete Dunne's Essential Field Guide Companion.* Boston and New York: Houghton Mifflin, 2006. Pete Dunne captures the essence of almost 700 North American bird species with rich, descriptive text designed to supplement the fine photographs and illustrations contained in existing field guides. The text emphasizes the color, shape, patterns, and behavior of each species and is intended to guide readers to look at the big picture of the bird, rather than the fine details of individual bird parts or plumage. Like for the other bird groups, the text on the gulls is outstanding, giving readers an excellent synopsis on what is unique and distinctive about each species without getting lost in the minutia.

Dwight, Jonathan. *The Gulls (Laridae) of the World: Their Plumages, Moults, Variations, Relationships, and Distribution*. Bulletin of the American Museum of Natural History 52, art. 3. New York: American Museum of Natural History, 1925. This classic book covers all the gulls of the world and remains a valuable reference.

Ebels, Enno B., Peter Adrianens, and Jon R. King. "Identification and Ageing of Glaucous-Winged Gull and Hybrids." *Dutch Birding* 23 (2001): 247–270. This article provides detailed information for identifying all ages of Glaucous-Winged Gulls, as well as the various hybrid combinations involving Glaucous-Winged Gulls.

Edwards, James L. "General Notes." *The Auk* 52, no. 1 (1935): 85. This account documents the first Lesser Black-Backed Gull record in North America.

Egevang, Carsten, and David Boertmann. "Ross's Gulls Breeding in Greenland: A Review, with Special Emphasis on Records from 1979 to 2007." *Arctic* 61, no. 3 (2008): 322–328. Breeding records of Ross's Gulls from Greenland are analyzed, with many of the records coming from the Disko Bay area of West Greenland and the Northeast Water Polynya in Northeast Greenland.

Ellis, Julie C., Mary Caswell Stoddard, and L. William Clark. "Breeding by a Lesser Black-Backed Gull (*Larus fuscus*) on the Atlantic Coast of North America." *North American Birds* 61, no. 4 (2007): 546–548. This paper documents the first breeding record of a Lesser Black-Backed Gull along the Atlantic coast of North America. A Lesser Black-Backed Gull was recorded breeding with a Herring Gull on Appledore Island, Maine. In subsequent years, some have begun to refer to confirmed or suspected Lesser Black-Backed × Herring Gull hybrids as "Appledore's" Gulls.

Finley, William Lovell. "Among the Sea Birds off the Oregon Coast, Part I." *The Condor* 7, no. 5 (1905a): 118–127. This fascinating two-part account documents a small group of scientists who camped on Three Arch Rocks off the coast of Oregon to document and photograph the seabirds that occur there. Gulls are featured prominently in the articles, both for their own sake and the grief they caused the other birds (the gulls are described both as "saintly-looking scalawags" and "freebooters and robbers"). A black-and-white collage of photos labeled simply "Gulls in Flight" captures their mastery of flight around the island. Elsewhere Finley writes, "One of the prettiest sights about the rock was the gulls that filled the air like so many feathered snowflakes. Their immaculate white bodies and soft, pearl-grey wings, tipped with black, are as catching as music strains wafted over the river."

Finley, William Lovell. "Among the Sea Birds off the Oregon Coast, Part II." *The Condor* 7, no. 6 (1905b): 161–169. Part 2 of the wonderful account of five days spent on Three Arch Rocks off the coast of Oregon. Part 2 focuses on cormorants and murres, but gulls are referenced several times related to their interactions with and harassment of the other birds.

France, R. L., and M. Sharp. "Newly Reported Colonies of Ivory Gulls in Southeastern Ellesmere Island." *Arctic* 45, no. 3 (1992): 306–307. Seven new colonies of Ivory Gulls comprising 330 adults were discovered on the nunataks emerging from the Manson Icefield, providing additional evidence that the rocky outcrops surrounded by glacial ice serve an important habitat for breeding Ivory Gull colonies.

Garner, M. and Mactavish, B (2001). "The in-between gull." *Birdwatch* 103 (January), 26–31.

Gilchrist, H. Grant, and Mark L. Mallory. "Declines in Abundance and Distribution of the Ivory Gull (*Pagophila eburnea*) in Arctic Canada." *Biological Conservation* 121 (2005): 303–309.

Gilg, Olivier, Hallvard Strøm, Adrian Aebischer, Maria V. Gavrilo, Andrei E. Volkov, Cecelie Viljeteig, and Brigitte Sabard. "Post-breeding Movements of Northeast Atlantic Ivory Gull *Pagophila eburnean* Populations." *Journal of Avian Biology* 41, no. 5 (2010): 532–542. This groundbreaking research used satellite transmitters to track the post-breeding movements of Ivory Gulls. Gulls were from three Northeast Atlantic populations (northern Greenland, Svalbard, and Franz Josef Land). The satellite transmitters provided new information on the postbreeding movements of these enigmatic gulls as they traveled between the breeding areas and their remote wintering grounds.

Gosselin, Michel, and Normand David. "Field Identification of Thayer's Gull (*Larus thayeri*) in Eastern North America." *American Birds* 29, no. 6 (1975): 1059–1066. This paper outlines features for identifying Thayer's Gulls (now ssp. *thayeri*) of all ages from Herring and Iceland (ssp. *kumlieni*) Gulls of the same age.

Grant, Peter J. *Gulls: A Guide to Identification.* 2nd ed. San Diego: Academic Press, 1986. Grant's classic book covers the gulls of Europe, the Middle East, and North America and sparked an interest in gull identification that continues to this day.

Hailman, Jack P. "Cliff-Nesting Adaptations of the Galápagos Swallow-Tailed Gull." *Wilson Bulletin* 77, no. 4 (1965): 346–362. This article summarizes the cliff-nesting adaptations made by Swallow-Tailed Gulls and discusses how they compare with adaptations made by another cliff-nesting species, the Black-Legged Kittiwake.

Hallgrimsson, Gunnar Thor, Norman Deans van Swelm, Hallgrimur V. Gunnarsson, Thomas B. Johnson, and Careron L. Ruti. "First Two Records of European-Banded Lesser Black-Backed Gulls *Larus fuscus* in America." *Marine Ornithology* 39 (2011): 137–139. This article documents that despite extensive banding of Lesser Black-Backed Gulls in Europe and Iceland, only two European gulls have been relocated in North America. This may indicate that the majority of wintering Lesser Black-Backed Gulls in North America are from Greenland, with Europe contributing few birds.

Hamilton, Robert, Michael A. Patten, and Richard A. Erickson. *Rare Birds of California: A Work of the California Birds Records Committee.* Camarillo, CA: Western Field Ornithologists, 2007. This book, and associated online resource, is the work of the California Bird Records Committee and is one of the most comprehensive compilations of a particular state's rare-bird records. While the book form is a beautiful work, the online resource is equally valuable and has been updated to reflect bird records and patterns of occurrence since the book's publication in 2007. Anyone interested in the birds of California or rare birds in general should utilize this exceptional resource.

Harris, Michael P. "Breeding Ecology of the Swallow-Tailed Gull, *Creagrus furcatus*." *The Auk* 87, no. 2 (1970): 215 – 243. This comprehensive article includes observations on the breeding ecology of Swallow-Tailed Gulls and provides insights into the reasons for its nocturnal behavior and the advantages that may be achieved by hunting at night.

Harrison, Peter. *Seabirds: An Identification Guide.* Boston: Houghton Mifflin, 1985. This book covers all the seabirds of the world, including gulls, and is based on Harrison's seven years of field research on working fishing boats and trawlers. This is a great resource if you regularly go on pelagic trips or take extended excursions at sea. Few people can match Harrison's experience with the birds of the open ocean.

Hjort, Christian, Gudmundur A. Gudmundsson, and Magnus Elander. "Ross's Gulls in the Central Arctic Ocean." *Arctic* 50, no. 4 (1997): 289–292. This fascinating article documents the Arctic Ocean 96 expedition, which used a Swedish icebreaker to access the Arctic Ocean and document its birdlife. Ross's Gulls were seen at 87 degrees north and were the most abundant bird species in the central Arctic Ocean.

Howell, Steven N. G., and Jon Dunn. *Gulls of the Americas.* New York: Houghton Mifflin, 2007. This is the definitive work on the gulls of North and South America. It illustrates all ages and plumages with high-quality photographs and describes how to separate gulls from potential confusion species. It also includes accounts for various hybrid combinations, from widespread hybrids such as "Olympic" and "Nelson's" Gulls to more rarely seen combinations such as "Appledore's" Gulls.

Howell, Steve N. G., and Martin T. Elliott. "Identification and Variation of Winter Adult Thayer's Gulls with Comments on Taxonomy." *Alula* 7 (2001): 130–144. This paper describes field marks and variation within Thayer's Gulls (now ssp. *thayeri*) and how to separate them from similar species of gulls, and includes comments on the taxonomy of the Thayer's/Iceland Gull complex. The variation of wingtip patterns is described and illustrated in great detail, and the photographs are instructive. The beautiful painting by Elliott depicts Thayer's Gulls with Herring Gulls and various hybrids.

Howell, Steve N. G., and Bruce Mactavish. "Identification and Variation of Winter Adult Kumlien's Gull." *Alula* 1 (2003): 2–15. A notoriously variable subspecies, "Kumlien's" Gulls can appear as pale as ssp. *glaucoides* to as dark as ssp. *thayeri*. Howell and Mactavish document this variation and give measures for assessing the wingtip patterns of adult Kumlien's Gulls.

Jehl, Joseph R., Jr. "Geographic Variation and Evolution in the California Gull (*Larus californicus*)." *The Auk* 104 (1987): 421–428. This article does a great job of documenting and explaining the geographic variation found within the two subspecies of California Gulls (*L. c. californicus* and *L. c. albertaensis*).

Jiguet, Frederic, Alvaro Jaramillo, and Ian Sinclair. "Identification of Kelp Gull." *Birding World* 14 (2001): 112–125. This article provides a wealth of information related to the molt, geographic variation, distribution, and identification of Kelp Gulls, with a goal of helping birders identify future vagrants.

Jonsson, Lars, and Bruce Mactavish. "American Herring Gulls at Niagara Falls and Newfoundland." *Birders Journal* 10 (2001): 90–107. This insightful article documents differences between populations of adult Herring Gulls at Niagara Falls and Newfoundland, suggesting that the two distinct populations might represent separate subspecies.

Kaufman, Kenn. *Kingbird Highway: The Story of a Natural Obsession That Got a Little Out of Hand*. Boston and New York: Houghton Mifflin Company, 1997. This fascinating book chronicles Kenn Kaufman's adventures as he crosses North America in search of birds. Few books capture the wonder of birds and the thrill of the chase better than this one.

Kenyon, Karl W., and Richard E. Phillips. "Birds from the Pribilof Islands and Vicinity." *The Auk* 82 (1965): 624–635. This article summarizes the birds observed or collected on the Pribilof Islands. Detailed information is provided on the gull species, including the Red-Legged Kittiwake, a Bering Sea specialty.

Leukering, Tony. "Smithsonian Gull: A Nomenclatorial Suggestion." *Birding* 42, no. 6 (2010): 40–43. This article makes a persuasive case for renaming the New World subspecies of Herring Gull (*L. a. smithsonianus*) as Smithsonian Gull. Because research indicates that *smithsonianus* is not closely related to "European" Herring Gulls, Leukering argues for a distinctly American name for a distinctly American gull.

Lonergan, Pat, and Killian Mullarney. "Identification of American Herring Gull in a Western European Context." *Dutch Birding* 16 (2004): 1–35.

Maftei, Mark. "Searching for the Ross's Gull in Canada's High Arctic." *Birding* 44, no. 3 (2012): 42–55. This article documents some of the groundbreaking research of the High Arctic Gull Research Group, which searched for and placed geolocators on Ross's Gulls in the Canadian Arctic. This research has led to a better understanding of the movements of this enigmatic species. Some of the most spectacular photographs of Ross's Gulls that I've seen are found in this article.

Maftei, Mark, Shanti E. Davis, Ian L. Jones, and Mark L. Mallory. "Breeding Habitats and New Breeding Locations for Ross's Gull (*Rhodostethia rosea*) in the Canadian High Arctic." *Arctic* 65, no. 3 (2012): 283–288. This article documents the splendid work of the High Arctic Gull Research Group on the seldom-seen Ross's Gull, by providing evidence of its breeding in the Canadian Arctic, including nests found via aerial surveys and on foot.

Maftei, Mark, Shanti E. Davis, and Mark L. Mallory. 2015. "Confirmation of a Wintering Ground of Ross's Gull *Rhodostethia rosea* in the Northern Labrador Sea." *Ibis* 157 (2015): 642–647. This groundbreaking work uses satellite and geolocator telemetry to confirm that some Ross's Gulls winter in the northern Labrador Sea. This is the first confirmation of where at least some of these little-known birds spend the dark, cold northern winter.

Maftei, Mark, Shanti E. Davis, Brian D. Uher-Koch, Callie Gesmundo, Robert Suydam, and Mark L. Mallory. "Quantifying Fall Migration of Ross's Gulls (*Rhodostethia rosea*) past Point Barrow, Alaska." *Polar Biology* 37 (2014): 1705–1710. The migration of Ross's Gulls past Point Barrow, Alaska, has been known to scientists since the late 1800s. This remarkable account quantifies this passage as the authors spent thirty-nine days at Point Barrow (every gull lover's dream) in September and October 2011, conducting a continuous survey of Ross's Gulls as they migrated past Point Barrow. The results are breathtaking—they recorded a total of 27,428 Ross's Gulls over the thirty-nine-day period, peaking with 7,116 gulls in a three-hour period of October 16! This is required reading for anybody thinking about going to Barrow in the fall to witness the Ross's Gull migration.

McKee, Tristan, Peter Pyle, and Nial Moores. "Vagrancy and Identification of First-Cycle Slaty-Backed Gulls." *Birding* 46, no. 6 (2014): 38–51. This article covers the latest identification tips for first-year Slaty-Backed Gulls, which had previously been considered difficult to impossible to reliably identify out of range. It is mandatory reading for anyone hoping to tackle this identification challenge, and includes never-before-published field marks for identifying this Asian rarity and separating it from similar-looking first-year gull species and hybrids.

McNair, Douglas B. "The Gray-Hooded Gull in North America: First Documented Record." *North American Birds* 53, no. 3 (1999): 337–339. This article provides an account and photos of the December 1998 occurrence of a wayward Gray-Hooded Gull in Apalachicola, Florida, a first North American record.

Newcomb, Raymond Lee. *Our Lost Explorers: The Narrative of the Jeannette Arctic Expedition as Related by the Survivors, and in the Records and Last Journals of Lieutenant De Long.* Hartford, CT: American Publishing, 1888. The Jeannette Expedition (1879–1881), as related by survivors, the journals of Lieutenant De Long, and expedition naturalist Raymond Lee Newcomb. While trapped in the ice of the East Siberian Sea, the crew saw flocks of Ross's Gulls, the first indication of their Siberian nesting grounds recorded.

Olsen, Klaus Malling. *Gulls of the World: A Photographic Guide.* Princeton, NJ: Princeton University Press, 2018. This book covers all the gull species in the world with clear and accessible text and a wealth of photographs. This user-friendly book's stunning photos and text tell you what you need to know to make an identification without getting into unnecessary details or cumbersome minutia.

Olsen, Klaus Malling, and Hans Larsson. *Gulls of North America, Europe, and Asia.* Princeton, NJ: Princeton University Press, 2004. This comprehensive reference includes both beautifully painted plates and large-format photographs for each species. In addition to being a great source of information, this book is a joy to leaf through, due to the paintings and the photographs. The text includes clearly written summaries of gull plumages, as well as all the "feather by feather" details you need for difficult identifications.

Olson, Clark S. "Band-Tailed Gull photographed in Florida." *The Auk* 93 (1976): 176–177. This brief article documents the remarkable sighting of a Band-Tailed Gull at Marco Island, Florida, in June 1970.

Patten, Michael A., Guy McCaskie, and Phillip Unitt. *Birds of the Salton Sea.* Berkley: University of California Press, 1997. This is the definitive resource to the ecology, biogeography, and birdlife of the Salton Sea. Anyone interested in this unique natural resource in general, or Yellow-Footed Gulls in particular, should read this book.

Pittaway, Ron. "Recognizable Forms: Subspecies of the Iceland Gull." *Ontario Birds* 10, no. 1 (1992): 24–26. This account covers the identification of the three subspecies of Iceland Gulls (*thayeri, kumlieni,* and *glaucoides*). It is an excellent synopsis of how first-year and adult birds of each subspecies can be distinguished in the field.

Pittaway, Ron, and Jean Irons. "Gull Watching Guide." *OFO News* 18, no. 3 (2000): 1–7. This is a great summary of the gulls of Ontario and where to view them. This guide was updated in November 2016.

Plyler, Cindy. "The Gulls of Niagara Falls." *Bird Watcher's Digest* 18, no. 2 (1995): 86–89. This enthusiastic and well-written piece extols the many reasons to look for gulls at Niagara Falls—one of the best gull-watching spots in North America. The diversity and number of gulls, in addition to the spectacular natural setting, are hard to beat in late fall or winter. If you haven't watched gulls at Niagara Falls, this article will make you want to go.

Reed, Tom. "Editors' Notebook / The Changing Seasons: Of Gales, Witches, and Gathering Storms." *North American Birds* 70, no. 1 (2017): 2–5. This column includes a detailed summary of the powerful November 2015 storm that displaced unprecedented numbers of Franklin's Gulls to widespread locations along the East Coast.

Retter, Michael. "Check-List Supplement Redux, v. 2017." *Birders Guide to Listing & Taxonomy* 29, no. 3 (October 2017): 37. This article includes a discussion of the decision to treat Thayer's Gull as a subspecies of Iceland Gull.

Sadler, Richard W. "Seagulls, Miracle of." In *Encyclopedia of Mormonism.* Edited by David H. Ludow, 1287–1288. New York: Macmillan,1992. This account provides documentation of the "Miracle of Seagulls," which occurred in 1848 when the crops of the Mormon pioneers were devastated by "Mormon crickets." When the outlook was at its bleakest, battalions of California Gulls descended on the area, feasted on the crickets, and salvaged what remained of the crops. As one observer noted, "The sea gulls have come in large flocks from the lake and sweep the crickets as they go; it seems the hand of the Lord is in our favor." The "sea gull" (or California Gull) is fittingly the official state bird of Utah.

Schnell, Gary D., Barbara L. Woods, and Bonnie J. Ploger. "Brown Pelican Foraging Success and Kleptoparasitism by Laughing Gulls." *The Auk* 100 (1983): 636–644. This study documents age-related feeding success for Brown Pelicans and gull-pelican interactions, with an emphasis on the kleptoparasitism performed by Laughing Gulls.

Schoettler, Carl. "Kelp Gull Draws Bird Lovers to Maryland." *Baltimore Sun*, March 11, 2004. This story documents the long-staying and much-celebrated Kelp Gull of Sandgates, Maryland. This famous bird was first spotted in 1998 and was a regular at a dock behind a restaurant in southern Maryland until early 2005, drawing thousands of visitors.

Scott, Michael J. "Interbreeding of the Glaucous-Winged Gull and Western Gull in the Pacific Northwest." *California Birds* 2 (1971): 129–133.

Shaffer, Fred. "The Gulls of Schoolhouse Pond: Gull Observations and Numbers from the Winter of 2002–2003." *Maryland Birdlife* 59, no. 1–2 (2003): 12–16. A summary of gull observations from Schoolhouse Pond, Maryland, during the winter of 2002–03 is provided here.

Shaffer, Fred. "Gull Observations at Schoolhouse Pond during December 2004." *Maryland Birdlife* 60, no. 3–4 (2004): 35–40. This article provides a summary of the many rare gulls observed at Schoolhouse Pond during December 2004. Included during the month were multiple white-winged gulls, a Black-Headed Gull, and a first-county-record Mew (now Short-Billed) Gull.

Sibley, David Allen. *The Sibley Guide to Birds*. 2nd ed. New York: Alfred A. Knopf, 2014. Sibley provides excellent coverage of the regularly occurring and rare gulls of North America, depicting a large number of plumages at rest and in flight. Sibley captures the shape and plumage of the gulls in flight better than anyone. If you are trying to identify flyover gulls at your local hotspot, this is the book to have at your side.

Smith, Joseph. *Essentials in Church History*. Salt Lake City, UT: Deseret News Press 1922. Includes details regarding the "miracle of the gulls" when thousands of California Gulls descended upon the crickets that were destroying the settlers' crops.

Smith, Neal G. "Commentary: Arctic Gulls 32 Years Later: A Reply to Snell." *Colonial Waterbirds* 14, no. 2 (1991): 190–195.

Snell, Richard R. "Status of *Larus* Gulls at Home Bay, Baffin Island." *Colonial Waterbirds* 12, no. 1 (1989): 12–23.

Snell, Richard R. "Variably Plumaged Icelandic Herring Gulls: High Intraspecific Variation in a Founded Population." *The Auk* 110, no. 2 (1993): 410–413.

Snow, Barbara K., and D. W. Snow. "Behavior of the Swallow-Tailed Gull of the Galapagos." *The Condor* 70 (1968): 252–264.

Soper, J. Dewey. "Ornithological Results of the Baffin Island Expeditions of 1928–1929 and 1930–1931, Together with More Recent Records." *The Auk* 63, no. 1 (1946):1–24, 223–239. This is a delightful and detailed account of the explorations and ornithological findings of Baffin Island. It provides a detailed inventory of the birdlife of the island and incorporates both Soper's personal observations and observations from the local Inuit population. It provides insights into the birds and natural history of a region seldom visited by birders or researchers.

Stelloh, Tim. "Rare Seagull Lands at Coney Island." *New York Times*, July 31, 2011. The excitement of a remarkable gull (Gray-Hooded) at an unlikely location (Coney Island) is summarized in this story.

Stevenson, Henry M. "General Notes." *Florida Field Naturalist* 8, no. 1 (1980): 21–23. A summary of the Florida records of Band-Tailed Gull is provided here.

Stokes, Donald, and Lillian Stokes. *The Stokes Field Guide to the Birds of North America*. New York: Little, Brown, 2010. This book includes concise species accounts of most of the gulls that occur in North America, with clear photos of each species at rest and in flight at all ages. It also contains some good identification tips for gulls and general patterns for aging four-year gulls.

Sutton, George M., and David F. Parmalee. "On Maturation of Thayer's Gull." *Wilson Bulletin* 90, no. 4 (1978): 479–491. This paper compares the maturation of Thayer's Gulls and Herring Gulls on the basis of observations of birds in the Canadian Arctic archipelago.

Thomas, V. G., and S. D. MacDonald. "The Breeding Distribution and Current Population Status of the Ivory Gull in Canada." *Arctic* 40, no. 3 (1987): 211–218. Aerial surveys were conducted from 1982 to 1985 to determine the size and distribution of the Ivory Gull population in the Canadian High Arctic.

Thompson, Bill, III, ed. *Identify Yourself: The 50 Most Common Birding Identification Challenges*. Boston and New York: Houghton Mifflin, 2005. This book includes a compilation of the popular bird identification column from *Bird Watcher's Digest*. Clearly written and beautifully illustrated, the columns on gulls include "*The Basics of Gull ID*" and "*Hooded Gulls*." Twenty years after its initial publication, I still think that Rick Blom's column on the aging and identification of gulls is the most enjoyable, well-conceived, and easy-to-follow approach to identifying the vast majority of gulls you see.

Tinbergen, Niko. *The Herring Gull's World*. New York: Basic Books, 1960. This delightfully written book covers the social behavior of Herring Gulls. It includes a detailed analysis of the behavior that makes gulls such a fascinating group of birds to observe and study. Tinbergen includes many firsthand diary accounts of gull interactions and social behaviors, many rendered in black-and-white drawings. This book is not written with a detached scientific viewpoint; Tinbergen's enthusiasm for gulls comes through in the text and the animated descriptions of their behavior.

van Dijk, Klaas, Date Lutterop, Rob Voesten, and Frank Majoor. "Black-Headed Gull of 33 Years and Re-appeal to Stop Using Aluminum Rings to Mark Gulls." *Dutch Birding* 36 (2014): 249–252. This paper presents information on a new longevity record for Black-Headed Gulls by documenting a bird that lived more than thirty-three years. Also presented is information on the wear and loss of aluminum rings on gulls (and other long-lived seabirds) and why they should no longer be used. The authors recommend that stainless steel or incoloy (a nickel-iron-chromium alloy) rings be used instead.

van Dijk, Klaas, Rene Oosterhuis, Benny Middendorp, and Frank Majoor. "New Longevity Records of Black-Headed Gull, with Comments on Wear and Loss of Aluminum Rings." *Dutch Birding* 34 (2012): 20–31. This article documents several long-lived Black-Headed Gulls, including one gull that was more than thirty-two years old, a new longevity record for the species.

Velarde, Enriqueta. "Breeding Biology of Heermann's Gulls on Isla Rasa, Gulf of California, Mexico." *The Auk* Vol 116 (1999): 513–519. The article provides detailed information on the breeding biology of Heermann's Gulls from Isla Rasa, where approximately 95% of the world's population nest.

Verbeek, Nicolaas A. M. "Comparative Feeding Behavior of Immature and Adult Herring Gulls." *Wilson Bulletin* 89, no. 3 (1977): 415–421. This study evaluates the feeding efficiency (or success rate) of immature, subadult, and adult Herring Gulls. It also documents some of the tactics immature gulls use (such as stealing food and aerial chases) to compensate for a lower success rate.

Wilds, Claudia, and David Czaplak. "Yellow-Legged Gulls (*Larus cachinnans*) in North America." *Wilson Bulletin* 106, no. 2 (1994): 344–356. Wilds and Czaplak document the three records of Yellow-Legged Gulls in North America up to the early 1990s. Identification features, comparisons with similarly looking gulls, and the potential for future records are discussed.

ONLINE RESOURCES

Audubon, John James. *Birds of North America*. London: Havell & Son, 1844. The John James Audubon Center keeps his legacy alive by maintaining a digital library of his paintings. Also available on this site is the text he wrote for each species in the accompanying *Ornithological Biography*. The spirit of exploration and discovery is conveyed in each account. http://www.audubon.org/birds-of-america.

Ayyash, Amar. *Anything Larus*. This indispensable site provides monthly updates on rare gull sightings, taxonomy, and identification, and gull identification quizzes. Few people can match Ayyash's knowledge and enthusiasm for gulls. http://www.anythinglarus.com.

Birds of the World. This wonderful online resource includes detailed information on all the breeding gulls of North America and was utilized regarding the biology, measurements, and identification of the gulls included this book. At the time the information was accessed, it was included under Birds of North America. However, in early 2020,

Birds of North America was merged into a new and more comprehensive global resource: Birds of the World. This larger, worldwide reference provides a wealth of information on every species and subspecies of the world's birds. The bibliography includes the updated references for the materials utilized for this book. https://birdsoftheworld.org/bow/home.

Burger, J. and M. Gochfeld. 2020. Bonaparte's Gull (*Chroicocephalus philadelphia*), version 1.0. In Birds of the World (A. F. Poole and F. B. Gill, eds.). Cornell Lab of Ornithology, Ithaca, NY. https://doi.org/10.2173/bow.bongul.01.

Burger, J. and M. Gochfeld. 2020. Franklin's Gull (*Leucophaeus pipixcan*), version 1.0. In Birds of the World (A. F. Poole, ed.). Cornell Lab of Ornithology, Ithaca, NY. https://doi.org/10.2173/bow.fragul.01

Byrd, G. V. and J. C. Williams. 2020. Red-legged Kittiwake (*Rissa brevirostris*), version 1.0. In Birds of the World (A. F. Poole and F. B. Gill, Editors). Cornell Lab of Ornithology, Ithaca, NY. https://doi.org/10.2173/bow.relkit.01.

eBird. This online resource and database of bird sightings from across the world is a great source of information on bird distribution, sightings, and rare-bird occurrences. It is also perhaps the best location to record your own bird sightings, because the records then become a part of a larger database available to others. As the largest citizen-science effort in the world, eBird compiles bird checklists from around the globe, archives the information, and freely distributes it for research, conservation, and educational purposes. Its many available tools include current comprehensive bird lists from specific localities, bird distribution maps, and rare-bird alerts for particular counties or states. It is also a wonderful source of up-to-date bird information for recreational birders. My initial notification of the Coney Island Gray-Hooded Gull came from eBird. Thanks to the rapid and widespread dissemination of information about the gull on this site, I and a lot of other birders got to see this spectacular rarity. Similarly, if other rare gulls or birds are seen in my local area or across the country, eBird is my first choice for information regarding location, photos, and additional details related to the sighting. https://ebird.org/home.

eBird News. "eBird and the Gray-Hooded Gull." eBird News, August 4, 2011. This story documents the role that eBird played in correctly identifying this unexpected and extremely rare gull, as well as how technology has revolutionized the speed with which information about rarities is disseminated.

eBird News. "Franklin's Gull Fallout of 2015." eBird News, November 13, 2015. This story summarizes the widespread fallout of Franklin's Gulls along the East Coast in 2015. These midwestern birds were seen in perhaps unprecedented numbers along the Eastern Seaboard for several days in November 2015, after the passing of a powerful weather front.

Ewins, P. J. and D. V. Weseloh. 2020. Little Gull (*Hydrocoloeus minutus*), version 1.0. In Birds of the World (S. M. Billerman, ed.). Cornell Lab of Ornithology, Ithaca, NY. https://doi.org/10.2173/bow.litgul.01.

Good, T. P. (2020). Great Black-backed Gull (*Larus marinus*), version 1.0. In Birds of the World (S. M. Billerman, Editor). Cornell Lab of Ornithology, Ithaca, NY.. https://doi.org/10.2173/bow.gbbgul.01.

Gull Research Organization. This is perhaps my favorite online source of information on gulls. The Gull Research Organization maintains a comprehensive library of research papers related to gull identification, biology, and taxonomy from around the world. Also included are links to various gull websites and additional information on gull topography, distribution, and gray scales. It even includes a forum for the exchange of information related to gulls. http://www.gull-research.org.

Hatch, S. A., G. J. Robertson, and P. H. Baird. 2020. Black-legged Kittiwake (*Rissa tridactyla*), version 1.0. In Birds of the World (S. M. Billerman, ed.). Cornell Lab of Ornithology, Ithaca, NY. https://doi.org/10.2173/bow.bklkit.01.

Hayward, J. L. and N. A. Verbeek. 2020. Glaucous-winged Gull (*Larus glaucescens*), version 1.0. In Birds of the World (S. M. Billerman, Editor). Cornell Lab of Ornithology, Ithaca, NY, USA. https://doi.org/10.2173/bow.glwgul.01.

Islam, K. and E. Velarde. 2020. Heermann's Gull (*Larus heermanni*), version 2.0. In Birds of the World (P. G. Rodewald and B. K. Keeney, Editors). Cornell Lab of Ornithology, Ithaca, NY, USA. https://doi.org/10.2173/bow.heegul.02.

Japanese Gull Site. This is another wonderful site that includes spectacular photos of the world's gulls in all ages and plumages. It is maintained by Osao and Michiaki Ujihara and is a great resource for gull photos, particularly of species of the Pacific Ocean region. This site can be used for information on the various vagrant Asian gulls that occasionally turn up in North America. http://www23.tok2.com/home/jgull/gullidentifi_.htm.

MacKenzie, Ken. "The Life and Travels of Ring-Billed Gulls." Massachusetts Department of Conservation and Recreation, Division of Water Supply Protection, 2013. This fascinating article describes the work of the Massachusetts Department of Conservation and Recreation to document the habits and movements of Ring-Billed, Herring, and Great Black-Backed Gulls by using wing tags, banding, and satellite tracking. The study was part of an effort to protect the water quality of reservoirs in the state by estimating the potential impact of the gulls on water quality. The results provide a detailed analysis of the movements of individual gulls. Gull 87428 (a Ring-Billed Gull) was fitted with a transmitter and recorded across the Northeast, with the majority of records at locations such as Boston, New York, Philadelphia, Buffalo, and Toronto.

While there were a smaller number of records at locations between cities, the vast majority came from urban areas. The study, as well as information on the movements of tracked birds, can be found at https://www.mass.gov/doc/the-life-and-travels-of-ring-billed-gulls/download.

Mallory, M. L., I. J. Stenhouse, H. G. Gilchrist, G. J. Robertson, J. C. Haney, and S. D. Macdonald. 2020. Ivory Gull (*Pagophila eburnea*), version 1.0. In Birds of the World (S. M. Billerman, ed.). Cornell Lab of Ornithology, Ithaca, NY. https://doi.org/10.2173/bow.ivogul.01.

Maynard, Bill. "Ivory Gull – Prince Edward Island." *PEEPS* (blog), January 27, 2009. This weblog summarizes the occurrence of an Ivory Gull on Prince Edward Island. The bird was first reported on December 26, 2008, and was the first Ivory Gull of what proved to be a much-larger and more widespread invasion into southeastern Canada and the northeastern United States.

Patten, M. A. 2020. Yellow-footed Gull (*Larus livens*), version 1.0. In Birds of the World (A. F. Poole and F. B. Gill, eds). Cornell Lab of Ornithology, Ithaca, NY. https://doi.org/10.2173/bow.yefgul.01.

Pierotti, R. J. and C. A. Annett. 2020. Western Gull (*Larus occidentalis*), version 1.0. In Birds of the World (A. F. Poole and F. B. Gill, Editors). Cornell Lab of Ornithology, Ithaca, NY. https://doi.org/10.2173/bow.wesgul.01.

Snell, R. R., P. Pyle, and M. A. Patten. 2020. Iceland Gull (*Larus glaucoides*), version 1.0. In Birds of the World (P. G. Rodewald and B. K. Keeney, eds.). Cornell Lab of Ornithology, Ithaca, NY. https://doi.org/10.2173/bow.y00478.01.

The Gulls of Appledore: Seabird Ecology on an Island in Maine. This site documents the gull banding and research taking place on Appledore Island, Maine, including ground-breaking documentation related to the Lesser Black-Backed × Herring Gull hybrids (or "Appledore's" Gulls). https://gullsofappledore.wordpress.com/about.

Tietz, Jim, and Guy McCaskie, eds. Update to *Rare Birds of California*. 2008–2021. This is the online update to the *Rare Birds of California*. This table updates the records included in the species accounts included in the 2007 book. The table is updated periodically and can be found at https://www.californiabirds.org/cbrc_book/update.pdf.

Weiser, E. and H. G. Gilchrist, 2020. Glaucous Gull (*Larus hyperboreus*), version 1.0. In Birds of the World (S. M. Billerman, Editor). Cornell Lab of Ornithology, Ithaca, NY. https://doi.org/10.2173/bow.glagul.01.

Winkler, D. W. 2020. California Gull (*Larus californicus*), version 1.0. In Birds of the World (A. F. Poole and F. B. Gill, eds.). Cornell Lab of Ornithology, Ithaca, NY. https://doi.org/10.2173/bow.calgul.01.

About the Author

Fred Shaffer worked for the Maryland–National Capital Park and Planning Commission for over 30 years and became interested in gulls by observing the large flocks that gathered each day at Schoolhouse Pond just outside his office. He enjoys observing gulls in all their diversity and plumages and has documented his gull observations from Schoolhouse Pond in *Maryland Birdlife*. He has studied gulls in their natural habitat across North America and photographed the many plumages of each species.